THE STUDEN

1992 EDITION

DYANNE GIBSON

The Student's Guide to Ontario Universities

1992 EDITION

UNIVERSITY OF TORONTO PRESS

Toronto Buffalo London

Printed in Canada

Toronto Buffalo London
Printed in Canada

ISBN 0-8020-6884-7

Canadian Cataloguing in Publication Data

Gibson, Dyanne
The student's guide to Ontario universities

ISBN 0-8020-6884-7

1. Universities and colleges – Ontario – Handbooks, manuals, etc. I. Title.

L906.05G52 1990 378.713 C90-094750-0

In remembrance of my mother,
Edith Ayres Gadd, whose support
made my university education possible.

Contents

Introduction

The Student's Guide to Ontario Universities is written for secondary-school students who are thinking about enrolling in an Ontario university. If you are one of these students, the decision you are considering may possibly be the most important one you will ever make.

One of the reasons this decision is so important is that a university education requires the investment of a large sum of money. Fees will be close to $2000, and residential expenses will cost approximately $6000 if you either cannot, or choose not to, commute daily to university from where you currently live. Add to this $8000 the $17,000 you might realistically earn working full-time after graduating from secondary school and you will see that a year's study could cost you $25,000. If you choose a four-year program at university, your degree will cost $100,000.

Will the investment be worth it? Yes, definitely, if you take the time to research the choices available within the university system and decide which one is right for you. That means you must look inward at your skills, interests and values to assess who you are and what you want from life. Only after you have done this can you begin to study what each university in the province has to offer and how it relates to your personal needs and career expectations.

I decided to write this book because I have learned from my own experiences, both as a student and as a part-time faculty member at a university, how important it is to define your eventual destination as well as the details of the journey you have to take to reach it. Too often I have seen students become disenchanted when university does not meet their expectations, or they find out, after graduation, that the program they took is wrong for the career direction they had hoped to take. They wasted not only time but a lot of money, because they did not bother to think about where they wanted their lives to go and how a university might, or might not, help them get there.

University is a three- or four-year commitment. Would you take off on a trip somewhere for that length of time and spend up to $100,000 without carefully planning each step of your itinerary? Of course you wouldn't. Yet too many students give their plans for university less thought than a weekend trip to a rock concert. If a concert bombs, only a few dollars and hours are lost. But if a university education does not live up to your expectations, a lot more damage is done to your bank-book and hopes for the future.

Attending university can be the best time of your life, as long as you know where your life is headed and how a university can help you get there. You can only be sure you are making the right choices by doing proper research. *The Student's Guide to Ontario Universities*, like any good travel book, offers suggestions on routes and locations you might want to consider before setting your itinerary for university. Read it carefully and you will improve your chances of having a wonderful trip.

Bon voyage!

THE STUDENT'S GUIDE TO ONTARIO UNIVERSITIES

1992 EDITION

1 *Researching your life work*

DEFINING THE SITUATION

Hamlet, as you probably know, pondered whether "To be or not to be." If you are in your last one or two years of secondary school, you should consider his query and formulate your own version of it: "To be or not to be **what**?" You know you can't continue as a perpetual secondary-school student. You'll have to move on to other options.

A number of possibilities are open to you:

1 Enrol in post-secondary studies.

2 Join the work force.

3 Combine work with post-secondary education on a part-time basis.

4 Travel.

5 Retire to live off the charity of your parents.

6 Become a beachcomber, which would be a laugh a minute in Ontario during the winter months.

If we consider that options 5 and 6 are remote, then you're left with four viable options. Travel is usually done for only a limited period and, when you run out of funds or countries, you'll still have to consider the other three possibilities.

Work is certainly a viable alternative if you want to leave the world of education to learn on the job and earn money while doing so. If this choice appeals to you, you should consult with your guidance office about the availability of jobs. If you leave school with the academic credits needed for university or community college, you can always apply to enrol in post-secondary studies later. Apprenticeship programs are also a good route to take. They often incorporate training at a community college with paid work terms, allowing you to earn money while going to school. Plumbing, cabinet-making and electrical or mechanical work are examples of occupations that are learned through apprenticeship programs.

There are other part-time educational options available to properly qualified students at post-secondary institutions. All community colleges have extension courses for people who wish to continue their education while working. Most universities also have either colleges or centres of continuing education that offer part-time degrees, diplomas or certificate programs. Thus, you can have your cake and eat it too by earning money and obtaining a degree part-time. But beware. This is easier said than done. One drawback is that part-time degrees take longer. Some others are:

- Most classes tend to be at night or on Saturdays, and after a tiring day or week at work, you won't be as bright or as eager as you might want to be. "Now, Ms. Smith, could you perhaps open your eyes long enough to focus on Darwin's evolution of the species? If you will explain one or two points about it, we won't disturb you again, will we, class? ... Class, are you listening?"
- A great many university programs are not available part-time, especially high-profile, limited ones. Business and nursing are exceptions at some institutions.

Although part-time studies can be enjoyable, as well as rewarding, they're not the same as immersing yourself in a full-time university career. When you choose university, you are committing yourself to learning as a way of life for a few years. This is done with society's blessing and support, and you will be in the company of others like yourself. Most people affectionately remember their time at university as being among the most memorable and valuable years of their lives. And when the time comes to sit around reminiscing, you can bet you'll be talking about the good friends you made during your years at university rather than the joy of learning Mazlow's theory of self-actualization.

Most of you who have bought, borrowed or swiped *The Student's Guide to Ontario Universities* are interested in university study. Would you be masochistic enough to read it otherwise? Do not, however, exclude the idea of attending an Ontario community college of applied arts and technology. You don't need six Ontario Academic Credits (OACs) to enter most programs at a community college. Although they don't grant degrees as universities do, their diplomas or certificates open doors to a wide range of careers.

The purpose of a community college is to give you training in the precise skills needed for a specific job. If, for example, you want to become an airline pilot or a mechanic who specializes in airplanes, then you'd enrol in a flight technology program. Or, you can train to handle a camera in a TV studio, work in a day-care centre or run an electron microscope in a research lab – just a few examples of how colleges train for specific careers. Their programs are designed to meet the needs of the market-place and are usually of one, two or three years' duration. The majority of the 23 colleges in Ontario publish graduate-statistics reports each year that list all programs, the percentage of graduates placed in jobs and what their starting salaries were. These reports are worth taking a look at if you're not quite sure that university is for you. To help you contact them, a list of the colleges, their addresses and telephone numbers is provided at the back of the *Guide* in appendix one.

Universities, however, do not guarantee that you will graduate with specific job skills. They were set up back in the Middle Ages to expand and disseminate knowledge. Cardinal Newman of England, writing in the 1800s on the "business of a university," said that its function is to educate the intellect and create an intellectual culture. A university, he said, "educates the intellect to reason well in all matters, to reach out towards the truth, and to grasp it."

Nary a word does Cardinal Newman write about preparing for the job market. He would probably have agreed with the idea that the primary purpose of education is not to teach you how to earn your bread, but to make every mouthful of life sweeter. That's a wonderful ideal, and suitable if you want to be a monk in a monastery, but we're talking about the real world here. Current surveys show that most students today see university as the route to a good job. And it can be just that, if you make the right choice of university and program.

Many professions require a university degree as a start in their particular career direction. A degree is often needed to get a place in a professional firm, which will then provide the training and on-the-job experience you'll need to write a professional exam. Chartered accountancy, for instance, requires a university degree before a company will accept someone for a period of "student-in-accounts" training. This training prepares you to write the exams you must pass to qualify as a professional chartered accountant. Law requires you to article with a law firm before you can write the bar exam.

Except for these types of professions, however, university degrees do not always prepare one specifically for a career. Increasingly, university studies have become a key to upward mobility in careers. Obtaining a general bachelor's degree often becomes a base on which to build a more specific career direction, such as teaching or business. How many jobs do you see posted for a philosopher or historian? And yet a degree in these disciplines can be worthwhile if you want to become a teacher. Courses that may seem to be unrelated to any real job are valuable too because they help round out your general knowledge about life.

A university education, properly assimilated, should allow you to develop thought processes that are crucial to making decisions in the working world. Remember that you'll be developing skills in analytical and critical thinking at university, and that the subject being discussed probably isn't as important as the process you'll be learning. University prepares you to reflect on human and social conditions, understand all sides of an issue and arrive at an informed opinion. When you enter the working world, you won't be paid to just blurt out the first thing that comes into your head, but to think like a worthwhile professional. University studies help smooth out the jagged edges around who you are now and shape the professional you'll become.

Are you still convinced that you should seriously consider enrolling in a university? If you are, then you would be wise to consider two questions:

1 Will you be successful at university?
2 In which program should you register to best prepare yourself for the future?

The route to the answers to these questions lies in defining your particular situation.

It has already been established that you must make some kind of decision about your future unless you want to haunt your secondary school's halls like the ghost of Hamlet's father. If you do nothing now, you'll decide by *not* deciding and end up passively accepting whatever fate brings. Did you know that the word "passive" stems from the Latin root "to suffer"? If you aren't into suffering, I suggest you spend some time considering whether you are suited for university study and what you should undertake as your life work.

Why call it "life work"? Because the idea of a career is too narrow to encompass all the variations brought about by personal and economic change over a lifetime. Although most people today end up having more than one career, there is usually a theme that ties the variations together. It's unlikely that you'll find many people choosing a line of work that's totally different from what they trained to do after university.

A computer graduate, for example, may have taken a job programming in a large company and then become a group manager, which requires personnel and management skills. Untimately, she could retire from some other computer company as its president. The nature of her work changed over the years, yet the tie to computers remained because it was the base of expertise on which all the other advancements were built. Or, someone may graduate in journalism, work at a newspaper for a few years and then enter public relations. He may end his career writing biographies of famous people. Once again, each job is very different, yet they are all tied to his talent for writing.

These kinds of related career changes are typical in life unless you stop your career dead in its tracks and go back to school to train for something else. That's why you have to imagine there is a "corridor" of life work along which you'll find several doors leading to other career options. Don't think that becoming a computer programmer means that's the label you'll wear for life. It's where you may start, but it's hard to imagine all the possibilities that will lead from it until you're actually involved in your life work.

By examining your skills, interests, personal realities and values now, a possible area of life work will be revealed. Once you've narrowed down your possibilities to such areas as teaching or science or business you'll be able to match those to areas of study at university that will suit you best. Further, you'll be prepared to make choices based on an assessment of who **you** are and what **you** wish to achieve.

Do I sense a murmur of resistance? I suppose you know, and have always known, that you want to be a doctor, Jane. And you a social worker, Eric? You may think you're sure about what your chosen career will be, but it doesn't hurt to prove how right it is for you by referring to your likes and dislikes as well as your recent work and educational experiences. Also, you should be aware that access to some professions is limited. Programs that lead to them may be tough to get into unless you're a truly outstanding student and person. It's always smart to have a second career option in mind if your first one doesn't work out.

So let's begin to define your particular situation. You may still be undecided about whether to enrol at university, enter a community college or find a full-time job. Consider the benefits and liabilities of these three options when you're doing your life-work assessment. The exercise will be beneficial. But don't think that you have to do it alone. Consult your guidance office about options at community college or the feasibility of being hired for a job out of high school that will satisfy your expectations.

Figuring out whether a university education fits with your future plans is an important part of your assessment. You must think of your involvement in post-secondary education over the next three or four years as a career in itself. If you don't think carefully about the decisions you are making before registration, you'll not only be wasting your time but a lot of money as well.

By filling in the blanks when you define your situation, you will have a much clearer understanding of your chances of being accepted at a university.

Defining the situation

– *I intend to have the necessary academic qualifications to enter*

university in ____________________________________
MONTH YEAR

– *I expect the overall average I will have in six or more OACs will be*

approximately ____________________________________

– *The OACs I will graduate with are:*

1 ____

2 ____

3 ____

4 ____

5 ____

6 ____

7 ____

8 ____

9 ____

Lines 7, 8 and 9 are optional, since only six OACs are required for university entrance. Universities, however, may base admission on your six *best* OAC marks unless the subjects with lesser marks are mandatory for entrance into the program of your choice.

A realistic estimate of your academic prowess based on past performance will place you in one of the following admission categories for university acceptance:

90% + The world is your oyster and there are several pearls for your picking. You will be accepted into virtually any program you select at all Ontario universities, possibly with a scholarship. The only negative may be the number of laudatory phone calls and letters you may receive extolling the virtues of the universities to which you have applied. Be a very cautious consumer and check out all promises carefully.

80–90% You are in a position of power for acceptance at all universities but, if your mark is at the lower end of this range, certain programs may be closed to you. As an Ontario Scholar, however, your credentials are impressive.

70–80% At the upper range you will gain acceptance at most universities in arts and science faculties and in some limited programs. At the lower end, you may be below the average required by some of the more academically exclusive universities.

60–70% Several universities will not consider you for any program, while others, who are committed to accessibility, will welcome you to programs that are not limited in numbers. Almost all professional programs, such as physiotherapy and engineering, will be closed to you. Decide whether to improve your OAC average or to accept an offer of admission from a university that welcomes you. Be prepared to work on your lack of study skills in special university sessions when you enrol.

50–60% Reconsider your desire to attend university. Barring a miracle, which only happens from time to time, you will not be accepted at a university in Ontario. If you are still determined to attend, consult with your secondary-school guidance office about how you can best improve your average so that you will be qualified at a later date.

It's also important to consider which OACs you will present for admission to university. You ought to have an OAC English (usually English 1) because many universities require it for all their programs and some require it for all but science-based programs. Do you have OACs in algebra and geometry and calculus? Most business-related programs demand those credits for admission. If you have no math or science OACs you will be unable to enter any science-intensive programs and many professional disciplines. It's a shock to students when they realize that the choice of courses they made earlier in their secondary school years seriously limits the range of careers they can prepare to enter. You may want to rethink your choice of OAC subjects now, if you still have the time to change them.

SKILLS

Your choice of OAC subjects gives you some insight into your skills. There are, however, many skills that are not reflected in academic subjects. Remember that a skill is something your are good at, not necessarily something you enjoy. For instance, you may be a fast and accurate computer operator, but you see this skill as the means to a satisfying end, such as a management position in the computer industry, rather than a job sitting at a terminal day after day.

Sometimes a skill in the past is like the tip of an iceberg; there's a great deal below the surface that needs to be considered. Suppose you're a good hockey referee. What skills are required to do this well? How can these skills be enhanced and applied to a specific career? If you're good at breaking up fights in a hockey game, then perhaps you could consider a career in criminology or as a labour negotiator. Or, if you enjoy arguing why you made a certain call during the game, you might have the kind of skills a lawyer or a business manager needs.

Try to remember that the skills you've learned in the past are like the roots of a tree. They provide the confidence that nourishes your present skills and are the foundation from which future ones will evolve. You've probably done a lot of things that you might not think are useful for deciding what direction your life work should take. But think again. Perhaps you've been a counsellor-in-training at a summer camp or have spent a fair amount of time baby-sitting. Those count as valuable skills. Also, skills don't always come from paid jobs. Volunteer work, such as being a teacher's aid in a lower grade at school or working as a candy-striper, may also have contributed to your current list of skills.

As an exercise, let's look at two jobs that you've done in the past. Through this process you'll discover some of the basic skills you are good at and enjoy. You can analyse these to narrow down the focus of your life work. To show you how this is done, let's use a fictional case. Tom is 18 years old and has worked in a retail store. While trying to figure out what his life work might be, he examines his past job, both the skills it required and the ones he was good at.

Job name: Salesperson

Function	*Good at*	*Poor at*
1 *Ringing up a sale*	X	
2 *Clinching the sale*	X	
3 *Helping people*	X	
4 *Cleaning the store*		X
5 *Marking mechandise*		X
6 *Learning about the product*	X	
7 *Handling complaints*	X	
8 *Sorting stock*		X

By looking at Tom's assessment, we can draw some basic conclusions. He's good at dealing with people and understanding product information, but not good at the general upkeep of the retail operation. One might conclude, therefore, that Tom should look at a life work that will incorporate and enhance his skills with people. He shouldn't contemplate a career that is built upon the orderly, day-to-day maintenance of things. His strength is in dealing with people, not organizing, and the kind of work he does in the future should recognize that, or else he's going to be very unhappy.

Now it's your turn to attempt a similar exercise based on your past experience. Make your judgements without worrying about the degree of expertise you acquired, just whether you were good or not.

Past job name: ____________________

Function	*Good at*	*Poor at*
1 ______	______	______
2 ______	______	______
3 ______	______	______
4 ______	______	______
5 ______	______	______
6 ______	______	______
7 ______	______	______
8 ______	______	______

This exercise tells you that you were good at the following skills:

____

____

And the skills you had in this previous job were in the following broad

areas of expertise: ____________________

____

____

Since there's little point in dwelling on negatives, you should note the areas you were not good at only if they are significant. We all know only too well what we don't do well.

Just as past jobs should be analysed, so should present employment be scrutinized for clues. You probably have a part-time job or have held a summer job recently. Try the exercise again using your most recent position.

Present job name: ____________________

Function	*Good at*	*Poor at*
1 ____________	______	______
2 ____________	______	______
3 ____________	______	______
4 ____________	______	______
5 ____________	______	______
6 ____________	______	______
7 ____________	______	______
8 ____________	______	______

I was good at: ____________________

____

____

Therefore, I can conclude that the present skills I possess and have used in this position are: ____________________

____

____

You can repeat this exericse for each job you have had in the past or present to begin to catalogue exactly what you are good at in the work environment. You should note any recurrent clustering of skills among the jobs so that you can build upon your strengths.

You may not, however, realise the areas in which other people think you excel. You may never realize that you have a skill that is evident to others unless you ask them. Make your day – ask friends and relatives what they think you're good at. The answers will be a suprise either by delighting or dismaying you. Perhaps someone will say, "You're good at making things happen," or "You're a good listener." These are the kinds of qualities you might not have thought of on your own.

Add these to your inventory of skills, incorporating the ones you've learned from other people with the ones you listed through your own efforts.

Now list all those great skills:

1 ______________________	9 ______________________
2 ______________________	10 ______________________
3 ______________________	11 ______________________
4 ______________________	12 ______________________
5 ______________________	13 ______________________
6 ______________________	14 ______________________
7 ______________________	15 ______________________
8 ______________________	16 ______________________

Now sit back and use your imagination to come up with careers that might possibly match your skills. Use Tom to practise. If we look at the complete catalogue of Tom's skills, we might imagine him in a business career. Because he is so good with people, he might even be a good politician some day. What other career might suit him? What kind of career profile could you draw up for a person with skills that match yours? If you have difficulty doing this, consult your secondary-school guidance office for help.

List below all the life-work areas that are open to someone possessing these skills. If your possibilities are really extensive, use a separate sheet of paper (or several sheets). The position of God doesn't count, but prime minister does.

1 ______________________ 5 ______________________

2 ______________________ 6 ______________________

3 ______________________ 7 ______________________

4 ______________________ 8 ______________________

Stuck? Okay, lots of people find it hard to translate mundane skills into professions or careers. Skills needed to teach hang-gliding can translate into the necessary qualities to become either a surgeon or an outdoor recreation leader. The skills of cooking, such as measuring and following directions, might mean you'd be a good chemist or nutritionist.

If you find that your skills seem to point to one career direction, like working with children, don't restrict yourself by thinking that teaching is your only option. Use your imagination to think of all the places where children congregate and what jobs people work at there. Perhaps you're an excellent skater. Why not consider running a school to teach kids how to skate, or become a pro who teaches at a recreation complex? Perhaps you're good at physics and chemistry, but you really want to help kids. Blend the two interests through a science teaching career or become a laboratory technician at a children's hospital.

When you've identified several areas of life work that you might be good at, look for similarities. In which career areas can your strongest assets be put to use?

1 ______________________________

2 ______________________________

3 ______________________________

4 ______________________________

Don't lose sight of the fact that you're going to embark on a career of university study for the next few years. Part of this exercise seeks to determine whether university is for you. Perhaps, then, you might look at what you are good at academically in secondary school. After all, if you lack academic skills you ought to know that by now. If you enter university underprepared you should run, not walk, to the upgrading programs that are offered by university counselling services to overcome these deficiencies.

Job name: University student

Function	*Good at*	*Poor at*
1 *Attending classes*	______	______
2 *Critical thought (analysis)*	______	______
3 *Reading quickly and effectively*	______	______
4 *Class discussion*	______	______
5 *Essay and report writing*	______	______
6 *Writing examinations*	______	______
7 *Seminar presentations*	______	______

If you have only one or two weak areas, you can address those at a university. But you'll want to find out which Ontario universities have oustanding remedial programs to help you with the kinds of problems you may be having. If, however, you are weak in several academic areas, you should think about overcoming these deficiencies **before** you enter university.

INTERESTS

Being good at something doesn't necessarily mean you like it. When personal interests are considered, the opposite is often true. You may like something very much but not be good at it. You may love music but have no musical talent or skills. Hockey may be the passion of your life but you trip over the stick every time you step on the ice. Nevertheless, life would not have the same zest if you didn't play hockey or listen to music. Interests, when combined with skills, can make for very satisfying life-work possibilities. Suppose your skills are in the area of business, but your interests all lie in the field of athletics. You might consider an undergraduate degree in physical education or kinesiology, followed by a graduate degree in business. Suppose you have similar skills in commerce but a love of music. Choose a university that allows the flexibility of combining a business major with a music minor. This might help you enter a music-related business such as a record company or music store. By planning carefully you can combine personal interests with a profession.

In a similar format to the one employed to discover skills, consider either the two or three jobs analysed previously or different ones, if appropriate, on the basis of what you enjoyed doing while employed in these areas. If we use again the example of Tom working in a retail environment, we might learn he discovered that what he was good at in his job wasn't necessarily something he liked to do.

Job name: Salesperson

Function	*Liked*	*Disliked*
1 *Ring up a sale*	X	
2 *Clinching the sale*		X
3 *Helping people*	X	
4 *Cleaning the store*		X
5 *Marking merchandise*		X
6 *Learning about the product*		X
7 *Handling complaints*	X	
8 *Sorting stock*		X
9 *Interacting with staff*	X	
10 *Boredom when not busy*		X

From this analysis, Tom can begin to draw some conclusions about what he excels in **and** what he prefers to do. It would seem that he both prefers and has skills in serving and working with people. Although Tom has skills in merchandising, he dislikes the process of closing a sale. Tom realized he has neither interests nor skills in the day-to-day organization of a retail business. Further, he suffered acutely from boredom when the store wasn't busy, a problem that was made bearable because he enjoyed the company of the other staff. Tom will probably enjoy a career that involves people and is active, but without mundane tasks attached to it. Remember that skills can be acquired if there is an interest and desire to do so. It's more difficult to cultivate an interest to enhance a facility.

Now it's your turn!

Previous job name: ______________________

Function	*Liked*	*Disliked*
1 ______________________	____	____
2 ______________________	____	____
3 ______________________	____	____
4 ______________________	____	____
5 ______________________	____	____
6 ______________________	____	____
7 ______________________	____	____
8 ______________________	____	____

Add new categories to the list of functions if they are important and appropriate. This is your personal assessment; you make the rules, so add to your heart's, or soul's, or wallet's, content. By looking at your most recent employment, you'll be able to chart similarities to, and divergences from, the skills pattern.

Present job name: ______________________

Function	*Like*	*Dislike*
1 ______________________	____	____
2 ______________________	____	____
3 ______________________	____	____
4 ______________________	____	____

5 ______________________ ____ ______

6 ______________________ ____ ______

7 ______________________ ____ ______

8 ______________________ ____ ______

Now consider both skills and interests together.

1 Functions in which I have **both** skills and interests:

____

____

____

2 Functions in which I have an interest, but lack skills:

____

____

____

3 Functions in which I have skills and no interest:

____

____

____

Now reread the functions that you have designated and asterisk those that you can enhance by further training or knowledge. Highlight those areas that you think could be of interest in the future as potential life work. Do the asterisks and highlights overlap? If so, a future career area may be crystallizing.

After considering both my skills and interests, I could undertake possible life work in the following areas:

1 ______________________________

2 ______________________________

3 ______________________________

4 ______________________________

Do these areas require post-secondary education? Probably most do, and many at the university level. You are interested in going to university or you wouldn't still be here (you are still here, aren't you?), so let's consider why you are considering university study. After all, you aren't going to enjoy the academic discipline if you don't like intellectual pursuits. A person rarely does well in something he or she dislikes. If you intend to gain entry into a faculty of education or business after first-year studies with high marks at the university level, how would you realistically rate your chance of success if you don't like learning? The worst lie is the one you tell yourself, so be scrupulously honest in your self-assessment.

Job name: University student

Function	*Like*	*Dislike*
1 Thinking	________	________
2 Reading	________	________
3 Discussing issues and concepts	________	________
4 Essay and report writing	________	________
5 Writing examinations	________	________
6 Attending classes	________	________

7 Social life ________ ________

8 Athletic pursuits ________ ________

9 Extra-curricular activities ________ ________

This is the section that you write in invisible ink so that your parents don't find out that you're really going to university to major in parties and a hot social life. If you are more inclined to party than to enjoy learning in a class-room session, realize that you'll pay a high price for those good times. Without the base of knowledge that first-year studies give you, your odds of getting through second year are greatly reduced. The University of Guelph reports that 15% of students leave before second-year studies, while over 10% fail.

If you're one of the few who intends to do nothing but study at university, you really should revise your criteria to include some social activities. It's the good times that are remembered long after micro-economics and the names of the prophets of Israel have been forgotten.

Which brings me to values.

VALUES

Values are cherished beliefs that make life worth living. They are part of your personality and play a big part in the choices you make. Everyone has a value system. A value can be so important that a person is willing to die for it. Students in China, for instance, risked and lost their lives in 1989 trying to overthrow a repressive political regime. They were fighting for freedom, a value we take for granted in Canada. But not all values are acted out to such an extreme. A value can also be a small thing that adds to your appreciation of life, such as unwinding with friends and a pizza on Friday night.

An assessment of your values is simply a stock-taking of who you really are. Perhaps you're outgoing and like to have people around all the time. Or, you enjoy people but need a certain amount of solitude as well. Although these aren't the kinds of values that will inspire you to political action, they are still important traits of your character.

Sitting down and taking a good look at your values will help you decide which career directions fit with who you really are. You may think you've already done this back in the skills and interests sections, but values add another level of insight into yourself. For example, Tom has good skills for business and he's interested in the people side of business, but one of his strongest values lies in believing that we must act now to save our planet. By adding some environmental studies to his business courses, he'll be preparing himself for career opportunities that suit his skills, interests and values.

If you don't examine your values before committing to a life-work direction, you may be in for some unpleasant surprises when you graduate and become employed. You may have thought that you wanted to enter social work because you're skilled at helping people and interested in improving social conditions, but you value the things that money can buy. Social work is a rewarding profession, yet it has very real limitations in terms of financial advancement. In cases like this, your values may make you take another look at how your skills and interests should be applied.

In the next exercise, mark an X in one of the columns opposite the listed values. Each column has initials at the top:

- **VI** stands for a value that is very important to you;
- **SI** for a value that is somewhat important to you; and
- **NI** for a value that is not important at all.

There's also room to add other values that aren't listed.

	VI	SI	NI
1 *Steady income*	______	______	______
2 *Prospects for advancement*	______	______	______
3 *Flexible working hours*	______	______	______
4 *Set nine-to-five hours*	______	______	______
5 *Chance to be creative*	______	______	______

6 *Being of service to others*	______	______	______
7 *Competitive atmosphere*	______	______	______
8 *Leaving your mark on the world*	______	______	______
9 *Having fun*	______	______	______
10 *Physical fitness*	______	______	______
11 *Being liked*	______	______	______
12 *Working alone*	______	______	______
13 *Working with people*	______	______	______
14 *Having a solid one-to-one relationship*	______	______	______
15 *Intellectual growth*	______	______	______
16 *Having many friends*	______	______	______
17 *Making lots of money*	______	______	______
18 *Being your own boss*	______	______	______
19 *Raising a family*	______	______	______
20 ______________________________	______	______	______
21 ______________________________	______	______	______
22 ______________________________	______	______	______
23 ______________________________	______	______	______
24 ______________________________	______	______	______

You will have found that some values are the opposite of others, such as working alone and working with people. Sometimes you can't get everything you might want out of one job. Unfortunately, most jobs that are of service to others, such as teaching, nursing and counselling, do not pay large salaries. A competitive atmosphere may be the kind of challenge you want, but if everyone around you is busy trying to climb the corporte ladder, don't expect your need to make a lot of friends at work to be fulfilled. Know what it is you need to be content within an employment field; your values operate at work, not just in your personal life.

To test your proposed career area against your belief system, consider the life work you are contemplating and evaluate it with regard to those values that you consider to be very important.

Possible life work: ______________________________

____

____

____

Incorporates these important values: ______________________________

____

____

____

Does not meet these important values: ______________________________

____

____

____

If your proposed career area incorporates most of your important values, you should feel encouraged. But remember, none of these exercises can be cast in cement to last for the rest of your life. They represent who you are now. Think about how much you may have changed over the past three years and you'll understand that the next three years at university are bound to bring other changes you can't imagine in advance.

University will challenge your current values by asking you to contemplate and question issues and concepts that you have previously taken for granted. A good university will stretch your mind and, as Abraham Lincoln stated, "a mind stretched by an original idea never returns to its previous dimension." Elasticity is guaranteed by the challenging of opinions, some of which you have cherished for a long time. It's the duty of a university to question prevalent social views so that students will examine both the basis and relevancy of their ideas.

Why then should you assess the values you currently hold if they're only going to change at university? One reason is that this period between secondary school and university is an excellent time to assess the person you have become. Evaluation of your values helps define who you are at this critical point in your life, and it gives you guidelines for determining who you want to be in the future. As you continue to learn at university, you'll be receiving new information that will broaden your perspectives. For example, you might be totally apathetic about global issues at the moment, but taking a course about the Third World may light a fire of passion in you that makes you want to get involved in international-development issues. Enrolling in a humanities course that questions traditional male and female roles in society may make you change your approach to relationships in your own life.

The examples of how your university leaning experiences might change you are endless. One thing you can count on is that your values will change as you change.

Another important exercise to do right now is to determine what kind of university environment will suit your current social, academic and personal values. Don't forget that this is a three- to four-year commitment.

	VI	SI	NI
1 Large urban campus (Windsor, Toronto, Ottawa, etc.)	____	____	____
2 Small city campus (Guelph, Trent, etc.)	____	____	____
3 Large student body (over 25,000)	____	____	____
4 Mid-sized student body (below 25,000, over 10,000)	____	____	____
5 Smaller student body (under 10,000)	____	____	____
6 Academic students	____	____	____
7 Fun-loving students	____	____	____
8 Co-ed residence	____	____	____
9 All-male/all-female residence	____	____	____
10 Townhouse/co-op residences	____	____	____
11 Ability to commute daily	____	____	____
12 Diverse student population	____	____	____
13 Students from a similar background	____	____	____
14 Close to home	____	____	____
15 Far away from home	____	____	____
16 Athletic activities/facilities	____	____	____
17 Extensive social activities	____	____	____
18 Outstanding library facilities	____	____	____
19 Excellent general reputation	____	____	____
20 Availability of my preferred programs	____	____	____

	VI	SI	NI
21 Student services useful to me	_____	_____	_____
22 Superior faculty	_____	_____	_____
23 Accessible faculty	_____	_____	_____

Now you should be able to describe the type of university that appeals to you. If the ability to commute is the most important factor, then your choice will be narrow. If, however, you are looking for a mid-sized university with an arts program and co-ed residence, as well as good social and athletic facilities with approachable faculty, you'll have several options. Taking into consideration those values that you designated as very and somewhat important to you, now describe the type of university that appeals to you.

My choice of university will be one that has the following:

____

____

____

____

PERSONAL REALITIES

If you thought an assessment of skills, interests and values was going to be the sum total of exercises, think again. There are certain facts of life, realities that pertain only to your situation, that you have to consider when making a career choice.

Everyone has limitations on their choices, even though none of us likes to think that we do. Maybe you have severe allergies, for example. If you do, it's unlikely that you will decide to enter a forestry or horticulture career where you'll be breathing in moulds and pollen all the time. Or, you can't be the veterinarian you dreamed of being because animal hair makes you sick. But, because you do have allergies and have listened to doctors say that you have to learn to live with them, maybe you'll decide to make your life work out of researching allergens with the hope of someday contributing to better treatment of allergies, or even a cure. For every down side of a limitation, there can be an up side too.

Besides health-related limitations, you may have to consider one that's personally important to you, such as a relationship. If you now live in a small community and want to continue living there after graduation to be close to your family and friends, which careers are possible in that community? If there's already an excess of lawyers, you'll have a hard time setting up a law practice there if you choose to graduate in law. Perhaps teaching law at one of the local secondary schools is a better choice if you really want law to be your career direction, and to return to your home community after graduation.

What personal realities do you have to consider when choosing a career?

My social realities are: ______________________________

____

____

My financial realities are: ______________________________

____

____

My relationship realities are: ___________________________

____

____

My "self" requirements are: ______________________________

____

____

Therefore, my personal realities are best met in the life work of:

____

____

because: ______________________________

____

Does this career direction require university study? If it does, you have one more exercise to do before you begin to investigate which universities are appropriate for you. What present personal realities will affect your choice of university? That is, you need to consider how your life will change when you graduate from secondary school.

One important reality to remember is that you'll be leaving a cosy nest that has for the past few years consisted of your home and school life. Once you launch yourself from this nest, there will be pieces of it that cling to you and, to a varying extent, influence how far you want to fly from it. Besides your emotional attachment to your nest, there's the important financial question of whether you can afford to leave it.

An unavoidable reality is that it is expensive to go to university. There is some help available through the Ontario Student Assistance Plan (OSAP), which finances post-secondary education through loans and grants to applicants who qualify. Thus, OSAP allows many students to enrol in a university or community college who otherwise would not be able to afford post-secondary education. However, because the loan portion of OSAP has to be paid back after graduation at 1% above the prime interest rate at that time, some people are reluctant to commit to such a debt. In a 1989 article in the *Toronto Star*, the chairperson of the Ontario Federation of Students, Shelley Potter, said that most students accepting OSAP loans had a debt of $12,000 to pay after graduation.

Where you choose to live will be a major factor in the cost of your university education. Many parents are willing to provide funds for tuition, but not for residence, if a student lives within commuting distance of a university. But the local institution is only feasible for you if it has an appropriate program that fits your career direction. If you have to leave home to get the right program, or if you simply want to leave, your educational costs will escalate by about $6000 because you'll have to include residence and food in your budget. This amount still doesn't include books, travel, clothing and other necessities of life (like pizza and liquid refreshments).

Cost isn't the only thing that can block your flight from the nest. Parents or teachers might question whether you're mature enough to go to university. They also might disagree with the career path you've chosen. ("Look, Lennie, with your marks you should be enrolling in business instead of music. Musicians don't have the kind of security financiers have. Don't you want the good life with prestige and lots of money?") What others may want for Lennie may not be what he wants for himself. Music is the driving force of his life, not making a lot of money. He has to stand up to the opposition and negotiate with his parents or teachers by pleading his case intelligently. This is *his* decision, *his* life, and he has to take responsibility for it.

A more subtle barrier to university might come from the limitations you place on yourself. Sometimes these aren't realities at all, but perceptions that you assume are true. You may think you're not smart enough or rich enough to go to university, and these kinds of perceptions are draining away the confidence you need to take this important step. Are you really being fair in your assessment of yourself? An inadequate understanding of your capabilities could be standing in the way of what you want to become.

Let's get those realities down on paper. Remember, this isn't a dress rehearsal. You'll never be making this particular decision at this time of life again.

These are the realities I face when choosing a university.

University realities (location, program, etc.): ____________________

____

____

____

Relationship realities (parents, friends, etc.): ____________________

____

____

____

"Self" realities (grades, finances, etc.): ____________________

____

____

____

MAKING A CONSIDERED DECISION

Remember our fictional student, Tom, from the sections on skills and interests? Of course, his values and personal realities would be intensely private, so we couldn't ask him to tell us his innermost thoughts on those issues. But he has completed his life-work assessment and is willing to share the conclusions he came to: "I'm interested in and good at working with people, and would like to be well paid and live in an urban environment after graduation. Therefore, I've decided to pursue a life work in the area of human relations. I'll keep other career options open in case I decide to go into personnel, public relations or marketing. I prefer to go to a medium-sized university that's strong in the social sciences and collegial in nature. I want it to be within 100 kilometres of my family. Because my marks are in the low 80s with no OAC sciences, I intend to enter a faculty of arts or social science. I'll major in a psychology degree and take some business courses as well. I have a good chance of being accepted by all the universities to which I'm applying, but because of my financial situation, I'd prefer to enrol in a co-op program, if possible."

What about you? As accurately as possible, write a similar profile for yourself.

Now that you have a good general outline of your realities and life work, let's move on to discover how to identify the Ontario universities that can help you satisfy your objectives.

2 *Researching Ontario universities*

If you've reached this section, you are serious about going to university. Having conscientiously assessed who you are, and what type of life work will fit your interests, you're ready to study the Ontario universities that offer you the educational experiences you require. Before you start, however, commit to memory the following rules.

GIBSON'S RULES FOR DECIDING ON AN ONTARIO UNIVERSITY

Rule 1: Listen to others

Everyone who has ever attended university will be happy to advise you. Your math teacher may be delighted to tell you about the superb math program at her alma mater. Your nearests and dearests will try to convince you that their choice is the only one to take. A grandparent may promise to reward you "when the time comes" if you follow tradition and register at "the only university in the province worthy of this family's attendance."

By all means listen to them and gather all the information you can. Become an informal sleuth, digging out any information about the general reputation of specific programs at all the universities that interest you. Ask alumni whether they would take their same program at the same university again, and why. Question current students about why they chose their university and what they like or dislike about it. The more you fill your fine computer brain with the options open to you, the better able you'll be to make your $100,000 commitment.

Rule 2: Trust your own judgement

You are not your math teacher. Her experience was based on her requirements. Your grandparents went to "the" university in another era. Their expectation of you following in their footsteps shouldn't sway your decision. And if you choose a university based on a nearest and dearest's persuasion, then he/she may quickly become your ex-nearest and dearest.

This is *your* life! You are the star of this production and don't lose sight of that fact. Ensure yourself a leading role by making up your own mind. Then, if you make a mistake, you own that error. You'll be immensely more confident about your ability to do well at university if you've made a rational decision based on personal research. Often, people who are pressured into an educational option or career by well-meaning others have a great deal of anger against those who swayed their decision if that choice turns out to be the wrong one.

Rule 3: Don't believe everything you hear

When you gather information about Ontario universities, you'll collect myths, assumptions, gossip and rumor about them. You may hear that University X is for snobs and independent school types (not necessarily the same thing, by the way), while University Y accepts any warm body who can pay the fee. Don't believe either good or bad reports until you check them out. Universities in Ontario are more than the sum of their reports. Both X and Y universities may be pleasant surprises. X may prove to have an orientation program that introduces you to other students who share your interests and enthusiasms, while Y has special academic programs that challenge your intelligence.

Rule 4: Be realistic

Are you having trouble maintaining a 75% average in the advanced stream at secondary school? If so, you're unlikely to get high enough

OAC marks to be accepted into a limited program that requires marks of more than 85% – at least, not without heroic dedication. You have two choices: lower your expectations or become a hero. The second choice is possible only if you know that you've never taken academic achievement seriously and that you've left a part of your brain lying fallow for too long. If your hidden brilliance only needs hard work and dedication to produce higher marks, then give it a try. You can't afford to bury your potential when Ontario universities admit only the most academically qualified students to their prestigious and professional programs. If, however, you erroneously comfort yourself with the thought you could do better if you really wanted to but, in fact, don't have any extra brain cells in reserve, it's better to recognize that now than later.

Rule 5: Listen to university representatives

Between September and December your secondary school will be inundated with university liaison officiers, unless you live in northern Ontario, where they'll be as rare as a year without tent caterpillars. At sessions with them, and at University Information Programs set up by your local board of education, you'll be able to hear what they think you should know about their institutions.

It's true that liaison officers are paid by their universities to say nice things about the institution, but they know they have to be honest with students too. There's little point in recruiting students who will leave because the university didn't live up to the rave reviews that liaison officers gave it. These people tend to be both knowledgeable and fair in describing their universities, and they're not paid, as is sometimes supposed, according to the number of students they attract. You should, however, never decide on a university based on this information alone.

Corollary 1: Attend information sessions about universities in which you are even vaguely interested, especially if they are far away. If you live in Toronto, you'll be able to learn more about Ryerson, Toronto and York at first hand without hardship. But information sessions on universities will let you hear about Lakehead or Windsor without travel and expense.

Rule 6: Remember, your commitment goes beyond the first year

"I would like to major in psychology," you say. "No problem," replies the liaison officer. "Enrol in Introductory Psychology and you'll have the prerequisite for majoring in that field." All very well, but what marks will you need to obtain in first year to major in psychology? Each university has a different set of rules for continuing in a program. If one has a higher grade requirement than another, better you should know now when you still have the choice of entering either institution.

"I would like to be in residence in first year," you tell the admissions representative, who assures you that "If you meet these requirements, there's no problem." But what about second and third year? Finding out late in first year that you're ineligible to continue in residence can be extremely upsetting. You might have preferred another university where remaining in residence past first year was guaranteed.

Surprises should be pleasant. Don't let your lack of research cause you anguish at a later date. Map out your academic and residential goals before accepting any university.

Rule 7: Visit, visit, visit before deciding

Would you buy a car without first driving it? Or rent an apartment without checking it out? Of course not; no sensible person would. But thousands of first-year university students invest their money and time in an academic and social commitment without ever looking at the university. By "looking" I don't mean taking a campus tour or attending another information session. I mean you have to study closely what the university offers. By visiting the campus alone or with a friend or your parents you can soak up its mood and culture. By meeting with faculty and staff, you can check what you've heard and read against what they tell you is true. The first day of classes is not the time to find out you've taken something for granted and have made a terrible mistake.

Corollary 1: See a residence room. If it's too neat, be suspicious that it might be hermetically sealed when prospective students aren't visiting it. There's nothing wrong with seeing a room's actual size, once cleared of the year's dirty laundry and test papers. But you should also see it as it is in real life, rather than still life.

Corollary 2: Attend a lecture. It's helpful to experience a lecture at the university level to prepare yourself for the difference from high-school classes. Check out the professor, the topic and the student's response to the lecture. If over 25% of the students are sleeping, you might consider the following reasons:

1 The professor or his/her topic is boring.
2 It's a great party university.
3 Under-funding has reduced the oxygen level.
4 All of the above.

So how can you assess this scene yourself? You'll need to pursue

Corollary 3: Talk to students. They'll know which of the four possibilities presented above is correct. Perhaps that particular professor was awarded the "Sleeper of the Year" trophy, but is not at all typical of the calibre of the faculty. Students will answer the questions that liaison officers dread; they are pleased to tell you what you want to know and are the best recruiters a university can have if they are satisfied consumers. Student input is invaluable.

Corollary 4: Have a standard set of quesions that you want to check at each university you visit. (See the next section for a suggested format.) Include a space for the answers as well as a section to record your "feeling" about the institution. This way you'll be able to compare one program with another by evaluating each university logically as well as recollecting your impressions of the campus. This codified research also comes in handy when you try to convince your grandparents that your decision is the right one for you.

How do you set up such a system? Read on!

QUESTIONS TO ASK ABOUT UNIVERSITIES

When I was a liaison officer meeting with secondary-school students visiting York University, I was most impressed with the ones who came prepared. It made my job easier because they knew exactly the questions they needed to ask to put together a comprehensive overview of what York offered them academically and socially. The following form, "Questions to ask about universities," can be copied (or modified, if appropriate) and taken to each university you visit. Sections 1 and 2 record information, while section 3 preserves your initial response to the areas you researched. After visiting all the universities you are considering, you will be able to assess the ones that you prefer based on facts and impressions. Then if you have to negotiate with the parental unit about your decision to attend University X, you have a documented argument that will be persuasive.

QUESTIONS TO ASK ABOUT UNIVERSITIES

Name of University: ______________________________

1 *I need to know about*:

a) Program of interest: ______________________________

OAC courses, etc., for admission ______________________________

____

Entry marks needed for admission ______________________________

Program begins (first, second, third year) ______________________________

Length of program ______________________________

Courses in first year ______________________________

____

Marks required in first year to continue ______________________________

Lecture I can attend? Professor's name ______________________________

Subject ______________________ Location ______________________

b) Residence

Acceptance procedures (lottery, marks, etc.) ______________________________

____

Cost of residence ______________________________

Type of residence ______________________________

Subsequent-year availability ______________________________

Meal plans ______________________________

____

Special options available (e.g., International House) ______________

____

Room I can visit? Location ______________________________

c) Student services

Registration (How do I pick courses?) ______________________

Counselling ______________________________

____

Clubs ______________________________

____

Athletics ______________________________

____

Orientation (when? type?) ______________________________

____

Who can I see? Name ______________________________

Location ______________________________

d) Financial considerations

Scholarships ______________________________

____

OSAP ______________________________

____

2 *How can I learn more?*

Upcoming liaison events ______________________________

____

Specific program publications ______________________________

____

3 *People I spoke to*

Name	Title	Phone Number
1		
2		
3		

4 *General impressions*

a) About programs ______________________________

____

____

b) About campus and students ______________________________

____

____

c) About residence ____

____

____

d) About teaching ____

____

____

e) Things I still need to know _______________________________

____

____

____

5 *Based on this research, this university is my* _______________ *choice.*

APPLYING TO AN ONTARIO UNIVERSITY

In the beginning

The beginning may have been when your parents leaned over your crib murmuring, "You will go to university, you will go to university." Or, maybe it was just a little while ago when you decided that you should look into what a university degree could do for you.

For practical purposes, you should be ready to begin your research when representatives from universities, community colleges and other institutions besiege your secondary school. This usually happens in the fall with the University Information Program.

A co-operative effort of all 15 universities plus Ryerson and the Royal Military College, this program sends out emissaries to secondary schools in Ontario as advance recruitement troops. Visiting at least two, and often three, communities a day, representatives from each institution gather at secondary schools to hold 40-minute sessions to which students, parents and guidance teachers are invited. Each session, repeated three times with eroding energy and vocal chords, is available to grade 11 and 12 students who want to hear all the details about the university.

Remember Gibson's rule 5, corollary 1, that you should attend sessions presented by all institutions in which you are vaguely interested (even distant ones), not just those to which you already intend to apply. You're given a staggering amount of information in a short time. This allows you to consider each option further or dismiss it. You can receive glossy publications extolling the virtues of each institution not only in the sessions you attend but in "walk-arounds" or "gym-style" programs.

In a walk-around, students roam the halls, grappling for every piece of information in what becomes a contest to win the "I've got more publications than you have" stakes. The gym-style program is worse. All the university reps stand behind tables barricaded by their hand-outs, awaiting the onslaught of students ready for the campaign to begin. The gym doors open and an army of students bears down to capture the hand-outs, leaving the battle field strewn with the inert bodies of fallen university officials. If you actually read the tons of material you collect, the effort will have been worth suffering through the prevailing mass hysteria, a large part of which is general student anxiety about the unfamiliar world beyond high school.

By all means, engage in this autumn ritual, but don't expect to get very much personalized information from the representatives. They're much more effective at responding to your questions in one of the information sessions that can be arranged at your school. If you hear from a friend that a university whose session you missed may be worth investigating, never fear. You can ask your guidance office to invite the representative from that university back to the school.

Liaison officers from universities try to visit as many secondary schools as they can to give information sessions. Some visit as many as five schools a day. They show videos of the campus and give out printed information. Their strategy is to keep prospective applicants informed and aware, as well as to convert some students who are undecided about their choice. Trent University tries to interview each student who has applied their individually, to give him or her a better understanding of the university and its programs. This process also helps the student determine whether Trent is an appropriate choice.

Generally, these organized sessions at your school consist of reps giving information that *they* think is important. You can ask questions of your own during the general discussion, however, and you'll learn from the questions of other students. Also, you'll get the name of someone at that institution you can contact if you have more questions at a later date.

The role of the Guidance Office

Back in the dark ages, when I was in high school, the role of the guidance office was to help students make a career choice. In a lot of schools, the guidance office is now called Student Services and does a great deal of social counselling as well as fulfilling its initial mandate to help students choose a vocation.

The counsellors are there to give you advice. They are aware of student assistance and scholarship programs, university OAC requirements and recommendations, entry marks and co-op programs, and other admission information for each university in the province. As well, they know who to contact within the university admissions offices to get specifics concerning programs and disciplines. A dedicated guidance counsellor can advise and help you make a good decision.

Unfortunately, many students don't discover the worth of guidance counsellors until it's too late. Students should check their career aspirations against their academic realities before deciding on a university program.

Angela: "Good morning. Mr Stanton, I'm just dropping by to tell you I've decided to apply to engineering."

Mr Stanton: "Excellent, Angela. I suppose you have, or are enrolled in, two OAC mathematics?"
Angela: "You mean you need math for engineering, Mr Stanton? I dropped math in grade ten!"

Does this sound far-fetched? It happens far too often. Many students don't realize that decisions made "way back when" have tremendous implications for future jobs. Therefore run, don't walk, to your guidance office and check out whether your course of OAC study meets the needs of the university program you are considering.

The guidance office has two indispensable publications to which you might want to refer. *Horizons: Guide to Post-Secondary Education in Ontario* is published annually by the Ministry of Colleges and Universities. Distributed to each school-board and inspected private school in Ontario, *Horizons* lists all post-secondary educational options in the province. *Info: The Guide to Ontario Universities for Professional Counsellors* is published twice a year by the Standing Committee on School Liaison, under the auspices of the Ontario University Registrars Association. A reference guide for secondary-school counsellors, *Info* often features new developments at Ontario universities.

Another duty of counsellors is to help you fill out the Ontario Universities' Application Centre Form 101. This should be done before Christmas.

The Ontario Universities' Application Centre Form 101

Mercifully shortened to OUAC 101, this form allows you to apply to three Ontario universities. It does not, however, allow you to apply to the Royal Military College (RMC), which has its own form. Thus, if RMC is one of your choices, you can still apply to three other institutions. (This information should be of particular interest to students who want to enter engineering. Because competition for these programs is tough, RMC gives you an extra iron in the fire.) The completed OUAC 101 goes to the Application Centre in Guelph, which then distributes the information to each university. The completed form alerts the three universities to your intention to enrol in one of them.

Filling out the form is not easy because of the multitude of codes that have to be entered and the "subject of major interest" that has to be decided. Don't despair. I've got help for you. With the University of Guelph's permission, I've reproduced their sample application to an Ontario university on pages 48–9. (This is an example of useful marketing on the part of a university, because this form not only explains how to apply to any university in the province, but educates the student about Guelph's programs, codes and requirements.)

In submitting the form, remember the following:

1 Make sure the fee accompanies the form or it will not be processed.
2 A code on the form signals special circumstances that may affect admission. A letter explaining these special circumstances should be forwarded directly to the universities to which you are applying. Send all supporting documents to the University Admissions Contact whom I've named in secion 5 of each university's profile.
3 Generally speaking, the order of choice for universities on the form makes no difference, except in an few limited enrolment programs. Scholarships and awards, however, may be affected by choice. At York University, you are only given a "Merit Award" of $250.00 in the Faculty of Arts if you put York as your first choice. So, most of the time it doesn't matter what the order of choice is, but sometimes it does. Check to make sure.
4 Note the number of the form. You are no longer a student with a name, but number 90-000-000-0. Whenever you contact the Centre about one of your university choices, use your application number.
5 Check the box "Residence Information Requested" if you are even vaguely interested in residence. That way you will be sent information on residences at each university.
6 You can change your choices after the form has been sent in to the Centre. During January and February, your school's guidance office will receive a verification/amendment form (OUAC 103). Use this form to remove universities and add others or to change the ranking if you wish.
7 Usually you choose three different universities, but sometimes you may want to choose two different programs at the same university. If you know, for example, that you must stay at home while attending university and your city has only one university, then you may wish to"use up" two of your three choices by applying to a limited and an open program. If you aren't accepted in a limited program, most

SAMPLE

RETURN TO: À RETOURNER AU:
ONTARIO UNIVERSITIES' APPLICATION CENTRE
CENTRE DE RÉCEPTION DES DEMANDES D'ADMISSION AUX UNIVERSITÉS DE L'ONTARIO
90 WOODLAWN RD. WEST
BOX 1328 GUELPH ONTARIO CANADA N1H 7P4

APPLICATION FOR ADMISSION TO AN ONTARIO UNIVERSITY
FOR APPLICANTS ATTENDING AN ONTARIO SECONDARY SCHOOL

DEMANDE D'ADMISSION À UNE UNIVERSITÉ DE L'ONTARIO
CANDIDATS PRÉSENTEMENT INSCRITS À UNE ÉCOLE SECONDAIRE DE L'ONTARIO

REFERENCE NUMBER NUMÉRO DE LA DEMANDE
90- 049-403 2
REFER TO THIS NUMBER ON ALL CORRESPONDENCE
NUMÉRO À INDIQUER DANS TOUTE CORRESPONDANCE

TITLE TITRE	LEGAL SURNAME NOM	ALL LEGAL GIVEN NAMES IN FULL (UNDERLINE NAME COMMONLY USED) PRENOMS (VEUILLEZ SOULIGNER LE PRENOM USUEL)	SEX SEXE	DATE OF BIRTH DATE DE NAISSANCE YR AN	MO MOIS	DAY JOUR	SOCIAL INS. NO. Nº D'ASSURANCE SOCIALE
MS	PASS	HOPE I	F	72	06	13	450-000-000

MAILING ADDRESS / ADRESSE DE CORRESPONDANCE
APT.# APP. Nº: 105 NO. & STREET Nº ET RUE: 1135 PINE STREET WEST
CITY VILLE: ANY TOWN PROV: ONT. POSTAL CODE CODE POSTAL: P4N 6B7 AREA CODE & PHONE NUMBER INDIC. RÉG. ET Nº DE TÉL.: (700) 200 - 1234

HOME ADDRESS / ADRESSE DU DOMICILE
☑ CHECK BOX IF SAME AS MAILING ADDRESS LA MÊME QUE L'ADRESSE DE CORRESPONDANCE
APT.# APP. Nº NO. & STREET Nº ET RUE
CITY VILLE PROV POSTAL CODE CODE POSTAL AREA CODE & PHONE NUMBER INDIC. RÉG. ET Nº DE TÉL.

MINISTRY IDENTIFICATION NUMBER NUMÉRO MINISTÉRIEL D'IDENTITÉ
COUNTRY OF CITIZENSHIP PAYS DE CITOYENNETÉ

STATUS IN CANADA / STATUT AU CANADA:
0 X CANADIAN CITIZEN CITOYEN CANADIEN
1 PERMANENT RESIDENT (LANDED IMMIGRANT) RESIDENT PERMANENT (IMMIGRANT ADMIS)
2 STUDENT AUTHORIZATION (STUDENT VISA) PERMIS DE SÉJOUR POUR ÉTUDIANT (VISA D'ÉTUDIANT)
3 OTHER AUTRE

IF NOT CANADIAN SI NON CANADIEN
DATE OF ENTRY INTO CANADA DATE D'ENTRÉE AU CANADA

MARITAL STATUS ÉTAT CIVIL: 1 X SINGLE CÉLIBATAIRE; 2 MARRIED MARIÉ

MOTHER TONGUE LANGUE MATERNELLE: 1 X ENGLISH ANGLAIS; 2 FRENCH FRANÇAIS; 3 OTHER AUTRE

LANGUAGE OF CORRESPONDENCE LANGUE DE CORRESPONDANCE: 1 X ENGLISH ANGLAIS; 2 FRENCH FRANÇAIS

COUNTY
C. OF CITZ.
DATE ADJ.

HIGH SCHOOL CURRENTLY ATTENDING
ÉCOLE SECONDAIRE FRÉQUENTÉE PRÉSENTEMENT
ABC HIGH SCHOOL 123456
ANY TOWN, ONTARIO (700) 200 - 1411

UNIVERSITY AND PROGRAM SELECTIONS — CHOIX D'UNIVERSITÉS ET DE PROGRAMMES D'ÉTUDES

CHOICE CHOIX	CODE COTE	UNIVERSITY NAME AND COLLEGE NAME (IF APPLICABLE) NOM DE L'UNIVERSITÉ ET NOM DU COLLÈGE (S'IL Y A LIEU)	PROGRAM TITLE TITRE DU PROGRAMME	SUBJECT OF MAJOR INTEREST LA MATIÈRE PRINCIPALE DU PROGRAMME	EXPECTED ENROLMENT DATE DATE PRÉVUE D'INSCR.	FULL-TIME PART-TIME TEMPS COMPLET TEMPS PARTIEL	IF YOU APPLIED BEFORE ENTER YEAR SI VOUS AVEZ DÉJÀ DEMANDÉ VOTRE ADMISSION, DONNEZ L'ANNÉE	RESIDENCE INFORMATION REQUESTED DETAILS SUR LA RÉSIDENCE
1	AQ	LAKEHEAD UNIVERSITY	ARTS HONOURS	ENGLISH	F90	F		X YES OUI / NO NON
2	WJA	ST. JEROME'S	ARTS	ENGLISH	F90	F		X YES OUI / NO NON
3	OXE	UNIVERSITY OF OTTAWA	ARTS - BA HONOURS	ENGLISH	F90	F		X YES OUI / NO NON

COURSE TITLES TITRES DES COURS			COURSE CODES CODES DE COURS	MARK % NOTE %	FR FR.	CREDIT VALUE ÉQUIV EN CR	YEAR ANNÉE	OPG AVAN
ENGLISH (FIRST LANGUAGE) ANGLAIS (LANGUE SECONDE)			ENG 4A	85		1.0	19 89	
FRENCH (SECOND LANGUAGE) FRANÇAIS (LANGUE MATERNELLE)							19	
GEOGRAPHY	GÉOGRAPHIE		GRE 4A	97		1.0	19 89	
HISTORY	HISTOIRE						19	
MATHEMATICS	MATHÉMATIQUES						19	
CHEMISTRY	CHIMIE		SCH 4A	82		1.0	19 89	
PHYSICS	PHYSIQUE		SPH 3A	76		1.0	19 88	
ENGLISH (FIRST LANGUAGE) ANGLAIS (LANGUE SECONDE)		GR 13/OAC	ENG OA				19 90	
FRENCH (SECOND LANGUAGE) FRANÇAIS (LANGUE MATERNELLE)		GR 13/OAC					19	
GEOGRAPHY	GÉOGRAPHIE	GR 13/OAC	GCE OA			1.0	19 90	
HISTORY	HISTOIRE	GR 13/OAC					19	
ALGEBRA	ALGÈBRE	GR 13/OAC	MAG OA			1.0	19 90	
CALCULUS	CALCUL	GR 13/OAC					19	
FUNCTIONS & RELATIONS	FONCTIONS ET RELATIONS	GR 13/OAC					19	
BIOLOGY	BIOLOGIE	GR 13/OAC	SBI OA			1.0	19 90	
CHEMISTRY	CHIMIE	GR 13/OAC	SCH OA			1.0	19 90	
PHYSICS	PHYSIQUE	GR 13/OAC					19	
GEOLOGY (GR. 12)			GGE 4G	92		1.0	19 89	
BIOLOGY (GR. 12)			SBI 4A	71		1.0	19 89	
MUSIC (CONSERVATORY)			AMX OA	81		1.0	19 88	
							19	
							19	
							19	
							19	
							19	
							19	
							19	
							19	
							19	
							19	

MOYENNE GÉN. (SI DISPONIBLE) POUR TOUS LES COURS: 88.4 | 83.4

NUMBER OF YEARS IN AN ONTARIO SECONDARY SCHOOL / NOMBRE D'ANNÉES D'ÉTUDES AU NIVEAU SECONDAIRE EN ONTARIO: 5

TOTAL CREDITS EARNED TOWARDS OSSD (EXCLUDING GRADE 13/OAC'S) / TOTAL DES CRÉDITS ACCUMULÉS POUR GAGNER LE D.E.S.O. (EXCLUANT LA 13E ANNÉE/CRÉDITS ACADÉMIQUES D'ONTARIO): 26.00

UPON COMPLETION OF CURRENT PROGRAM APPLICANT WILL BE QUALIFIED FOR
À LA FIN DU PROGRAMME D'ÉTUDES ACTUEL, LE CANDIDAT DÉTIENDRA (LE)

☐ S.S.H.G.D. / D.E.S.S.O. ☒ O.S.S.D. / D.E.S.O. ☐ NEITHER / NI L'UN NI L'AUTRE

SCHOOL OFFICIAL / MEMBRE DE LA DIRECTION DE L'ÉCOLE

NAME / NOM: MRS. J. SMITH

TITLE / TITRE: HEAD OF GUIDANCE

DATE / DATE: Dec 2/89 SIGNATURE / SIGNATURE: J Smith

HAVE YOU EVER ATTENDED A POST SECONDARY INSTITUTION?
AVEZ-VOUS JAMAIS FRÉQUENTÉ UNE INSTITUTION POST-SECONDAIRE?

☐ YES / OUI ☒ NO / NON

DO YOU AUTHORIZE THE UNIVERSITY TO FORWARD TO YOUR SECONDARY SCHOOL ACADEMIC DATA REGARDING YOUR PERFORMANCE WHILE AT UNIVERSITY? THIS INFORMATION WILL BE KEPT CONFIDENTIAL AND WILL BE USED BY THE SECONDARY SCHOOL FOR CURRICULUM RESEARCH AND GUIDANCE PURPOSES ONLY.
PERMETTEZ-VOUS À L'UNIVERSITÉ DE TRANSMETTRE À VOTRE ÉCOLE SECONDAIRE LES RENSEIGNEMENTS SCOLAIRES RELATIFS À VOTRE RENDEMENT À L'UNIVERSITÉ? CES RENSEIGNEMENTS DEMEURERONT CONFIDENTIELS ET SERVIRONT UNIQUEMENT À L'ÉCOLE SECONDAIRE À DES FINS DE RECHERCHE DANS LE PROGRAMMES D'ÉTUDES ET DANS LES SECTEURS D'ORIENTATION.

☒ YES / OUI ☐ NO / NON

I HEREBY CERTIFY THAT ALL STATEMENTS ARE CORRECT AND COMPLETE INCLUDING MY DECLARATION OF CITIZENSHIP AND STATUS IN CANADA. I UNDERSTAND THAT I MAY BE REQUIRED TO SUPPLY DOCUMENTATION AT SOME FUTURE DATE TO SUBSTANTIATE MY CLAIM, AND THAT ANY MISREPRESENTATION OF THIS DATA MAY RESULT IN THE CANCELLATION OF MY ADMISSION OR REGISTRATION STATUS. I AUTHORIZE THE SECONDARY SCHOOL AND THE MINISTRY OF EDUCATION TO FORWARD ALL ACADEMIC INFORMATION, SCHOOL RECORDS AND RECOMMENDATIONS TO THE APPLICATION CENTRE AND TO THE UNIVERSITIES OF ONTARIO.

JE CERTIFIE QUE LES RENSEIGNEMENTS DONNÉS SONT EXACTS ET COMPLETS Y COMPRIS MA CITOYENNETÉ ET MON STATUT AU CANADA. JE SAIS QU'ON POURRA ME DEMANDER DE FOURNIR DES PREUVES À L'APPUI ET QUE TOUTE FAUSSE DÉCLARATION PEUT ENTRAÎNER L'ANNULATION DE MON ADMISSION OU DE MON INSCRIPTION À L'UNIVERSITÉ. J'AUTORISE L'ÉCOLE SECONDAIRE ET LE MINISTÈRE DE L'EDUCATION À FAIRE PARVENIR MON DOSSIER SCOLAIRE AU CENTRE DE RÉCEPTION ET AUX UNIVERSITÉS DE L'ONTARIO.

DATE / DATE: Dec 1/89

APPLICANT'S SIGNATURE / SIGNATURE DU CANDIDAT: Hope I. Pass

APPLICATION WILL NOT BE PROCESSED WITHOUT APPLICATION SERVICE FEE. LES DEMANDES REÇUES FRAIS ADMINISTRATIFS NE SERONT PAS PRISES EN CONSIDERATION universities will offer admission in an "open" program. Queen's, however, does not do this, so if you want to ensure a place at Queen's, designate your preferred option and then your alternative.

... and then you keep on studying and wait.

On the whole, the universities grant admission based on your OAC marks, although some (and the number is growing) require a supplementary information form. This is used to determine how a student will fit in a particular discipline and to consider athletic, social and community interests in relation to the chosen academic option. At the University of Toronto, this information is given closer consideration when program spaces are very restricted. The information form is used to make final selections among many highly qualified candidates.

In fine arts faculties or departments, a portfolio of work or an audition is usually requested. At York, each department within the Fine Arts Faculty has its own special requirements. If you do not read the instructions and make the appropriate response you will not be considered. Of course, the universities vary. You should learn all the requirements before organizing a portfolio or scheduling auditions.

Back to marks. To be accepted by an Ontario university you will need a minimum of six OACs at 60% overall. With extenuating circumstances, however, there are rare exceptions to this rule, and sometimes applicants who score below 60% or are missing a sixth credit are admitted. It's more usual, though, that a university will require a higher percentage, around 70% for entry into a liberal arts or science program. Although liaison officers and guidance counsellors can sometimes predict the entry rate fairly accurately, there are no sure bets. The universities set the entrance mark in late winter or early spring on a supply-and-demand basis, and there are only so many spaces available in each program.

If there are a great number of applicants, the university administration consults statistics, logarithms, Ann Landers and the entrails of chickens to decide which grade will give them the number of students they need to ensure they'll get enough provincial funds to balance their budgets. You, gentle readers, are each worth a certain number of government dollars to a university; what you pay out of your pockets doesn't cover the cost of your education. The government funds the university according to a complex formula. Each student guarantees a dollar value that fluctuates depending on the program of major study. For instance, an education student is more valuable than an arts student when it comes to ministry grants. Because all universities in Ontario are funded by public money at this time, they all operate by the same rules.

The trick to being accepted by the three universities of your choice is to earn the highest OAC marks you can. Some universities get a bit pickier, though. They'll look to see if this is your first attempt at an OAC subject or if you've taken a night-school course. Some also might exact slight penalties if it is not a highly academic OAC, such as mathematics, history, English or science, but a less demanding one, such as theatre arts or family studies. Most universities, though, look for the basic requirements. OAC English 1, for example, is almost universally required by Ontario universities for arts programs. Universities check what is needed for the specific program and admit students who have appropriate OAC marks and subjects that meet the entry requirements.

If you think you're going to have trouble being accepted and there are extenuating circumstances for some low OAC marks, you should document the reasons for them as soon as your school has done the interim grades in April. Some universities require a letter from you and your school plus a doctors's report (if appropriate) before they will consider entry-level marks that are below their requirements. Reasons ranging from time spent on athletics or student council to personal problems will be considered, confidentially, by admissions personnel. Send the documentation in early so that you will still be eligible for early admission and residence.

If you are completing your six OACs in the June prior to going to university, six interim grades will be sent to the Application Centre in April. You will be admitted on the basis of these grades and even offered scholarships if they are high enough. Then you must finish your OACs with marks in the range for which you were admitted to maintain your acceptance and your scholarship.

If you are in a semestered school where you completed three OACs in the fall and are continuing with three in the winter, the three final and three interim grades will be forwarded in April. Any variation on these two themes is acceptable as well.

If you've finished your final OACs by January, and six final grades are forwarded in April, some universities will give you admission immediately, and perhaps preferential treatment for residence in September.

The universities to which you have applied will continue to send you printed material about the campus and services as well as specific information about the program you have chosen. All university publications will urge you to visit the campus for special programs during March Break or on weekends in the early spring. Some will even have sessions in your city hosted by alumni, faculty and current students.

In spite of all the recruiting procedures, though, most secondary-school students have to wait until mid-June to find out which universities will accept them.

Early admissions

Strong young men and women quake as mid-June approaches, when they will find out which universities have accepted them. Around June 15, you can expect to receive letters of acceptance, rejection or deferral from each university to which you have applied. Several scenarios are possible.

1 *Oh, Happy Day! You receive offers to all three universities in the program of your choice.* The secret here is to know which university is the preferred choice before experiencing this delightful state of affairs. Then you can send your acceptance back immediately, your parents can spread the news and you can start making residence plans. If you're offered a scholarship at your second and/or third choice, you'll have to decide if the prestige and monetary considerations are enough to sway your choice. If you are undecided, make a speedy return visit to the competing institutions to ensure that you're making the right decision for the right reason.

2 *You receive an acceptance to the university of your choice but not to the program in which you wanted to enrol.* The tough situation here is that your third-choice institution offers you the limited program you really want, but you've decided that your first choice, which won't let you into the program you want, is the only university where you

will be happy. The consensus of experts seems to be that if you are committed to the program, go for it. Your regrets about not having gone to your first-choice institution will be minimal if the career decision is the right one. An undergraduate degree is basically the same at any university in Ontario; even some university presidents I have interviewed thought this was true. But remember, if you consider several scenarios *before* acceptance, you will probably know how you'll react when you come to the point of making a decision.

3 *You receive one acceptance.* Your choice here is to accept the offer and begin your university education or go back to secondary school and improve your marks. The problem is that if you choose the latter course of action, the marks for entry next year may also have risen. Further, to raise a 68% average to a 70 means you have to raise your lowest mark by 12% if you need to upgrade one OAC subject out of the required six. Many students are bored in their last year of secondary school. If you're in such a yawning state now, why would you be such a masochist as to go back a second time? If you only receive one acceptance and it's not your first choice, remember that you can transfer from one university to another later if your university marks are satisfactory. There are some disadvantages to disrupting your education this way, but it's still an option to consider.

4 *Despair – no offers are forthcoming.* A university deferral letter may say that although your mid-term marks were unsatisfactory, you will be admitted if your final marks meet the requirement. So if you succeed on this point,drive, fly, or courier a copy of your final marks, with an imprint of the school's seal on it, to the university's admissions office so you can be admitted immediately. You can also check the availability of suitable programs still open at other universities by calling OUAC's "Hot Line," which operates through the summer. The same advice applies if you enrol in summer school to improve an unacceptable mark in order to gain a September admission. Ask yourself, though, whether you can improve your OAC marks sufficiently to be accepted. Even if you do, you have to consider whether there will be a broad enough choice of courses open to you by the time you are finally admitted and whether residence space will still be available. The answer is frequently "no." The most popular courses are filled first and the students who are enrolled

in June stand the best chance of getting into courses that fit their career goals. If a September admission means you are taking courses that don't interest you, you're probably better off taking another secondary-school semester. Entering university in January or February may be an appropriate option or, if the increase in percentage needed is slight, a year of work. You can take night or correspondence courses to improve your marks and enter university the following September.

After reading about how the system operates,it probably seems that you don't have many rights as a consumer. The procedures are rigid in principle but not half as bad in practice. When you understand the principles you can manoeuvre inside them. If all else fails, and you think you have a case for admission or that a mitigating circumstance has been overlooked or discounted, call the director of admissions. It's the squeaky wheel that gets the grease, but only wheels that have a well-prepared, rational and polite argument are lubricated. Pulling rank (so your father *is* chancellor of the university) may work, but the ill will you stir up is rarely worth the price of admission.

3 *Using the university profiles*

In the previous chapter of *The Student's Guide to Ontario Universities*, you were advised to research the universities in which you were interested. The purpose of the profiles (chapter 4) is to provide specific information about the universities that will help you decide which are the most appropriate ones to meet your career requirements. The profiles are based on a questionnaire that was filled out by each degree-granting institution in the winter of 1991. All the information relates to the academic year 1990/91 unless it is stated otherwise. Also, the academic requirements only refer to OACs and not to grade 13 credits, which, although still accepted, are now almost totally phased out.

The numbered sections of this chapter correspond to the sections of the profiles. If you don't feel like reading this whole chapter yet, do make sure that you refer to the sections here that refer to the profile information in which you are most interested. That way you can make the most of the profiles.

As soon as you have formed some preliminary opinions about which institutions most interest you, request current publications from them and visit those that become a distinct enrolment possibility.

Read on to find out how to narrow your choices.

1 OVERVIEW

Each university was asked to provide a 50-word overview of itself. Read this preamble to each university's profile carefully. Because the descriptions were kept short, you'll get a good idea of what each university thinks is truly notable about itself. Waterloo, for example, writes that it "boasts the world's largest co-op enrolment of more than 9,600 students." This type of information lets you know that Waterloo is famous for its pioneering efforts in this form of education. If co-op study is important to you, then Waterloo should be investigated further. Carleton, to highlight its outstanding programs, writes that its "architecture, Canadian studies, social sciences and journalism are known world-wide." These types of descriptions may help you narrow down your choices.

Rule 3 of Gibson's Rules of research (chapter 2) warns you that assumptions often work two ways. You may have formed positive or negative impressions about a particular university that aren't based on actual fact. For example, you may have a preconceived idea that a university in Windsor would be ugly because the city's image is less than beautiful. Yet, the University of Windsor has a green, clean campus tucked in close to the Detroit River. McMaster also suffers from the image of Hamilton being a lunch-pail, industrial city. The campus, however, is more suggestive of picnic hampers filled with pâté and Perrier than of peanut-butter sandwiches and colas.

Use the 50 words provided by each university as a background to your research. Remember that a picture is worth a thousand words and these sections aren't nearly long enough to give you the clear image you'll need to choose a university. Don't judge a university solely on its brief overview. The best picture you can have is the one you snap into your memory when you visit the campus of a university.

2 PRESIDENT

The most important person at a university is its president, because that person sets the tone of the university. Some are so successful that it's not uncommon for a president of one institution to be hired by another when his or her term of office is completed. Brian Segal, for example, was head of Ryerson before becoming president of Guelph.

I've included the presidents' names not only as a courtesy to the institutions, but also because it could be useful to you if you have trouble getting your application processed. It never hurts to know the name of the person at the top.

3 ENROLMENT

This section of the profiles gives you an overall picture of the type, and number, of students who attend each university, broken down into males and females. Appoximately 51% of full-time undergraduate students in Ontario are female. Many universities that teach primarily arts subjects attract larger numbers of female students, while professional programs requiring math and science backgrounds have more male than female students. Waterloo, with its emphasis on math, science and technology, has a ratio of almost six men to every four women.

Full-time and part-time

The difference in the number of full- and part-time students may be important and worth further research if you're thinking about working and pursuing a degree part time. All three institutions in Toronto meet the post-secondary educational needs of a large urban population and have extensive part-time programs. Universities in smaller cities, like Laurier and Laurentian, offer distance and outreach education programs within their broad geographical region. Part-time studies fill a real educational need and provide extra funding for universities, but full-time enrolment is the academic and financial backbone of a university. You may not be able to get the exact courses you want at each university on a part-time basis, however. If a university has a large number of part-time students, it probably has a wider selection of courses.

If a particular university has a large number of part-time students for no obvious reason, such as serving a diverse area like Toronto, you should question why so comparatively few students are enrolled in full-time study. It could be that there are different standards for part-time admission to a particular university. For instance, you can apply to Queen's in the Faculty of Arts and Science as a part-time student, taking no more than $3\frac{1}{2}$ courses a year with a 60% average. If you are admitted on this basis, however, you won't be considered for residence and can't play sports for a varsity team. But it's a way to enter a university whose admission standards are among the highest in the province.

Graduate studies

A graduate program leading to a master's or doctorate degree requires an undergraduate degree for entrance. Not all Ontario universities have graduate programs, and some that do offer them only at the master's level, which is the next degree you can obtain after a bachelor's. You'd have to go elsewhere to advance your studies to the doctoral level.

In the profiles of each university, the number of graduate students enrolled in advanced degree programs at the institution is given, as well as the breakdown of males and females enrolled in them. Toronto, for example, has the largest number of students enrolled in graduate programs in Canada. Although these numbers are an indication of academic prestige in certain fields of study, you shouldn't use them to reject an institution if it has only a modest graduate program, or none at all. Ryerson, as a polytechnical institution, doesn't have graduate programs because it has the special function of training people to meet specific employment needs in society. Despite the absence of graduate programs, however, Ryerson has an excellent reputation at the undergraduate level. Trent has a few graduate students, but it has a strong emphasis on providing outstanding undergraduate teaching in small classes, with caring faculty. Most students who choose to take graduate degrees do so at a university other than the one at which they earned their bachelor's degree. Again, the choice is yours and, after weighing all the pros and cons, you should enrol in the university that meets your particular needs.

Commuters and residential

Another important question to ask when you're looking at this enrolment section is whether or not a university is predominantly made up of residential, off-campus or commuting students. These figures indicate whether students live in accommodation associated with the university (residential), rent places on their own (off-campus) or live in the family home (commuting). You should know if a university is heavily residential or commuter when you start your selection process because universities tend to cater to the majority of their clientele.

Generally, the larger the city in which the university is situated, the more likely the university will be a commuter institution. If you commute to a university where almost everyone is in residence you may find it harder to become involved in student activities. The main campuses of York and Toronto are largely commuter while their satellite colleges are less so. At the other extreme, RMC insists that all its cadets live in residence. The only students who commute are part-time ones.

Some universities have large numbers of students who live off campus but not with their parents, and when filling out our questionnaire, some couldn't show this group separately from commuters.

In section 14 of the profiles, "Residences," there is more specific information about residence and off-campus accommodation. If you're serious about immersing yourself in the university experience, moving out of your parents' home is a good way to go about it.

4 ADMISSIONS TO FIRST YEAR

Most first-year students start their studies in September. They finish secondary school in June, work for the summer and enter university in the fall, richer and refreshed. Most universities operate on a September-to-May schedule, offering either five full courses (approximately 26 weeks, or one year, of instruction) or ten half-courses (approximately 13 weeks, or one half-year, of instruction). Some might even offer a combination of these two choices. Others, such as Guelph, are semestered (September to December, January to April, May to August) and offer five half-courses a semester.

An ordinary, or general degree, requires 15 full courses (30 half-courses), usually taken over three years. An honours, or specialized degree, normally takes four years to complete 20 full courses (40 half-courses). Every institution has variations in pattern, as you will see once you start reading about specific programs in the profiles.

Entry dates

Each university has a September starting date, with the first term, or semester, ending in December. The second term, or semester, begins in January and ends in April. If you enrol in a university that operates on a system of 13-week semesters, you take five half-courses in September, five more in January and perhaps more in May, if you're a masochist or in a hurry to graduate. At Ryerson, for example, you need eight semesters of study to earn a degree, two per year. At Waterloo, classes are scheduled over three four-month periods to accommodate co-op programs. It's possible to speed up a degree by including summer courses.

From the admission Entry Dates section in the profiles, you'll be able to find out whether a university is semestered and to what extent. Usually, the autumn point of entry will be the one with the highest enrolment and the summer will be the lowest. At semestered universities, some programs are open to new students at the beginning of each semester. Thus, you can begin degree studies in the winter and spring sessions. However, secondary-school exams aren't written until late January and the winter semester begins in early January. So if you enter a semestered university, you may have to forgo your secondary-school graduation diploma or try to be at two educational institutions at the same time. Guelph will, however, grant a matriculation certificate if students are not eligible to receive their Ontario Secondary School Diploma (OSSD) from their secondary school because they declined to write their final exams in favour of entering university.

Other entry dates

There are other entry dates as well. After semestered secondary schools became more popular in Ontario, and more students were graduating in January, some universities initiated a special first-year program to meet their needs. These programs start in late January or early February. They allow students to pick up courses in the winter and spring that will enable them to continue into second year the following September at that university. They can also transfer the credits to another institution.

Other universities that are not semestered have special first-year programs for incoming students:

- Toronto's Erindale College started a 13-week program in 1988 that allows students to enrol in the February session and take a maximum of two and a half full credits. Most students in this program actually register in fewer courses, however, because of the compact nature of the learning experience and the work it requires.

- Both campuses at York have a winter / summer program running from February to June. Glendon College admits a small number of students to bilingual Liberal Arts study, while the main campus admits approximately 1000 students into its Faculty of Arts and Faculty of Science. Both locations advise students to take no more than three full credits under this program.
- Lakehead has a February admission program through which three full credits can be gained by the end of April. The program is mainly for arts and science students and Lakehead describes it as "intense." Residence space is available and a six-week session is offered in May so that students who wish to obtain further credits before breaking for some holidays can do so.

These special winter programs have both good and bad points. One advantage is that through them a student can earn two or three university credits in three to five months. They are particularly appropriate for students who improved their OAC marks in the first term at a semestered secondary school in order to become admissible to an Ontario university. They are also good for non-traditional students who are eager to pack in as much learning as possible in the shortest time, or for someone who got stranded while travelling and didn't return to Canada in time for the September entry. Their disadvantages are that there is little choice in courses, only a limited period to adjust to university before final exams, and a scarcity of residence accommodation.

How to decide? It depends on how motivated you are. Are you willing to work very hard with no extended holiday, such as the Christmas vacation, to ease the academic agony of first-year university study? If you accept that challenge, you have the chance to earn some university credits sooner. You'll also have the possibility of taking summer courses to further shorten the time spent gaining your degree. The choice is yours, but consider your goals carefully before deciding. University is best savoured, not gulped.

If your decide to work or travel between January graduation and entering university in the fall, some institutions will offer you admission before the early admission date in June. That means you will be accepted before the students who are still working for their OAC requirements, and sometimes you can even be guaranteed residence. Such advance admission is usually granted for programs that don't have limited enrolment. For professional programs, you'll usually have to wait until June for a decision. But, if you're an outstanding candidate in the 90% and above range, universities will be very eager to enrol you. Deans may call you personally. Special-delivery letters and engraved invitations to select soirées may arrive at your home. What power you have! But don't be swept away by their flattering interest in you. Check out the university for yourself!

By looking at the number of students who enter a university in first year, you'll get some idea of the size of the entering class. Where universities have provided this information in the profiles, you can also see the number of applicants to first-year studies, the offers of admission that were made, as well as the number of students who accepted the offers.

A university with a modest number of applications, a relatively large number of offers of admission in comparsion to those applications, and then a considerably lower number of enrolled students is probably not the first choice of many secondary-school students. In contrast, a university with a large number of applications, fewer offers of admission and a comparatively large group of enrolled students is a more frequent first choice.

Of course, you must take into account the size of the institutions when you begin to make comparisons. This information in the profiles indicates the relative "popularity" of the universities you are contemplating. Although a university's size shouldn't be crucial in your considerations, it might be a factor when you're having a difficult time making a choice

Community-college transfer requirements

Secondary-school graduates aren't the only applicants to Ontario universities. As many as 15% of first-year students may have either transferred or graduated from a Community College of Applied Arts and Technology (CAAT) or decided to enter university after working for a few years. Each university has a separate admissions policy for students from community colleges and for the non-traditional student.

When considering community college students for admission, the universities look at their college marks, the number of courses taken, whether OACs were earned and whether or not the students graduated from their program. They may even be granted advanced standing, depending on their academic achievements. Advanced standing means that academic credits earned elsewhere are accepted at value by the university and count towards a degree. For example, instead of needing 15 credits to graduate, a community college student might only need 13 or 14.

There is a great deal of interaction between the universities and the community college system. Sometimes a university and a community college will co-operate to provide a unique program. Here are some examples:

- York University and Seneca College have combined forces to offer an Early Childhood Education Program in psychology that awards both a degree and a certificate. It's taught at both institutions, with York providing the theory and Seneca the practical experience.
- Lakehead allows applicants with a Diploma in Technology from a community college, Lakehead or Ryerson to apply to their post-diploma program in Engineering, as long as they have an average of 70% or above in their final year.
- Durham College, in Oshawa, signed an agreement with several universities in its immediate region to allow access to one another's programs. If you're a community college student or graduate, look closely at the section in the profiles on Community College Transfer Requirements to see which university, of those you are considering, is likely to give you the greatest credit for your previous academic experience.

Mature students

Mature students, whom I prefer to call non-traditional, are applicants who don't meet the published academic requirements. This special status is available to people who didn't have the opportunity to go to university directly from secondary school and want the chance to do so now. Even someone with a secondary-school honours graduation diploma from the 1940s will be granted admission based on that document. If the marks are lower than current acceptance requirements, credit will be given for years of experience.

Mature-admission requirements vary from institution to institution, but at most you must be at least 21 years of age and a Canadian citizen or permanent resident living in Ontario. You must also have been out of full-time attendance at secondary school for two years. Most universities want you to have completed grade 12, but work experience is considered as well. Other universities require documents such as a personal letter, letters of recommendation, a period of probation, and bridging-course marks before they will make a decision on admission eligibility. Some programs, such as nursing at certain universities, have Challenge Exams. Mature students who can pass the exam in a required course without going to lectures are awarded a credit even though they haven't taken the course.

The process for admission for a mature student isn't as onerous as it sounds. Most universities have special information sessions just for such students. You'll feel more or less at home in the sessions, depending on how self-conscious you are about returning to school. Here are two examples of the kind of help that's available:

- McMaster has a day-long session that provides not only information about admission requirements but a study-skills workshop as well.
- Scarborough College presents seminars to hone writing skills over the summer prior to university entry and during the university term as well.

Mature students whose writing experience over the past ten years has consisted only of compiling "things to do" lists will find that these types of seminars help them feel more comfortable about how they'll keep pace with a class filled with recent OAC graduates. In fact, after a few classes, mature students often realize how much their experience adds to a typical university seminar. So gird your loins and get that application off to the university of your choice.

At this point, let's take another look at the word *mature*. If you are a mature student, does that make all the secondary-school graduates of eighteen and nineteen immature? Just how mature are you? Really, you're a *non-traditional* student, one who didn't continue directly from secondary school to university. Therefore, from now on, the term "non-traditional" will be used to describe this type of student.

Non-traditional applicants fill out an OUAC 105 form, rather than an OUAC 101. To receive one, call the admissions office of any university. The form and information on how to apply will be sent to you. A rule of thumb regarding which form to ask for is that daytime undergraduate programs, part-time or full-time, are applied for with an OUAC 105 form. Extension courses, which are often presented by specific sections of a university, on or off campus, are usually Saturday or evening programs and have a separate application form. Often, centres for continuing education or part-time studies offer degree courses as well. They generally have a separate admission form. A call to the admissions contact at the university will get you going in the right direction.

5 ADMISSIONS CONTACT

The name of the university contact designated in the profile of each university is very important to know regardless of what type of applicant you are. This is the person to whom you will address any documents concerning your admission or application status.

If you can't speak to the contact person directly when you call, accept a substitute. Registration and admissions offices are very busy and the contact listed may not always be available. Ask your question of whoever answers the phone, but make sure you record the name and extension of the person with whom you are speaking. If you are given incorrect information, you'll need to know who gave it to you if you decide to complain later. It's more likely, though, that the person who helps you will be polite and accurate and you'll want to keep his or her name handy in case you need more information at another time.

6 STRUCTURE AND DEGREES

Board of governors

In section 6 of the university profiles, you'll find a description of each university's board of governors, or its equivalent. The primary task of this body is to make policy decisions.

Governors are often chosen for their ability to attract donations to the institutions during a fund-raising campaign. Thus, the ideal board member is a president, or chairman, of a large corporation and an alumnus of the institution. Most universities, however, try to balance the membership of their boards with representatives from the constituencies that make up a university. Even though slightly more women than men attend university, no institution is even close to having 50% women as governors. Staff and faculty are also important representatives on a board because they know the institution from a work-place perspective and provide a balance to the corporate governors.

When you are looking at this section in the profiles, also look to see if students are represented on the board and, if so, how many there are. This is important because student membership means that the concerns of students will be brought to the board.

Universities sometimes go beyond their governing board to get direction on their plans for the future. Queen's, for instance, has a University Council composed of senior academic and financial administrators of the university and an equal number of graduates. The graduates are elected by their peers to represent them at an annual meeting where a theme of major interest to Queen's is discussed. In 1989, the University Council focused on the future funding of Queen's. The council assessed the needs of the institution and considered what might be the best way to meet those needs through federal, provincial and corporate funding. Dr David Smith, principal of Queen's, believes the council is unique because it allows alumni who care deeply for the university to contribute their knowledge and experience to decisions about policy.

Faculty make-up

Another important part of an institution's structure is its teachers. Teaching is mainly done at university by full-time faculty. All universities employ part-time faculty who are either hoping for full-time appointments or are involved in other work that precludes their teaching full time. This subsection in the profiles lists the total number of full-time and part-time faculty, male and female.

When you compare the ratio of full-time to part-time faculty, you'll notice that it differs considerably from institution to institution. Sometimes location, size or funding restrictions force a university to employ a larger number of part-time faculty, but that doesn't mean the faculty are inferior. If part-time faculty are dedicated and knowledgeable, they bring some advantages to the class-room by teaching while working in their profession. Because they are working professionals, they understand how class-room theories, in business or law for example, can be applied in the work-place. In other instances, part-time faculty are young and trying to obtain a full-time position. Students benefit from the enthusiasm and contemporary outlook these faculty members bring to the lectures.

Finding out which professors at a university are outstanding is often difficult. At Toronto, the Arts and Science Student Union (ASSU) publishes the "Anti-Calendar," which evaluates most of the professors in the Faculty of Arts and Science. One professor in a past issue of the Anti-Calendar was described as being very boring. Most students found that he went off topic and rambled on about irrelevant points. He showed little enthusiasm for his subject and neglected to provide class discussion. In addition, there was little structure to his course outline. In spite of all that, some students did enjoy the content and found the course interesting. Obviously, a student enrolling at Toronto shouldn't pick a course before checking out the professor's rating in the Anti-Calendar.

Many universities rate their faculty, but few make the results available for students to use when making course choices. The best way to find out about a professor's reputation is to ask upper-year students at the university. Once you know who the highly rated professors are, be prepared to have to fight your way into their courses.

Did you know that in medieval times, when universities were very new, teachers' wages came from tips the students gave them? Perhaps a return to this antiquated system of payment might rid some of the universities of their teaching duds by starving them to death. It would also be amply rewarding for the informed, accessible and interesting professors.

Another intriguing bit of information on the subsection on faculty is the male-to-female ratio. If half the undergraduate students at universities are women, why are there so few full-time female faculty members? Why are there usually more female members among part-time faculty? One of the answers is that slightly more men than women pursue graduate degrees, particularly at the doctoral level. This means that fewer women are qualified to teach at university, where a Ph.D. is almost always a requirement for a full-time teaching appointment.

You'll also notice there are very few women teaching at universities that are particularly strong in science and technology programs. Only 9% of Waterloo's full-time faculty are female. Women who decide to enter a science-related discipline should be prepared to band together with others of their sex for mutual support. Barbara Leslie, assistant registrar of RMC, said that the first women to enrol in RMC had a very difficult time in the all-male environment. It's a much easier situation now, though, because women have been incorporated into all four years of study. Other Ontario universities are also actively trying to address the male-to-female imbalance in some of their programs and in the make-up of their faculty, but it's not a simple situation to change. There are cultural and administrative issues at work here and it will take time for new recruitment procedures to increase the number of female faculty members and female students in science-related programs.

Faculty/student ratio

The figures in the profiles that give faculty / student ratios will show you how many students there are to each faculty member. These figures indicate how many faculty members are employed by the university, but note that not all of them are teaching. Some faculty members are involved mainly in administration or research, which greatly reduces the time they actually spend in the class-room or lab. Of course, it's the quality of teaching, not just the quantity of it, that finally adds up to a superior learning experience. This aspect is pretty hard to gauge from these figures. However, this section does give some indication of the number of faculty members who are likely to bump into students on any given day. You'll see that in most cases you aren't in any danger of being crushed by the sheer number of professors on any campus.

Degrees conferred

Finally, in this section of the profile there is a list of undergraduate degrees granted by each institution in 1989/90. Check the degrees to see if the one in which you are interested is available at an institution before turning to section 15. At first glance, there seems to be considerable difference in the types of degrees awarded, but sometimes it is because they are only labelled differently. Carleton, for instances, grants engineering degrees, while Toronto awards degrees in applied science; none the less, graduates from both programs are professional engineers. The same is true with business degrees, which are granted in administration or commerce. All universities grant degrees in the arts and in the sciences except for Ryerson, which, being a polytechnic, awards applied arts and technology degrees. No matter what the degrees are named, you will find them in section 15 under the proper code for the discipline; for example, 15.3 is always business, 15.7 is always engineering.

7 TEACHING FACILITIES

Class size

Teaching is the backbone of every university. Ideally, it takes place in a setting that is conducive to learning, such as small, intimate classes where the professor gets to know each student. But those kinds of classes aren't always possible for university courses that are in big demand. Huge classes are most common in first year, because students who try to keep as many career options open as possible enrol in introductory courses, such as psychology, that are basic to several possible careers. Thus, popular first-year courses often have to be held in the largest class-rooms on campus to accommodate the hundreds of students who want to take them.

The University of Toronto has the largest teaching facility in Ontario. Some 2000 students attend introductory psychology lectures in Convocation Hall – hardly the kind of excellent facility where valuable learning can take place. Keep a balanced perspective, though, when forming an opinion. The class-room is only one part of the learning experience. Toronto does have excellent facilities and resources available to make up for the size of some classes. And remember, it's only the first-year courses that can swell to monstrous sizes. In subsequent years the courses are more diversified and much smaller classes are the result.

Sometimes, universities tape lectures for simultaneous broadcast on television monitors in adjacent class-rooms. A monster-sized class with a real professor is certainly far better than a smaller one with the professor glimpsed indistinctly on a television set. Choose a real, live professor (well, it might be hard to tell from where you sit), speaking in front of a full house at the SkyDome, over an ectoplasmic form on a television screen.

Many universities that resort to large classes hire part-time faculty, or graduate students, as tutorial leaders. At York, a first-year humanities course may have 450 or more students attending a lecture, but the larger group is divided into tutorial groups of 30 to allow for discussion and amplification of the subject.

There are several Ontario universities that don't need tutorial groups because their enrolment is smaller and they are able to maintain a commitment to small classes taught by full-time professors. It's up to you to weigh the advantages of one system over the other. A larger university will have a broader offering of programs and a different ambiance on campus. A smaller one may have a program that suits you and a cosier campus atmosphere that you prefer. A visit to a first-year class will help you make up your mind.

Facilities

One point that guidance counsellors throughout Ontario stress in talking to students is to check out the facilities of professional schools and faculties of science. Because of chronic underfunding, the universities have been unable to renew laboratory equipment, renovate facilities or purchase *up-to-date* equipment as much as they would like. Queen's, for instance, has a serious shortage of class-room teaching equipment in its undergraduate Applied Science program. Dean David Bacon was quoted in *Queen's Alumni Review* as saying that "more than $12 million is needed to refurbish and purchase new equipment." Queen's is not the only Ontario university facing this problem.

As a consumer of what the universities are offering, you should find out which ones have appropriate laboratory facilities so you can weigh the quality of equipment with other important factors in your decision. Some universities have high-profile scientific facilities, like the nuclear reactor at McMaster, which is pretty impressive, but also look at their bunsen burners and laser equipment to ensure that your needs in those particular educational areas will be met as well.

Research

Universities play a very large role in research in Canada. Toronto is "among the half-dozen major research institutions in all of Canada," wrote former President George Connell, in *Renewal 1987: A Discussion Paper on the Nature and Role of the University of Toronto*. Most Ontario universities obtain large amounts of research grant money and it isn't necessarily allocated according to their size. Gerry Quinn, Guelph's director of external relations, is proud that his university "ranks third as the most research intensive university among the mid-sized institutions in Canada."

Faculty members at universities are encouraged to become involved in research within their field regardless of whether it's a scientific orientation such as physics or an arts discipline such as literature. Often, faculty promotion and tenure depend on the publication of research results in scholarly journals. This is not something that is done just for the prestige and personal recognition. Publishing in scholarly journals promotes scientific communication and contributes to academic advancements that become part of the curriculum over time.

Some universities have affiliations with other institutions and corporations in their area. This not only encourages the exchange of research ideas, but it's also helpful to a student's future career. It's important for someone contemplating a career in health sciences, for example, to know what alliances universities have with professional institutions in the community. Toronto has its own hospital, Sunnybrook, and has access to several other hospitals in the city for teaching purposes. If the quality of your education depends on practice, as well as theory, you'll want to inquire about the companies that are associated with the on-the-job-training component of your program.

This is also true of concurrent programs in education. You'll want to check out where, when and who you will be teaching.

Graduate programs

Graduate programs probably seem of little interest right now, because you know you have to get through four years of study before you'll be eligible to enter one. More and more university graduates, however, are deciding to go on to graduate studies because so many people now have undergraduate degrees. In the 16 years from 1971 to 1987, the number of students enrolled in Ontario universities grew by 57% even though the population of the province increased by only 22% (Statistics Canada). As a result, to have a career edge, many people now take either a graduate degree in their area of expertise or a second undergraduate degree in a career-related field. Those with a degree in English, for example, may decide to take a business degree as well so they will have the skills of communication and administration.

The graduate-studies section in the profiles tells you the number of graduate programs a university has, as well as what its enrolment is for master's and doctoral programs. This information adds to the overall profile of the institution. The older, larger universities generally have a wider offering of programs at both graduate levels, but there are exceptions. If you think graduate studies might be a part of your future, this section will be important in your research into universities.

Libraries

Libraries are places where you will spend more time than you can now imagine. All universities have libraries and they're not just filled with books. They also have scholarly journals, films, maps, microfilms, magazines and newspapers.

Each fall, universities hold orientation tours of their libraries so you will become a knowledgable user of these facilities. Some universities have more than one library and divide their collections according to specific disciplines. The social sciences and arts library will be in one location, medicine and science in another. Others have rare-book collections and the working papers of eminent writers. McMaster, for example, has the Margaret Laurence collection. The unique strengths of a university's library system might be important for you to know about if they apply to an area of study you intend to enter.

Some university libraries also make it easy to find material you need by having sophisticated computer systems. Librarians at Scarborough College, for instance, can help you research a topic by providing computer print-outs of all journal articles pertaining to a specific subject. So if you want to find out what has been written about the greenhouse effect, for instance, all you have to do is ask for it.

By learning as much as you can about a university's facilities, there will be few surprises when you start classes. The old saying "knowledge is power" is especially true in this situation. It's within your power to pick the university that has the facilities you'll need to accomplish your life-work goals. You'll only get the power to make a wise choice by acquiring all the knowledge you can about what facilities a university offers.

8 STUDENTS

Teaching may be the backbone of a university, but students form its heart. The information in this section of the profiles tells you how many students attend an institution, what the enrolment is in any one year of a four-year program and what portion of the student population is made up of Ontario Scholars or students on scholarships. There are also figures to show how many students receive financial help from the Ontario Student Assistance Program (OSAP).

Enrolment

You will see from the enrolment numbers that the first year has the largest group of students. This figure usually drops in second year because some students choose to drop out or "stop out," which means they leave after first year but eventually return. In a study of first-year students at Guelph, Dr Sidney Gilbert found that 10% of the students transferred to another university for second-year studies and approximately 5% left to enter a community college; relatively few students left in first year to enter the work force. Guelph's findings are typical of many Ontario universities, though very few publish the rate of student departure and the reasons for it.

When you look at the difference between first- and second-year enrolment for each university, you can see how many students did not continue at that institution. This number includes those who chose to leave, those who failed and those who weren't allowed to return because of low marks. If you're considering a university that has a 20% drop in enrolment between first and second year, you should ask what the reasons for it are when you visit the campus. Ideally, if you follow the rules for researching a university in this book, you'll be satisfied with the choices you've made and you won't drop out or transfer elsewhere.

The difference between enrolment levels in third and fourth years is also interesting. At some universities, a greater number of students register in four-year honours degrees that in three-year general, or ordinary, programs. As a result, these universities have a higher percentage of students in the fourth year. Also, some universities offer more four-year programs than three-year because virtually all professional programs demand the extra year of study. If you're interested in taking a four-year honours degree, these figures will be important to you. When you see less than 20% of a university's total enrolment continuing past third year, it probably has a limited number of honours and professional programs. Check it out, especially if the university reported that the figures were not available.

Ontario Scholars and class make-up

There is also a line in this section on the number of Ontario Scholars attending the university. Ontario Scholars graduate from secondary school with an average of 80% or above, and universities take pride in how many of them enrol at their institutions. Recently, the number of Ontario Scholars has escalated considerably. Optimists suggest that this is because students are smarter, while cynics argue that, as the university entry marks rise for limited programs and scholarship qualification, the marks of students graduating from secondary school are being given a nudge upwards as well.

The most recent Ontario Ministry of Colleges and Universities statistics (1987) on Ontario Scholars enrolled at each university give figures that are often quite different from those that the universities report. The percentages shown in this section of the profiles come from each university's statistics for 1990. They haven't been checked for accuracy.

Why is the number of Ontario Scholars enrolled at one university important to you? If there is a large percentage of Ontario Scholars at a university, you know you'll be in the company of many students who did very well on their OACs. This may not seem like a big deal, but consider the effect that many very bright people can have on one class.

Good teaching depends on receiving well-informed and intelligent responses from students. A faculty member at Waterloo said that if the best teacher in the world was asked to teach a herd of cows, no amount of skill, charisma or knowledge could make the lecture memorable for those cows because what they're capable of learning is too limited. If a teacher has a lot of Ontario Scholars in a class, several average students and a few "moo's," it's very difficult to present a learning experience that's meaningful to everyone.

Some students who have been in enriched classes, or read widely on their own, will be bored with a professor who has to present basic theory to a group of less educated students. For example, a well-read student might be able to speak with knowldege about nuclear fission, while others in the class need some introductory lectures before they can grasp Heisenberg's uncertainty principle.

By the way, you don't fall into the cow category just because you can't make an informed comment on a subject you haven't studied. But if you're in a class where a great deal of knowledge on the part of the student is assumed, you'll be lost in the subject very quickly. That's why it's important in the profiles to look at the percentage of Ontario Scholars at a university as well as the line that indicates how many students won scholarships. When a university requires higher marks for admission, it also requires higher marks to qualify for a scholarship. (The ins and outs of scholarships will be explained in the next section.) The purpose of the Ontario Scholar and scholarship numbers is to alert you to the percentage of these types of student at each university. It may, or may not, play a part in your decision-making process.

The same reasoning is true for the next line of figures in the profiles, which shows the percentage of students who require OSAP loans. Many students in Ontario qualify for OSAP, and if you're one of them, you'll be part of a large group of students at most universities. The profiles include this information where possible, but the figures were not available from several universities.

9 ENTRANCE SCHOLARSHIPS

Scholarships vary as widely in Ontario as the universities that offer them. In this section of the university profiles, several types of scholarships are listed, ranging from the most prestigious to smaller ones that only pay partial tuition.

An example of a most prestigious scholarship is the National Scholarship at Toronto. To be considered for this full-tuition and free-residency scholarship, you have to be nominated by your secondary-school principal. Each school in Ontario is allowed to nominate only one student, so academic performance must be excellent. You also must show proof of creativity and how you've served your community and school. If you're selected as one of the strong contenders, you'll be given an expenses-paid visit to Toronto's campus. During the visit, you'll meet the other scholarship nominees at informal sessions with faculty and administrators. If you succeed, and some years as many as nine awards are made, you'll receive $5000 plus your residency. The finalists are awarded an Arbor Scholarship, which covers tuition. At their secondary-school graduation, first-round contenders are given a book inscribed by a Toronto graduate to commemorate their candidacy for such an illustrious award.

There aren't very many prestigious scholarships available in Ontario, but both full- and partial-tuition scholarships are somewhat more numerous. Many of these are decided solely on the basis of marks, which are automatically submitted by secondary schools. All applicants to a university who have marks over a certain average are offered scholarships. Other types of scholarships require supporting documentation from either the school or the applicant.

Another scholarship available at all Ontario universities is the Canada Scholarship. This is a trial program started in 1988 by the Ministry of State, Science and Technology. Its intent is to try to lure academically qualified men and women into science-related programs. An equal number of men and women are selected each year as scholarship recipients. The number of scholarships available to each university is decided by how many students graduated from science-related programs in a previous year. A university with large science and technology programs, such as Waterloo, would have more Canada Scholarships available than a university with a strong arts focus, such as Trent.

Many scholarships, including Canada Scholarships, are renewable after first year if your marks remain at a high level. But don't take for granted that this will be true for you. It's difficult to attain an 80% or higher average at university, even though you may never have had a grade below that level in your life. A higher level of academic performance is expected at university because only the brightest students are allowed to enter. The academic ante rises, and as it does, average grade levels go down. Statistics indicate that the overall average of many students drops as much as 10% in first year. Figures on Canada Scholarships also show that the number of students having scholarships renewed after first year is far below the number who received them when they entered university.

The scholarship section in the profiles gives a brief outline of how many awards there are, and how much money is available, at each university. Finding out the full details of awards can only be done by studying a university's calendar closely or asking about them during a campus visit.

RMC, for example, doesn't have scholarships because there are no individual tuition or residency costs for students who are accepted. This is a military school and students who enrol must make a commitment to military service in exchange for a free education. The Regular Officer Training Plan requires an RMC graduate to serve five years as a full-time officer in the Canadian Forces. But RMC does award some students special status. Being accepted as a Reserve Entry Cadet at RMC means a graduate is only required to serve as an officer in the volunteer reserve forces for five years after graduation. There are fifteen Dominion Cadetships available to anyone whose father or mother died or was severely disabled as a result of service in the Canadian Armed Forces. The cadetship provides for up to four years of residence and recreation club fees, as well as college fees for first-year studies.

Sometimes, financial need is also considered in a scholarship at a university. At Laurentian University, $500 Alumni Entrance awards are available to three students entering first year if they have an average of over 70% and need financial help. McMaster has the Jury Scholarship, which is awarded to a student from a Bowmanville secondary school. McMaster prefers that the recipient is preparing to enter the Faculty of Humanities or the Faculty of Social Sciences. There are several of these types of scholarships that are not very well known but can provide some monetary security for anyone with a solid, though maybe not brilliant, academic performance at secondary school.

There are more than just financial benefits available to a scholarship winner, however. A place in residence is sometimes guaranteed. You still have to pay for it, but a guarantee means that regardless of how close you currently live to the campus, you'll have first choice over non-scholarships students. As well, many universities have receptions for scholarship winners in the first week or two of classes. Others have enriched courses taught by prestigious professors that are only available to scholarship recipients. After you graduate, being a scholarship winner also looks great on your résumé.

Scholarships are, of course, a way to entice well-qualified students to a university. If you're offered one at University X, which is your second- or third-choice university, you may want to rethink your decision to go to your first choice, University Y. If money is a real problem for you, being offered a scholarship will add a new factor that wasn't considered when you reached your previous decision. In that case, go back to the notes you made when you researched your university choices and add this unexpected financial windfall. If you're convinced that your future career path will be seriously affected by not going to University Y, then the scholarship shouldn't be significant enough to sway you from your choice. If, however, you're an arts or science student who wants a solid educational experience, and you're convinced you can obtain that from either institution, follow your financial nose and switch to the one offering a scholarship. Before making a commitment, though, make sure you know the terms of the scholarship offer. Is it only for one year? If it's available throughout your university career, what grades are needed to ensure it will be renewed each year?

This section in the profiles also shows the number of scholarships offered, compared to the number accepted. You'll probably see that there's a correlation between the mark at which scholarships are awarded and the number of scholarships that are accepted. A larger percentage of scholarships will be accepted at universities that attract highly qualified candidates and are thought to be very prestigious.

Finally, the surveys include a figure for the total amount of funds available for undergraduate scholarships. If it is large, it's quite possible that:

1 The university is well endowed with scholarship money because it has been in business longer. It also might attract more corporate donations because of its professional programs.
2 There is a campaign to attract more top-notch scholars to the university.
3 Scholarships are an important component of the university's philosophy.

The large funds may also result from a combination of all three of the above possibilities.

Ontario universities have agreed not to offer scholarships to more than 10% of their first-year full-time student class or to spend operating funds on scholarships. Even within these guidelines, there is considerable money available for outstanding scholars. And remember, scholarships don't have to be paid back like the loan portion of OSAP.

10 INTERNATIONAL STUDENTS

If you're attempting to research Ontario universities from outside Canada, this book can help point you in the right directions. You might be able to get more information on post-secondary education options form the Canadian consulate in your country or from education fairs. Representatives of Ontario universities attend these fairs in Hong Kong and some other cities around the world. Your school will probably know if such an event is held in your country. Also, there may be alumni chapters from Ontario universities in your country that you can approach for information. The International Students section in the university profiles will help you assess the types of programs available to you and determine what qualifications are required.

All Ontario universities accept international students with the exception of the Royal Military College, which enrols only Canadian citizens. In some instances where programs have limited space, applications from international students either aren't accepted or are subject to higher academic requirements for admission. Toronto's pharmacy program, for example, has such a high Canadian demand for admission that international applications cannot be considered.

All Ontario universities require international students to pay a tuition fee that is almost four times the amount charged to Canadian students. Because so much of the cost of a university education is paid for by Ontario taxpayers, an international student must spend more on tuition. But the other costs remain the same regardless of a student's country of origin. Therefore, make sure you're going to receive your money's worth by looking at each university carefully.

Language requirements and assistance

Universities require proof of competence in the English language. In the university profiles, you will see the language requirements for admission. All Ontario universities require Test of English as a Foreign Language (TOEFL) scores within a range of 550 to 600 for admission. Some also accept Michigan English Language Assessment Battery (MELAB) scores. Usually, if you are applying from abroad, the TOEFL test will be universally accepted as proof of your English proficiency. If you are applying within Ontario, you may be asked to write a particular university's test, not only for admission, but also to determine how well you listen and write in a language other than your native one.

Universities that require a score of over 580 on the TOEFL test may do so because they want to make sure you can cope with all the language instructions being in English. This level of competence is required because universities want you to succeed at your studies.

I've taught many international students. Some have been so concerned about their ability to understand the lectures that they tape them to make sure nothing is missed. Although one student doing this isn't disruptive, it does get annoying when ten or more students get in and out of their seats during class to flip over the tapes in their machines. When this kind of commotion is going on, the professor and other students are distracted and lose the lecture's train of thought. But this class-room inconvenience is slight compared to the frustration a professor feels when marking the papers of intelligent students who can't express themselves in English. Even if their arguments can be pieced together through a thicket of poor language and grammar, how does a professor grade the work? What is a fair grade when the paper is inferior and barely readable compared to the efforts of the rest of the class? So you can understand that a university isn't doing anyone a favour by admitting students who don't have the prerequisite English skills. If you doubt your ability to learn in a difficult, alien language, then I suggest you hold off enrolling in an Ontario university until you've improved your English.

All Ontario universities have either a special office, or staff within student services, to help students adjust to Canadian culture and to the university, especially in the first few weeks of classes. Some universities have international student advisers who will meet you at the airport and help you get settled. At McMaster, for example, these advisers also send out information on such important details as visas, university fees, accommodation and clothing requirements. This is sent well in advance of the student's departure for Canada.

There are a variety of other programs to help international students. Brock has one in which international students are tested for English proficiency. If there language skills are at a level where they can manage a full course load, they're allowed to enter a degree program. If there is doubt about a student's ability, though, three or more courses can be taken for degree credit in one year, while non-credit, remedial courses are required to increase the student's language ability.

York has English as a Second Language (ESL) tutorial sessions attached to many of its first-year courses. These give extra help, in smaller classes, to students who are having language difficulties. At Ottawa, which is a bilingual French and English university, the Centre for Second Language Learning offers advanced courses in both these languages for students who have passed first-year ESL courses. These courses can be counted for credit towards a degree. As well, the Centre, in collaboration with several departments in the Faculty of Arts, offers "sheltered" courses that enable students to incorporate improvement of their language skills into their studies in particular disciplines.

If you are interested in enrolling in arts at Laurentian, another bilingual university, you'll be involved in its Writing Across the Curriculum (WAC) program. Laurentian's program, like Ottawa's, is meant for students who don't speak English or French as their mother language, as well as for Canadian students who need to upgrade their language skills. As a condition of graduation, Laurentian requires all of its arts students to achieve specific competency levels in either English or French. This can be done by either passing a particular test for writing proficiency or taking a degree credit course with a writing component. A program of this sort can, at first, look onerous, but a university that requires writing skills of this calibre usually provides a support system for improving these skills.

The availability of basic language-skills programs is an important consideration when choosing a university. Another thing you should look at is what percentage of the enrolment is made up of international students. If there is a large percentage, there will be more students facing the same adjustment problems as you are and you won't feel so out of place. But you'll have to be careful not to use this source of comfort as your only social life. Making new Canadian friends will force you to speak more English and that will help you improve your language skills outside of a class-room situation. This experience will enhance your study program and give you a bit of fun at the same time.

Services

Some universities are extremely sensitive to the needs of international students and provide support services and social activities for them. Lakehead has a buddy system to help international students orient themselves to campus life. It also has a host-family program which places you with a Ontario family that takes an interest in you during your stay in Thunder Bay. The host-family concept is becoming popular and more universities, especially in smaller cities, are beginning to organize similar programs.

An opportunity to live and study with Ontario students is available through The International Program (TIP) at Trent. More than 400 students from over 50 countries and across Canada have been involved in this program. Its social and cultural activities include bringing both foreign and Canadian students together once a week for an International Affairs Colloquium. Trent President John Stubbs calls TIP the "yeast within the Trent system," because it gives students of many cultures a variety of experiences. He remembers the time an African dance troupe performance included two blonde Canadian students. In his view, this kind of cultural interaction adds a unique dimension to Trent, which is one of the smallest of the Ontario degree-granting institutions.

If you decide to apply to an Ontario university, ask for an application form from:

The Ontario Universities' Application Centre
90 Woodlawn Road West
P.O. Box 1328
Guelph, Ontario
Canada N1H 7P4
Telephone: 1-519-823-1940

Remember that you must allow 11 months for processing your application. So if you want to begin university in September 1991, you must apply by October 1990.

When you've completed the application form, you must include an international money order for the amount requested. The money order is payable to The Ontario Universities' Application Centre. All other documents needed for admission, such as TOEFL scores and transcripts of marks, should be sent directly to each of the universities to which you are applying. The name and address of the person to whom you should send these documents is listed in section 5 of each university profile.

11 ATHLETIC FACILITIES

Be careful not to judge a university too harshly if you think it doesn't have the flashiest athletic facilities. In many cases, the facilities of a university aren't nearly as important as the people behind them. The ingenuity and dedication of the staff and faculty in physical-education departments are what really count when it comes to worthwhile recreational and athletic experiences at university.

This is especially true for Ontario universities, because many athletic complexes are far below the standard of most American universities. In the United States, intercollegiate football and basketball leagues are a big business and attract huge crowds. Universities there can afford to pour more money into facilities and programs because they can get big revenues in return. Only a few Ontario universities have stadiums and gyms large enough to accommodate large numbers of spectators. But, as I suggested, look at the quality of the programs rather than the glitz of the facilities.

There are very few new athletic complexes under construction. Guelph opened a new one in 1990 and Laurentian has a new outdoor track, left from the World Junior II Track and Field Championships hosted by Sudbury in 1988. Some universities, like Brock, share their athletic facilities with the community on a regular basis. York has first-class facilities such as the National Tennis Centre and the Metropolitan Toronto Track and Field Centre. These facilities aren't owned by the university, however, though students have access to them.

If you're a competitive athlete who wants to continue training while enrolled at university, take a close look at which varsity sports are offered. Queen's offers all inter-university sports, while other universities offer only a few. At each university, you'll have to contact the coach of the sport in which you are interested to get details of the inter-university training available. As well, you might want to ask what the competitive records of the teams have been over the past few years. If the academic program you want is not offered at the university with the best athletic credentials, you'll have to decide whether your academic or athletic priorities will play the most important role in preparing you for your future career.

Unless you're an excellent athlete, you won't be torn between choosing the best athletics or the best academic programs. If there are organized teams within the university, that will probably satisfy your competitive or physical-fitness requirements. Also, these intra-faculty sports are enjoyable social outlets that enable you to meet people from other faculties, departments or colleges. Usually, a student can sign up for a team at the athletic office and be placed.

Besides these intramural competitions, there can be recreational teams formed mostly for the simple enjoyment of playing the game. Scarborough College has indoor baseball, played in the gym with a "mushball," that has rules of its own. On selected Fridays in the winter, a Blitz Baseball Tournament is scheduled. Teams of ten members, each with no more than six of either gender, have one inning to score runs. No bunting is allowed and a ball caught in the rafters means the player is automatically called out. This is typical of the kind of recreational sports offered by universities.

Out of almost 5000 full-time students at Laurier, about 3000 signed up for intramural sports in 1988/89. Queen's gives varsity letters for athletic involvement, based on a system of points awarded for each team on which a student plays. This is a neat way for Queen's to encourage students to participate, and it boosts university spirit at the same time. If you want to keep fit with aerobics, weight training or swimming, all universities have recreational programs that are either free or available for a small fee. Students at Laurentian and Lakehead are avid cross-country skiers. They clamp on their skis and stride out from campus.

To find out whether a university has the kind of athletic programs you want, drop into the athletic office and question the staff and students about what is available and readily accessible. You wouldn't join a health club or a squash complex without finding out exactly what's included in the price, would you? Apply the same smart-shopper mentality to researching universities. Athletic facilities and programs are included in your university fees and it costs you nothing to ask questions.

12 STUDENT LIFE

While academic experiences are of great importance, they do not, on their own, make a university experience memorable. A lot of time has to be spent on keeping up with demanding courses, but there also has to be leisure time when you relax and blow off steam. Universities are wise enough to know that students who have a balanced academic and social life will be satisfied with their university years when they graduate. That's why a university does much more than just deliver courses. There are campus pubs, dances, clubs, student councils and organized themed activities such as Homecoming.

University social life is a blend of the good times that just happen and the ones that are planned. Universities are usually very supportive of the social life they can control and a little less enthusiastic about spontaneous Thursday night revels. But those students pranks and impromptu parties are part of an institution's tradition too and they add to the overall spirit of a campus.

Student administration

The students I talked to during my tour of Ontario universities thought the amount of student involvement with the administration was an important thing to look for when shopping for a university. Where there is significant involvement it means there's a network in place for communication among faculty, staff and students. This allows problems to be solved together, with each side's point of view getting a fair airing.

All universities, depending on size and complexity, have one or more student councils. How active students are in university issues varies from campus to campus. At Windsor, for instance, students occupied President Ron Ianni's office to make sure he heard their concerns about the university's investment in stocks that were linked to South Africa. As a result, Windsor sold its stocks. Ianni took pride in the confrontation because he felt the students showed a certain amount of trust in the administration by thinking their complaint would be listened to and get the action they were demanding.

When students are involved in the administration of a university, it can create a spirit of accomplishment and goodwill. Students at Queen's have sponsored incoming scholarships for a refugee student, as well as for one from South America. At Waterloo, the engineering class of 1989 pledged $94,000 for a long-term program of buying undergraduate teaching equipment. Making a financial commitment that will last several years certainly shows that these students were satisfied consumers of what Waterloo had to offer.

At Queen's, its 130-year-old volunteer Alma Mater Society runs several social functions and services that either don't exist at other universities or are run by staff. It arranges bus services from Kingston to Ottawa, Montreal and Toronto at reduced rates so students from those areas don't have an excuse for not going home for a weekend or two during the term. The society also publishes a book that lists current students' names, addresses and phone numbers. It's handy for keeping in touch with students, and for finding others from your past. ("You'll *never* guess who's here, Sally! Remember that hunk of a camp counsellor? Well, he's at Queen's in his fourth year. I think I'll go hang out on his porch tomorrow.")

Many universities have an ombudsperson to handle student concerns. Most are paid by the administration but in some instances, such as at Carleton, half the salary comes from student funds. At Queen's, the position is called the Rector and the imcumbent is elected by the students. The Rector sits on Queen's Board of Trustees and acts as a mediator between students and administrators.

Another vital link in campus communication is its radio stations and newspapers. They are usually funded through student fees, so they have to stay relevant to their student listeners and readers to keep their financial support. Radio and newspapers not only report all the news about the university, but also provide training for students who want to enter media-related careers.

Clubs and student centres

Campus clubs come and go depending on how many students can be grouped together during any one year to support a certain issue or personal interest. (Universities made up of affiliated colleges have a greater number of groups.) You can find out whether a university has organized activities that match your interests by looking at a list of the clubs and groups on campus.

Another focus for campus activities is the student centre. It often has lounges, pubs and space for clubs, as well as a range of student services. McMaster, for example, has a special room in which commuting students can congregate and get to know each other. These types of centres are springing up at several universities across Ontario. The oldest, and most prestigious one, is Hart House at Toronto. The warden of Hart House, Richard Alway, says the centre's main role on campus is to provide informal educational programs ranging from debating to tai chi. Committees controlled by students plan and evaluate the activities and organize fund-raising campaigns that support the programs. Hart House also has one of the oldest small theatres in Toronto, as well as an art gallery. It is unique among student centres in Ontario, but then, it's been around a lot longer than any of the others. Good facilities take time to develop.

Pubs

All universities have pubs on campus. Brock has Alfie's Trough, named after General Brock's horse, and Waterloo has Federation Hall, which can accommodate 1200 people. Live concerts are also played here and are often sold out. Thursday nights are the big evenings at pubs because Fridays tend to be light teaching days and some students like to take off early for the weekend.

There is concern about underage drinking on campus, as well as in the communities surrounding a university, and this makes it virtually impossible to be served if you're underage. Some pubs, like Federation Hall, allow underage students to enter but they won't be served alcoholic beverages. Others refuse to admit anyone under the age of 19. There's also concern about excessive drinking and most universities have very active drinking awareness programs in place.

Orientation

Orientation programs at university are the most important events you'll attend before sitting down in your first classes. They are your introduction to both the social and academic life you're about to begin. Without these programs, you'll feel like an alien on a foreign planet when classes start. Orientation helps you find out where things are and what academic expectations you will encounter. It also allows you to have a great time socially while you're getting acquainted with your new surroundings. Depending on the university, orientation may last most of the summer or for only a few days immediately before the start of classes.

At RMC, all accepted applicants are required to attend an eight-week, pre-academic Basic Officer Training course. Because of the discipline required to meet the rigorous demands of RMC's educational program, this form of orientation is a mandatory test of an incoming student's stamina. Some find the discipline too much to take and drop out. But those who succeed are then required to face a schedule that RMC's principal and director of studies, Dr B.J. Plante, says is like trying to keep "three balls in the air and catch the axe." Here is an outline of one day in the life of an RMC student:

6:30 a.m.	Reveille, wash, dress, defaulter's parade, room inspections
7:00 – 8:00 a.m.	Breakfast
8:00 – 11:30 a.m.	Classes
11:30 – 12:40 p.m.	Lunch
12:40 – 4:10 p.m.	Classes
4:25 – 7:00 p.m.	Sports (Tuesday to Friday) or Tutorials (Monday)
5:00 – 7:00 p.m.	Dinner
7:00 – 10:00 p.m.	Study period
11:00 p.m.	Lights out for recruits

Weekends for first-year students aren't always kept open. Special sessions, such as learning survival skills for Canada's inclement climate, are sometimes scheduled.

Prior to its orientation, Guelph offers a Start Program. This gives incoming students a choice of three, two-day sessions during which they can get familiar with the campus. The program, which costs approximately $100, includes residence, four meals and all program materials. Start's aim is to give students a glimpse of residence living and the academic expectations they'll be facing, plus the chance to become familiar with campus resources and extracurricular activities. In the process of becoming comfortable with the university, Guelph hopes these students will find old friends and meet new ones. Parents are also encouraged to attend a special session that acquaints them with the university and discusses some of their concerns. Parents stay off-campus in nearby accommodation, much to their children's relief.

There are many approaches to orientation but its main goal is to get as many students as possible to attend. Commuter students who live close to the university they're about to enter often skip orientation because they think they know everything there is to know about the campus. They couldn't be more wrong. They may know the university from an observer's point of view, but not as a consumer of its services.

Orientation is the introduction they need; by skipping it, commuter students make their first couple of weeks on campus much harder than it has to be.

Universities have different ways of attracting commuter students to campus before the first day of classes. When it found that only 20 per cent of its new commuting students were attending orientation, Laurier pitched tents so that they could stay overnight and join in the activities. Generally, Laurier's orientation includes information sessions, auditions for the Faculty of Music, and later registrations. Laurier, along with Waterloo, also enlists the high spirits of freshmen for community service: the students shine shoes and wash windows in the Waterloo community to raise money for the fight against cystic fibrosis.

When I was a student at Toronto, around the time the glaciers receded from Lake Ontario, one of our orientation activities included scrubbing Bloor Street sidewalks with a toothbrush while wearing outrageous clothes. Most universities have abandoned this demeaning type of activity at orientation.

If you skip orientation you'll only be hurting yourself. Obviously, universities think the process is worthwhile, as do the students who attend because many become volunteers for the next year's orientation program. All the students I talked to were convinced that orientation was one of the main reasons they were able to adjust to the social and academic changes of university. It's a relaxed few days of fun before the crunch of classed begin. Don't miss it.

13 STUDENT SERVICES

Orientation helps you adjust to your arrival at university, but throughout your years there a wide range of student services are available to help you get through troubled times or to give guidance if you are stumped by a difficult decision.

Counselling

At some universities, psychological counselling is available by appointment only. Other universities have a counsellor available on a drop-in basis during office hours, and someone may be on call during the evening hours. These services are more critical than you may think. November and March are suicide months at university. This is the time you realize you haven't done all those things you were supposed to do, and you're frantic about blowing your year. You got a D on an essay, there are two reports that had to be done yesterday, there is a seminar presentation for tomorrow and, to top it off, your romance is on the rocks. You can't cope! Going home isn't going to help, but going to get counselling will help put things into their proper perspective. When you're researching universities, make sure the services you might need are available. They can make a big difference.

Career counselling is also available at all universities. Matching job aspirations to academic choices is a process that should be undertaken very early in first-year studies. University career centres have information on careers, salaries and the anticipated supply and demand of jobs in the future. As well as career counselling, staff present workshops on résumé writing, interview skills and job-search techniques. Often the career centres will invite employers on campus for employment fairs, which often lead to student jobs. For those students who don't have a clue about what they want to do, testing is available that highlights their interests and skills and then suggests what possible employment directions they might consider.

Career centres are often helpful when a change in a career goal occurs in first year. Students who are sure they want business in the first semester may consider changing to a philosophy major in the second. Business courses may not be what the student expected and philosophy, a subject they'd never taken before, may have become their reason for living. The career centre can help that student decide whether the change of focus is a transitory aberration or a divine revelation for his or her future. You want to be sure that you're really more interested in becoming an existentialist philosopher than president of IBM before you write home to tell the family. Such changes in life-work direction have caused parental howls of anguish, followed by a cessation of funding.

Peer counselling at university isn't as common as the first two types of counselling, because peer counsellors are usually volunteers who need to have counselling experience as well as the time to spend with students. It's a very useful service, however, because sometimes it's easier to discuss personal problems with someone your own age. At

Western, there's a special Peer Advising Program for off-campus, first-year students to help them with the transition from secondary school to university. The advisers draw on their own experiences of integrating into university and provide support and direct contact with services at Western. The program starts during orientation week and continues until the exams before Christmas. At Windsor, the students government runs a peer counselling service that includes a hot line for upset students who need to reach a friendly, informed student volunteer.

Medical services

It's comforting, especially to parents, to know that there are medical services on each university campus. Some have nurses and doctors available every day; others have nurses on staff and doctors on call. Most universities, like Laurier and Windsor for instances, provide a full range of services such as health counselling, birth-control advice and allergy injections. At Laurier, each new student is required to submit a medical form and be enrolled in OHIP. Did you know that once you're 21, you must carry OHIP independently of your parents? You have 30 days after you reach 21 to apply. If you don't, there may be a three-month waiting period for coverage depending on individual circumstances.

Special needs

There are also services, provided in varying degrees by the universities, for students with special needs. All universities have services for hearing-, visually- and mobility-impaired students. In the summer of 1989, grants were made to Ontario universities to allow them to improve their existing services. Therefore, there are more, and better, services available for students with disabilities.

The rule of thumb, again, is to check the situation out. In the case of wheelchair accessibility, don't take it for granted that a university claiming to be 90% accessible is going to meet your needs. That 10% of unaccessible space may prevent you from attending a prerequisite course, or enrolling in a program, because a building may not be wheelchair-accessible.

But universities do try. Here are a few examples:

- Toronto is not as wheel-accessible as some universities constructed more recently. Toronto does, however, try to relocate courses to meet the needs of students confined to wheelchairs.
- In its Accessibility and Resource Guide, Carleton has provided a manual for disabled students that helps to inform the special-needs student on all aspects of university life, even access to Oliver's Pub.
- Residence is an important consideration for disabled students. Dependence on transportation to and from the university, the scarity of off-campus housing designed to accommodate wheelchairs, and distances between class-rooms all conspire against mobility-impaired students. Scarborough College has accommodation in new townhouses that integrates two disabled students into a group of six residents.
- Carleton has a Residence Program for the Disabled that allows severly disabled students to live in specially renovated rooms with an Attendant Care Program. As a Carleton student wrote, "discovering the importance and significance of belonging and socializing is an integral part of a successful independence."
- When Canada's winds blow and snow ices the sidewalks, it is reasurring to realize that a tunnel system lurks underneath the walkways. Carleton's system of tunnelling permits almost total access without going outside. Other universities such as York have a similar system.

The bottom line, however, is how much support you're going to get from the university as a disabled student. Starting university studies is always a challenge; to begin your post-secondary degree with disabilities puts even more pressure on you. Make sure you can count on the university to help integrate you successfully. This can only be done by visiting the campus, talking to the co-ordinator for disabled students and verifying what services are in place.

A total handbook could be written about access for disabled students, with a subsection for those students who come to university with learning disabilities (LD). York has a Learning Disabilities Program that is a model in the province. Not only does this program provide support to students with identified learning disabilities, it also develops clinically sensitive diagnostic and screening procedures that clearly identify LD students who have the ability to succeed at the university level. To help LD applicants to York with admission requirements there is a modified admissions procedure that is implemented by the Admissions Office and the co-ordinator of the Learning Disabilities Program.

Other universities may not have as extensive a program, but all of them have services available to LD students. They will negotiate with faculty on testing procedures and counsel students regarding appropriate learning techniques.

Writing/study skills

It is becoming much more common to have remedial academic services available for students whose performance, particularly in English and mathematics, is below the university level. At York, there is a Mathematics Learning Centre that provides a student with a diagnostic test and, if necessary, a series of assignments to raise mathematical competence. For more than seven years, Western has helped students adjust to campus life through a program called the University Life Project. This is a non-credit course available only to first-year students. It explores such educational components as learning skills, note-taking, textbook comprehension and exam survival techniques. In this nine-week course students commit two hours a week beginning the first day of classes. Approximately 175 students enroll for a modest fee; students describe the course as being "informative, educational, fun and good stuff."

Some universities have an English-requirement component that a student has to pass before graduating. At Laurentian, you may either pass a competency test, which is given twice a year, or successfully complete a full credit course with a writing component. If you choose to take one of Laurentian's Writing Across the Curriculum (WAC) courses, you'll first write a test to find out what your language problems are. A WAC course can be incorporated into most arts subjects and it includes professional coaching throughout the exercise of writing an essay. Laurentian argues that academic writing "is an integral part of [the] learning process. A paper is not an isolated lump of work – it is one of many necessary steps in becoming educated."

Western agrees. Its degree requirements for earning a three-year B.A. (15 courses) include the successful completion of two designated essay courses, only one of which may be a first-year course. Extensive writing assignments are required, which are overseen by professors trained to help students with their weak points. This requirement, like the one at Laurentian, may be satisfied within a wide range of subjects.

Most universities offer remedial services for writing. At Scarborough College, a Writing Laboratory offers instruction ranging from coping with grammar and punctuation to the organization and rhetorical development of essays and reports. You can even sign up in May for a four-week, two-nights-a-week course at Scarborough to strengthen your grammar skills before entering university. Queen's has a Grammar Hotline for when the chips are down and the unavoidable essay needs some guidance. How comforting it is to know that help is at the end of the line when you're faced with the finer points of grammatical construction.

Why do I stress these services? Not just to take up space in *The Student's Guide*, but because you may need them. Even excellent students often experience a decline in marks of 5 to 10% when they go from secondary school to university study. Borderline students who have honestly assessed their need for help can avoid a similar and, in their case, often disastrous drop in marks by using study-skill services at the start of first year. You may have been a star in East Whimplesnail Collegiate, but that could change once you cross the threshold into the world of advanced education. Make sure there's a parachute available for you at the institutions you're considering. It's a matter of academic life and death.

Mature student association

You may not think it's important now to have access to a mature student association, but wait until you're enrolled as a non-traditional student. When I returned to university, I wore jeans and walked backward, hoping I'd fool everyone into thinking I was a regular student. Forlorn hope! If it hadn't been for other equally noticeable non-traditional students, I don't think I could have coped. If you enter straight from secondary school, your path is traditional, and a natural progression. Non-traditional students are reversing the usual order of school followed by work, especially if they're pursuing their studies full-time. They often feel out of step with the majority of university students.

Non-traditional students need a group of other like-souls to talk to about their immersion into university studies. It's not necessarily harder, but it is certainly different to return to school. ("What do you mean you only got a C in logic, Dad? I think you'd better be grounded for two weeks until your marks improve.") The change of role from bread-winner to full-time student, from home-maker to essay writer, sacrifices security for the risk of academic failure. This switch in life roles can be a traumatic experience. Some universities offer counsellors for non-traditional students, lounges for them to meet in and special courses to help them cope. There are also scholarships available. York has several for entering first-year non-traditional students.

Off-campus housing

Off-campus housing registries are very important if you don't get into a residence, or choose not to live in one. They're especially important too if you're a non-traditional student and know you're past the stage of enjoying Animal House-type antics in residence.

Off-campus housing provides a viable alternative to residence and should be seriously considered when applying to a university. Some of the points to consider when researching it are:

- Is there a definable student ghetto? There certainly is at Queen's. Ottawa has the Sandy Hill district, which is currently undergoing Yuppification. The ghetto may not be cheap, or even attractive, but it is the place where students live, and parties occur. You're living with the mass of students who can't be, or don't want to be, accommodated on campus. If there isn't a student ghetto, where is viable accommodation? Check on how far it is from the campus. Do you want to travel 30-plus minutes every day to classes? Often, accommodation further away from campus will be cheaper, but it's a trade-off in terms of your time.
- What about cost? In Toronto the availability of apartments is at a premium and, if you can find one, they're expensive. In other university areas, this problem doesn't exist. It's important to know

what is available because, even though you're accepted into residence your first year, you may not be able to remain there for subsequent years. Therefore, if you intend to continue your degree you should consider whether you may have to find alternative housing after your initial year. Is it available? If it isn't, you may have to transfer to another university.

- Off-campus housing is not necessarily all bad. It can be the best of all worlds if there are other students close by who provide companionship when you need it and leave you alone when academic necessity requires solitude. You've always wanted independence, right? Off-campus housing is the real test of maturity, but you may want to wait until second year to immerse yourself in that kind of total freedom. Most universities will help you find housing, and if that's the direction you want to take, check to see if such a service is available.

14 RESIDENCES

There are as many variations on the theme of residences as there are universities. You can choose to be in an all-male or all-female residence. Brescia College at Western, for instance, is an all-female college and its residence is, of course, just for women. Many are co-ed, but even here there are vast differences, ranging from one floor male, one floor female, to shared bathrooms. Talk about culture shock! Most first-year accommodation is shared in residence, except where the university has townhouses or apartments available. In these instances, accommodation often resembles a co-op, with tenants getting separate bedrooms while sharing a common living space and domestic duties.

Some residences are attached to colleges, which means that when you choose a college for either academic or social reasons, you enter the residence affiliated with that college. At Trent, there are five residences, two located in downtown Peterborough and three on campus. Each college has special programs and facilities as well as distinctive residence accommodation. Toronto's St George campus has a system of seven arts and sciences colleges that includes a great diversity of residence accommodation. How does one choose? Obviously it's difficult because, as a Toronto publication states: "Each college has its own unique tradition, atmosphere and array of activities ... [which]

range from the stately and historical to the modern and informal." Add to that social and academic considerations. Trinity, for example, attracts highly academic students from fairly affluent homes, while St Michael's College maintains a strong Catholic tradition. Obviously, a lot of research is needed to make a wise choice. Toronto will offer you an alternative college affiliation and residence if there is limited space for admission into the first college you choose and you don't meet the requirements. Beware, however, that if you don't specify your order of priority for all colleges at Toronto, your application may be returned as incomplete.

Some universities, such as Western and Toronto, have satellite housing available at fraternities and sororities that are close to the campus. There are pluses and minuses to fraternal orders on campus. If you are sure of being asked to join ("pledged") and can afford the cost of membership, the friendships you'll make could add to your overall enjoyment of university life. If, however, you either reject the idea of fraternities and sororities, or think you'd be rejected by them, don't force the issue. The status you think you might gain from a membership won't be worth the personal turmoil it will cause if you're not right for them, or they're not right for you. So if you're not sure a sorority or fraternity is for you, put it on your list of things to check out when you visit a campus. After you get a variety of opinion from alumni and students, you'll know whether this is an option for you.

First-year availability

Research the availability of residences by finding out the percentage of undergraduate students who are in residence. By referring to section 14 of the profile, you can determine the number of places reserved for first-year students. Some universities reserve places for scholarship winners, and many deny residence to applicants whose home address is within a certain distance of the campus. Once you've sorted through these data, you'll begin to see what your chances are for getting a residence space at certain universities.

RMC and Guelph are among the universities that assure a place in residence for all first-year students whose applications are accepted early. But other universities have limited residence capacity and select students based on marks, lottery or a first-come, first-served basis.

McMaster, for example, guarantees residence to its applicants with an 80% or better grade average, as well as to out-of-province applicants with a similar average. It then has a lottery to decide which applicants get the remaining places. Ryerson, which currently relies on off-campus housing for accommodating students, will have a 550-bed residence by September 1991. Many other institutions are building new residences too, so there will be more on-campus accommodation available over the next few years.

Another wrinkle in this accommodation dilemma is that when you accept a university through the Applications Centre, you may not know if you are guaranteed residence. By confirming one of the offers of admission, the Centre automatically cancels the others. Thus, if you find out in mid-July that you have lost the lottery for a residence space, you can't fall back on your second university offer. Even if the program you want is still available at your second choice, it's unlikely that spaces in residence will be.

After first year

If you are sure of a residence space in first year and think you'll want to remain in one throughout university, then consider what the rules are for getting a place in subsequent years. Remember that you are entering a three- or four-year contract with a university and you have to think about the long-term implications. How many residence spaces are allocated for students after first-year? If the number is low, that means most residence students will be in first year and your chances of getting a place after first year will be slim. Also, the absence of older and wiser second- and third-year students means you won't have the support in residence you might want to guide you through first-year traumas. ("I know, Kathy, four essays in the next three days seems like an impossibility, especially when one in on the implications of free trade in the 21st century, but it can be done if you banish sleeping, eating, and Ralph from your life.")

Support systems

Good residence complexes do have a support system in place. Consider McMaster as an example of what you can expect in a well-run residence. As a first-year student there, you can choose from male, female and co-ed accommodation. You can even apply to a Lifestyle Residence, of which there are three choices: La Maison Française, designed for students with French as a first or second language; International House, for both Canadian and international students who want to learn about different cultures; and Quiet House, where the operative word is *shhh* ...to ensure silence for the dedicated sleeper, the serious studier or those who prefer less noise on principle.

All universities have experienced people in control of university living. At McMaster, the residences are governed by Hall Members elected by students of each residence (unlike dons, who are usually chosen by the university). They are responsible for discipline, the observance of rules and regulations, the organization of social and athletic events, damage control and the general welfare of the residence members. McMaster is proud of this residence administration because it depends on the students electing representatives they trust. The elected Hall Member works within a constitution to provide counselling and advice on policy. McMaster administrators say this system of self-government is unique among residences in Ontario. Through it, the administration and student representatives have been able to negotiate compromises on disciplinary matters that could otherwise have been contentious.

Ideally, in any residence, you'll have a room-mate you can get along with. ("I'm sorry, Mick, but you can only play your Mozart in equal time with my Stones." If Mick is deaf to both compromise and the Stones, and he's driving you crazy, request a transfer.) The general housekeeping routine in a residence includes supplying clean bed linen once a week, but you're expected to provide your own towels and keep your room clean. There are laundromats in them too for your personal washing. You'll probably study in your room or the library, although there are common rooms you can go to within the residence. A communal phone is provided, but you can have a private telephone installed in your room, if you're flush enough to afford one.

Meals

Meals are served in dining-rooms either connected to the residence or close by. A meal plan is purchased at the beginning of the year. Some universities offer choices of meal plans based on the number of days or meals you'll be taking in residence, or the amount of food consumed. The flexibility of these plans allows the university to cater to the person who wants three meals a day, seven days a week, as well as to those who prefer to have a set, dollar amount that suits their appetite or erratic eating schedule. Some students will require a less extensive meal plan if they choose to go home each weekend to eat courtesy of their parental units and return to school with a CARE packet of food for the week. Of course, if you choose to share an apartment or townhouse at Scarborough, Erindale or Lakehead, check out the girth of your house-mates to see if you'll get your fair share of the co-operative food purchase. Food was something you learned to take for granted at home, but once you start paying for it yourself, it becomes a sole possession rather than a shared commodity.

Your choice of residence requires careful research. Being able to get accepted into residence may be the deciding factor in choosing a university if all other factors are the same, but it's rarely that simple. The program you want, the mix of students and the general academic reputation of the institutions will play a part in your decision. There are usually enough options within the residental offerings to allow some flexibility. If you want the program and approve of the faculty and students, then you can afford to give a little on the residence.

Try to go for the type of residence you want, such as co-ed or a single room. But if the university has everything else you need, don't reject it just because it offers a single-sexed residence or a double room.

15 PROGRAMS OF UNDERGRADUATE STUDY

Basic information

Each university needs a structure for offering courses and it does this by grouping subjects together into faculties. When you first start looking at faculties, and the courses they offer, it can get confusing because each university has a different way of organizing its programs. To keep this organization straight in your mind, compare it to shopping in a large store.

The store (university) organizes its products (courses) into departments (faculties) so the consumer (student) benefits from all the related products being close together. A store puts tennis rackets in the sports department, and stereos in appliances, with sales specialists in each area who know what they're talking about. If every product was stuck anywhere in the store without departments, shopping would be a nightmare. You'd also have a hard time finding sales staff who specialized in what you wanted to purchase. It's similar at a university. Courses and programs are clustered together, according to the relatedness of their subjects, into faculties. You know, if you're walking down a hallway of chemistry labs on campus, that you're not likely to find someone who will talk to you about English courses. You've stumbled into the science faculty when you should be looking for arts.

You'll notice there are several variations on how faculties are structured among the universities. Trying to sort them out can get frustrating, but remember that faculties are important because, in the end, the majority of courses that make up your degree will have been taught by one faculty. If you majored in engineering, for example, you'll have more credits from the faculty of science than anywhere else. Except that some universities group engineering within a faculty of engineering instead of a science faculty, and there's one (Lakehead) that teaches it through a Faculty of Professional Studies. See how confusing it can be ? Don't be discouraged. It's easy once you get the hang of it.

Picking faculties

At some universities you can choose to major in a subject in one of two faculties. Let's use geography to show how this set-up can affect your career direction. At York, for example, you can major in geography either in the Faculty of Arts or the Faculty of Science. If you're in Arts, most of your courses will be in Arts, whereas in Science you will be taking science and mathematics as part of your program. The geography courses are the same regardless of which faculty you are in; only the supporting courses that surround your major are different. Thus, in this case, when you're deciding which faculty to enter, base your choice on the subject area you do well in and enjoy. But also remember that each faculty is preparing you for a different career direction. Your career will be rooted in your knowledge of geography, but the courses you support it with make a big difference. A faculty of science direction gives you a B.Sc., leading you into a science-related field such as research, medical geography or demographics. A faculty of arts choice gives you a B.A., which could be a ticket into urban planning, teaching or land development.

Here are five guidelines for deciding which faculty might be right for you:

1 If you know the academic area in which you are going to major, then check out the department within the faculty that is responsible for the program at each university you are considering. For instance, if you intend to major in mathematics because you want to become an actuary, then make sure the courses offered will enable you to meet your goal. You can always check with the professional association to make sure that the courses are the appropriate ones for your professional accreditation.

2 If you're told that there are renowned faculty members in the mathematics department, make sure they teach at the undergraduate level. Some high-profile professors teach only at the graduate level, if then, while others have only select seminars for small numbers of students. There's no point in hoping to have the expertise of an outstanding professor in mathematics if the only time you see him or her is seated on the platform at your graduation.

3 If classes are large, find out if there are tutorials. Although small classes taught by dedicated full-time faculty members are usually preferable, it's still possible to have a good learning experience if the class size is large. Much depends on the subject-matter and the accessibility of the faculty to the students. Remember, there should be tutors available to augment the lecture with small discussion groups.

4 Some prerequisites to the most popular and prestigious programs at the university are "killer" courses. If you can't pass the killer with a certain average, you can't continue with second- and third-year courses that rely on the killer for basic knowledge. If you are preparing for actuarial accreditation, for example, there will be an introductory mathematics course that you must take. Inquire into the mark that's needed to continue from that course into actuarial stream courses. If you also ask about the failure and drop-out rate, you'll know before you decide on that university what percentage of

students successfully enter the upper-year actuarial program, compared to the number who attempted to do so but failed.

5 If you want a particular program, research the kinds of choices that are available at each university. Again, using the example of actuarial science, you would have the choice of entering a faculty of arts and/or science at most Ontario universities or, possibly, enrolling in the Faculty of Mathematics at Waterloo. Waterloo's Actuarial Science program has a co-op option, and approximately 80% of the enrolling students choose it. If you prefer not to be a co-op student, of don't have high enough marks to apply, there is a regular system of study. To be considered for entrance to the Faculty of Mathematics, however, an average of 75% is required. In 1985, 78% of the successful candidates at Waterloo were Ontario scholars with an 80% average or higher.

Now, to muddy the waters even further, let's talk about the difference between three- and four-year degrees within faculties.

General or ordinary degrees

There are three-year degrees that allow you to place the coveted B.A. or B.Sc. behind your name, but they don't carry enough credits to let you continue on to graduate school. You'll need a four-year, "honours" or "specialist," degree to do that, and I'll tell you about those in a minute. Three-year degrees require 15 full courses at a specific grade-point average (GPA) to be completed before you graduate. Referred to as "ordinary" or "general," or even "pass," degrees, they are available, in one form or another, at all Ontario universities with the exception of Ryerson, which usually grants three-year diplomas instead.

Most general-degree programs require you to take more courses in one area than any other. (This isn't always true, but we'll get to that later too.) This route gives you a degree and general knowledge about one or two disciplines. If you are intending to teach at the primary level in the education system, or use the degree as an entrée into the job market, general degrees are a good way to go.

As I said above, a general degree needs 15 courses to be completed. If you decide to have your course concentration, or major, in English, you might be required to pass six courses in English, the other nine being "electives" chosen outside of your main area of concentration. Within an ordinary degree it is sometimes possible to have two areas of concentration, say English and history. This means you may have to have five courses in each discipline, which leaves you five electives to complete the degree.

Honours degrees

The four-year honours or specialization degrees are a bit different from general ones because you'll need to take a larger number of courses in your major field of study. This degree usually requires 20 courses, though some may vary up or down from that number by one or two courses.

If, for example, you wanted to major in English at the honours level, you would need to take approximately 10 courses in English. If you decide to enrol in a combined major, English and history, or take a specialization in English and history, you need about seven courses in each subject. The honours approach would be of interest to you if you wanted to teach at the secondary-school level, intended to continue with graduate work or wanted a greater knowledge about one or two particular subjects.

To enrol in, or stay in, an honours program, you have to accomplish a better than average standing in first-year university studies. The regulations for graduation at the honours level are also stricter than those for obtaining a general degree. The rule is to always strive for honours because:

1 It allows you more latitude in the future in relation to both work and education.
2 It's easier to opt for a general degree while in an honours program, rather than the reverse, because the requirements aren't as tough for the former.
3 Since most professional degrees are also of four years' duration, an honours degree is considered to be more prestigious in the business world.
4 You want to keep your options open.

All these points are important, but you won't have wrecked your whole future if you haven't figured out how they might relate to you before you step into your first class on campus. Your first year will give you plenty of opportunities to understand the intricate ins and outs of the university system. One important thing to keep in mind, though, is that you can upgrade a general degree to an honours one later, if your marks warrant it. You may have a good reason right now (poverty perhaps) for graduating with a three-year general degree. Don't worry about this choice limiting the educational directions you might want to take in the future. If your marks are good enough, you can continue studies towards an honours degree at a later date, either on a part-time or full-time basis.

Another question to think about when you're confronting the general-versus-honours issue is: How do you want to use your degree? If you want to be an economist you need a four-year degree. A three-year degree in that subject will condemn you to being on the sidelines (possibly in the bleachers) of your discipline. It really depends on your life-work goals. To be over-qualified academically is better than being under-qualified. If all else fails, at least you'll be an interesting taxi driver.

Finally, don't lose sleep about the difference in degrees at this point. Things will become clearer (not like crystal, but like frosted glass) when you're in first-year studies. Just remember to check out the university options and see if they fit with your requirements. Make sure you know what special academic requirements are needed for honours programs. That way it won't come as a shock when you find out you have to have a certain percentage in required courses before you'll be admitted to an honours program.

15.1 ARTS
15.2 SCIENCE

All universities in the province teach arts subjects such as languages, anthropology, sociology and philosophy. Their science subjects include biology, chemistry, geology and physics. There are more students enrolled in arts and science programs in Ontario than in all the other, professional faculties combined. This isn't too surprising since professional programs such as dentistry, or law, accept a limited number of students and have stricter admission requirements, while arts and science programs are more flexible. They form the main core of universities, and many of you will enrol in one, or both, of them.

At some universities, such as Toronto, both arts and science subjects are taught by one faculty, called the Faculty of Arts and Science. Other universities prefer to separate the arts from the science courses and have separate faculties for each. York has both a Faculty of Arts and a Faculty of Science, but not all universities have such a simple division. Western, for example, has a science faculty, but instead of an arts faculty it divides these subjects into two distinct sections called the Faculty of Humanities and the Faculty of Social Science. Humanities includes such subjects as languages and philosophy, while Social Science includes sociology and anthropology.

Don't let the names confuse you. As mentioned in the introduction to this section, faculties are simply a way of organizing courses and programs, though they aren't always simple to understand. The set-up of faculties won't be the same at all universities. The main thing you have to figure out is which slot of study fits you, and then determine where that slot is within each university. If you are more suited to arts-type programs than to sciences, then start shopping for the specifics of what arts courses might appeal to you. But if you're not sure which faculty suits you best, remember that you can mix your choices in first year and make a more solid commitment to one faculty in the next.

Arts and Social Science

At most universities, the first year of study in an arts faculty is one that stresses breadth of knowledge, so don't panic if you think you're limiting your options by having too many credits in one faculty. Western insists that each entering student take at least one course in the Humanities and Social Science faculties. Choosing one faculty for registration in first year does not rule out switching to another faculty for second year. You may decide to change your major from languages (Humanities) to psychology (Social Science) at a later date. You can do that as long as you don't wait too long to switch. Think of the courses you're taking as building a path in one direction. If you decide to change directions too late in the game, you may lose credits if they aren't related to the new faculty you want to enter. Faculties have academic requirements for admission too, so if I seem to be nagging too much about planning your courses carefully, it's for a good reason.

In a faculty of arts or social science, you don't always have to choose one or two subjects of major interest. Some universities have programs that meet a wider spectrum of academic needs. Trent's Special Emphasis programs allow students to define a program of individualized study within Trent's existing course offerings. A student can approach the university towards the end of first year with a request to study, for instance, religion and medieval studies. The Special Emphasis Program will only be granted if the proposal meets the university's degree requirements. Tutors are available in the desired disciplines and there is an academic adviser available to be responsible for the student's course of study. For those students who are inspired to pursue special academic areas, there are options at other universities as well as Trent. Most students, however, can be accommodated within the existing academic structure of interdisciplinary courses at Ontario universities.

Science

The faculties of science at some universities also have departments that divide science into applied or pure (which doesn't mean "applied" is impure). A pure scientific course is one in which the treatment is highly theoretical and doesn't easily translate into a solution to a practical problem in the real world. The study of subatomic particles in physics, for example, is extremely fascinating if you're interested in the peculiar behaviour of quarks or muons, but can you build a light bulb out of that knowledge? That's not what pure science is all about.

Applied sciences, such as engineering or environmental studies, put the theory to work to solve practical problems. If you want to build a better light bulb, you'll have a better chance of doing it in an applied science like electrical engineering. Pure science refines and expands the theories of how everything in the real world works. Applied science puts those theories to work in the real world.

Science programs aren't very popular right now with Ontario secondary-school students. Initial applications to university science programs fell almost 10% from 1988 to 1989. Some professional faculties are also experiencing a decline in applications. One of the reasons for this decline may be that faculties of science require mathematics and science OACs for admission, and many students drop these subjects in secondary school as soon as they can. Anyone who hasn't lived in a cave for the past ten years should know that science and technology is one of the biggest growth industries in the world and there is a hugh demand for employees with science backgrounds. Too many Ontario students are missing the boat for some of the highest-paying jobs by failing to see the value of math and science studies at secondary school.

Now that you can tell the difference between arts and science faculties, here are a few highlights of them:

1 There are limited co-op programs available in arts-related disciplines. Waterloo has an arts co-op program that has more than 1000 students enrolled in each academic year. Ottawa has co-op programs in Translation and Leisure Studies. Scarborough, the only university in the Toronto area to offer a co-op arts program, does so in three arts programs: Administration, Arts Administration and International Development Studies (IDS). IDS has a 10- to 12-month work placement with a Canadian-sponsored development agency after third year.
2 There are more co-op possibilities for science studies. While Scarborough College has two co-op choices in the science field, Computer Science and Physics and International Development Studies, other universities offer more options. Waterloo has many options for co-op study in science; however, the Liberal Science program, which is unique in its goal of producing graduates with the ability to understand more than one field of science, is not a co-op possibility. Waterloo's Honours Psychology program in the Faculty of Science, however, can be co-op. It's geared to the student who wants to apply knowledge gained in biology, chemistry and physics to problems in neuropsychology, neuroscience, cognitive science, and developmental and clinical psychology. Waterloo publishes a list of its science alumni and their current professional status, which can give you an idea of the variety of jobs available to graduates. McMaster

now offers a new Honours Biology and Pharmacology program given jointly with the Faculty of Health Sciences. This is the first science co-op program at McMaster.

3 The Integrated Science Studies program at Carleton allows students to combine science with subjects from other faculties. For instance, you could combine journalism with science if you had a career as a science writer in mind. As an option after first-year studies in the Faculty of Science, the program is "designed by the student around a special focus," according to Tom Ryan, Carleton's past vice-president, academic. With the help of an adviser, the student can use this flexibility to customize his or her program.

4 McMaster University has an extremely prestigious Arts and Science program that admits only 50 students to first year. Offering a Bachelor of Arts and Science degree (B.Arts Sc.) after three years of study, or an honours degree after four, the goal of the program is to integrate studies in both arts and sciences. This program offers preparation for advanced study in medicine, law and business, as well as other professional fields. Developing skills in the use of the written and spoken word and considering current social issues are two important objectives of this innovative course. Guelph offers similar programs, Akademia and MPC^2 that also allow considerable latitude for independent study. They too will accept only a limited number of students.

If you are aware of the options available to you in arts or sciences, as well as the special programs that certain universities present, you'll know what credentials are necessary for admission. You probably think, by now, that you deserve a degree in Advanced University Terminology, and you're right. Onerous as this process is, however, take your time to find the fit that's right for you before you accept an offer of admission. Doing extensive research is the only way you'll get a basic understanding of the regulations that affect all the combinations of arts and science programs.

15.3 *ADMINISTRATION, BUSINESS AND COMMERCE*

Each year more than 12,000 students want to enrol in business-related programs at universities in the province of Ontario. Courses such as economics, marketing, accounting and management seem to carry the scent of money and success. Only RMC does not offer courses that have a business-career component.

If you are thinking of studying business, be aware that there are two types of programs: the ones you're admitted to in first year and those you're admitted to after one or two years of undergraduate study. In the first case, you have to work very hard to stay in the program. In the second, you have to undertake the labours of Hercules to be admitted on the basis of your grades from university study.

Universities that have a general year or two, either within the business program or in an adjacent faculty, require another hurdle before you break the tape. If you're a high achiever who enjoys hurdles, you may not mind taking a chance that your marks may drop in first year. If your average does drop because of partying, infectious mono, not enough or too many love affairs, or just adjustments to university study, you've put yourself at a serious disadvantage.

For instance, you may read in the admission requirements: "Upon completion of the first (or second) year a student may apply for admission to Business (Commerce, Administration). Students may also transfer to the Faculty of Arts and Sciences provided they have the necessary marks and prerequisites ..." You should realize at this point that the number of candidates is far in excess of the number of places. This is called the Freshman Crunch. The questions that ought to be asked are: How many students are accepted into pre-business courses in first year? How many finally enter the business program? If there is a wide divergence, do you want to take this chance? All I want you to be aware of is that there's many a slip 'tween cup and lip and a lot of them occur in first year. Be very careful you don't get your future hopes "crunched" by the discrepancy between the number of applicants and the number of open spaces.

If you're unsure you will have the OAC marks necessary to be accepted into a business program that demands an 80% OAC average or better, then look at some of the universities that do give you a chance to prove yourself in undergraduate studies. York and Western both require two qualifying years in undergraduate programs before you can apply to their Business Administration faculties. Both require similar prequisites: economics, computer science, statistics and either calculus (York) or business (Western). If you have a 70% average or better, you'll be considered for the qualifying years. Laurentian accepts students from Algoma and Nipissing, which have programs to provide the prerequisite courses for third-year entry into Laurentian's Bachelor of Commerce degree. Of course, each university will accept transfer students from other universities if they have the appropriate prerequisites. Ask, though, whether they give preference, and how much, to their own students.

Carleton's Bachelor of Commerce is an example of a university program that admits students directly into first year based on OAC marks. Carleton attracts almost 2000 applications and accepts only 300 students with averages between 70 and 90%: a 20% latitude for individual consideration. To be accepted to this four-year honours program in the School of Business you need OACs in calculus and algebra and geometry. The first year is devoted to the enhancement of basic skills, courses in relevant disciplines (such as psychology and economics) and an introduction to management and organizational behaviour. Second year continues with courses in business areas and related disciplines. In third year, courses are selected according to the student's preference in one area of major interest: accounting, human resources, management, marketing, operations management, information systems or finance.

The general outline of Carleton's Bachelor of Commerce program is similar to others in Ontario. At Ryerson, you qualify for a Diploma in Business Administration after three years of successful study, and then enrol on one year of study to secure your degree (B.B.M.). Windsor has a Bachelor of Commerce with emphasis on administration, policy and strategies related to business and a Bachelor of Commerce combined with economics. Universities that admit directly on the basis of OAC marks demand a high level of performance from students to enter the program but, once the students are admitted, the universities try to keep them by making sure they'll be successful. Queen's, for instance, has a Brain Trust, which is a buddy system to keep students afloat during adjustments to a demanding first-year program.

To be successful in business you have to be smart. To get into a business-related program you have to be smart and lucky. Go for the course, no matter where it is, if it gives you the credentials you want.

Here are some observations on business programs at the universities:

- Laurier offers co-op Honours Business Adminstration as well as a regular program. Career Services at Laurier reported that 93.9% of 1988 Administration graduates were employed at an average salary of $27,155. C.A. students earned less on the average, only $23,383.
- McMaster has a one-year general program before students continue into their subsequent three years of study leading to one of a Bachelor of Commerce, Honours Bachelor of Commerce or Honours Bachelor of Commerce and Arts degree.
- Brock offers degrees in Business Administration, Business Economics and in Accounting; the latter is offered through a regular or a co-op program.
- Waterloo has a co-op School of Accountancy that presents a Professionally Accredited Studies (PAS) accounting sequence, which is specially accredited by the Institute of Chartered Accountants of Ontario and the Society of Management Accountants of Ontario. Graduates are awarded both B.A.'s and Master of Accounting degrees.
- Guelph's Business and Management Studies presents programs in Management Economics in Industry and Finance, Hotel and Food Administration, Agricultural Business, Institutional Foodservice Management and Marketing. Some of these are co-op programs.

By not mentioning all universities I don't mean to infer that those not mentioned are any less worthy. All should be considered. Graduating with a business degree is rather like memorizing a manual on sex. When it comes to practice, you'll probably have to improvise. That's why those two years of liberal arts and science studies before entering a business major are worthy of consideration. Improvisation demands imagination and general knowledge as well as a grasp of the theory of commerce. However, if a degree in business, like the sex manual, will get you to first base, it'll be worthwhile.

15.4 ARCHITECTURE AND DESIGN

Architecture goes back to the origins of humanity, when decisions about the design of caves had to be made ("Neander, I don't like this particular cave. Its entrance isn't wide enough to carry a Mastodon haunch through. Change it!") Design has kept pace with Neander's evolution, and there are courses at many universities that build on the old and grow with the new.

Architecture is available at Carleton, Ryerson, Toronto and Waterloo. Architecture is a five-year program at Carleton and Toronto, and a four-year program at Ryerson. Waterloo's School of Architecture is part of the university's Faculty of Environmental Studies and requires completion of a pre-professional, three-year Bachelor of Environmental Studies Program, plus a two-year professional program of study for the Bachelor of Architecture degree. Because both sections are on the co-operative system, a Bachelor of Architecture degree at Waterloo takes six years. Waterloo's extra length of study can be alleviated by a fourth-year option to study in Rome.

It's not too useful to design a building and then not have a site for it. Ryerson complements both its program for an Architecture degree and Landscape Architectural Technology diploma with a technical degree program in Survey Engineering. Erindale College also has a special program, Survey Science, which is a Faculty of Arts and Science major because "surveying is both a science and art." An almost 100% employment rate is enjoyed by graduates from these programs.

Carleton's School of Industrial Design is the only one in Ontario. This four-year program trains experts in the methods, techniques and skills of modern design, either brand-new (a better mousetrap) or improvements to existing products (a dryer that doesn't destroy one out of every pair of socks). Only 35 students a year are admitted to this inventive program.

Landscape architecture degrees are available at Guelph and Toronto. Toronto's program, part of the School of Architecture, is a five-year program leading to a B.L.A. According to the school's fact sheet, the program is "based on the idea that human survival and sanity depend on a healthy setting in harmony with nature." Guelph, as part of its commitment to ecological and environmental issues, offers a 10-semester program in the School of Landscape Architecture.

For students interested in indoor landscapes, Ryerson has a four-year degree in Interior Design. It begins with the fundamental theories of design and progesses to a major interior design project. A Ryerson publication says this approach "utilizes both written and visual information [and] is presented publicly before a jury of professional designers and faculty."

Ryerson approaches design from a very different perspective with its degree program in Fashion, the only four-year degree program of its kind in Canada. One of two streams within the program, Fashion Design or Fashion Merchandising is chosen after a general first year.

You can choose, therefore, to enrol in a program of study to design something as large as the SkyDome or as small as a microchip, as tangible as a park or as fragile as a scarf. There are many options available to match your personal interests. However, the faculty or school will want more than OAC marks to make an admission decision. To maximize your chances for acceptance, make sure you meet their extra requirements in the area of supplementary information forms, interviews or portfolios.

15.5 COMPUTER SCIENCE AND APPLICATIONS

Computers have come, seen and conquered all universities. Each university in the province uses them extensively in its day-to-day processing of information. RMC has a Computer Engineering program that combines electrical engineering with computer science. There are similar programs in other faculties of engineering. At Waterloo, the Faculty of Mathematics is responsible for the computer-science programs, while many universities have schools or departments of computer science in the faculty of science and, less often, the faculty of arts.

Here are a few words of advice about researching the universities before considering specific computer programs. There is a shortage of computer facilities at most universities. Because of the limited funding available, many have entered into co-operative research agreements with major corporations that have provided hardware and software resources, but some haven't been able to do this. Look very carefully at the availability of computers before enrolling at a university. Sometimes facilities are so strained by the number of students trying to complete assignments that it's necessary to book a 3 a.m. computer time-slot. This lack of computer facilities can be extremely onerous. So don't just ask administrators; go to the computer rooms and question current students.

Also, if you intend to major in computer studies, make sure the program is flexible enough to allow for a liberal education. Computers are fascinating instruments, but a full grasp of their capabilities doesn't automatically include an education in the arts and science areas. Do you know how boring people with computeritis can become? The computer has helped solve many problems, but it has not yet determined the purpose of human existence. Therefore, look for a university whose program lets you grow in other disciplines as well as in computer science.

However, after warning you about getting too involved in computers, it is important to alert you to their pervasiveness. Make sure that courses and facilities are available that will allow you to become, or remain, computer literate during your years of university. You may wish to enrol in two or three elective courses, even if you don't major in computer science, to make sure that both you and your resumé are current at graduation.

Some of the areas you may want to consider studying are the design and implementation of computer programming languages, the design of complex computer systems, the use of computer resources, as well as the organization and management of data in business applications. Computer graphics is the application of a computer to the analysis and generation of information presented through pictures and graphs. You might even enrol in a course on "artificial intelligence" and the limits of the computer in comparison to human intellectual behaviour.

Because all universities have computer programs available, only some that seem to be out of the ordinary or to have an unusual twist will be mentioned here. You will, however, have to do some real research to uncover the university that best fits your precise interest in computers.

(No, Jim, you can **not** research the university by relying only on your computer. I know you can access their system, but you must visit the university to see for yourself. Computers never lie, you say, and they will send you graphs and renditions of the computers? Jim, trust me. Go for a visit. If you feel more secure with your lap-top in tow, do take it along when you go on campus. I'm sure you'll impress the professors.) Some impressive programs include the following:

- Waterloo has basic honours computer-science programs that combine two disciplines. Computer Science with Electrical Engineering Electives or Pure Mathematics with Computer Science are two of many options offered as co-op studies.
- Queen's and York are among the universities that allow computer-science degrees as either B.A. or B.Sc. options.
- Carleton has five options in its School of Computer Science B.Sc. degree: Software, Hardware, Computer Theory, Scientific Applications and Management and Business Systems. This is a five-year co-op program combining academic study and work terms.
- Ryerson has not only Applied Computer Systems but a program in Graphic Communications Management that teaches computerized typsetting systems as well as the role of computers in printing operations.
- McMaster has a Department of Computer Science and Systems that has several honours programs, including an Honours Computer Science and Psychology major that is entered after one year, with courses in psychology, mathematics and computer science.
- In its undergraduate calendar, Western publishes many interesting minors that can be taken with a Computer Science major. One of them is Philosophy. I wonder if a computer might challenge Descartes's famous dictum "I think, therefore, I am" by becoming rational.
- Ottawa presents a Specialized Program in Management and Information Systems (MIS) for students who are interested in the analysis of business systems or in computer science and applied quantitative methods; the degree granted is either a Bachelor of Commerce or a Bachelor's degree in Management Science.

15.6 EDUCATION

The desire to teach is similar to being "called" to the priesthood. The old adage "many are called, but few are chosen" has great relevance to becoming a teacher.

Currently, it's very difficult to enter an education faculty or school. For one thing, the number of teaching jobs fluctuates depending on demographics and retirements within boards of education. Therefore, there may be a great need for teachers foreseen in one year, only to have a surplus of graduating teachers in another. Universities respond to these trends, taking more students when there is a demand and curtailing entry into faculties of education when teaching positions are scarce.

There are two ways to become a teacher. One is the consecutive program, which is a one-year degree program entered into on completion of an undergraduate degree; this is the time-honoured path to a teaching degree and is available at many universities across Ontario. There are also the undergraduate concurrent programs, which allow you to proceed towards two degrees at once, usually a B.A./B.Ed. or a B.Sc./B.Ed. These programs are described here. The consecutive ones are not included because an undergraduate degree is required to qualify for them.

There are three levels of teaching: primary-junior (kindergarten to grade 6), junior-intermediate (grades 4 to 10), and intermediate-senior (grades 9 to 12). If you choose the primary-junior field, a generalist degree is sufficient. If you prefer one of the other two classifications, it's necessary to have one teaching subject for junior-intermediate specialization and two for intermediate-senior. The specialization depends entirely on the ages and stages of the children you wish to teach.

Choosing between the two methods of obtaining a faculty of education undergraduate degree is rather like deciding between a dish of chocolate ripple ice cream and a chocolate sundae. The chocolate ripple ice cream has the vanilla undergraduate degree with a chocolate education degree rippling through it, making an integrated concurrent-education dish. The chocolate sundae is a scoop of vanilla undergraduate degree later topped by a dollop of chocolate consecutive-education sauce.

Remember, in the first section, when you tried to determine whether you were a prime candidate for any program? If you're an exceptional student, it's always better to cash in the academic chips you're already gained when you are choosing an undergraduate program. In this case, they might allow you to enter directly into an education faculty.

Queen's University will consider students with marks in the mid-80s for its concurrent Education program. You'll be discouraged to find that there are about 12 applications for each accepted registration. But, if you consider that each applicant has applied to three universities, your spirits will rise considerably.

- Queen's Faculty of Education co-operates with the Faculty of Arts and Sciences to award B.A./B.Ed., B.A.(Honours)/B.Ed. and B.Sc.(Honours) /B.Ed. degrees. During the first three years students take 15 of the courses required for an arts and science degree and complete approximately 30% of the requirements for the Bachelor of Education degree. If an honours degree is sought, a full fourth year of arts and science courses is undertaken. In either case, the student enrols in a final year, taking any further required arts and science courses as well as the outstanding courses needed to fulfil the B.Ed. degree requirements. During the winter term of the final year, students complete a four-month internship. (Students can complete a similar program at Trent, which has a co-operative program with Queen's, in which case the fall semester of their final year will be spent at Queen's.)
- Brock and Lakehead also have concurrent education programs, with Lakehead presenting, as well, a Native Teacher Education Program. To enter this program, the applicant must be of native ancestry and be recommended by a native organization. The purpose of the Native Teacher Education Program is to meet the social and cultural needs of native communities.
- Laurentian offers a program leading to the certification of French-speaking teachers for the French-language classes and schools of Ontario. There is a three-year program in the Faculty of Arts, with a concentration in Education. An evaluation for competency in French is required before admission to this program is granted. This course of study is not concurrent, however, and graduates still have to gain their Bachelor of Education degree and teaching certification after graduation.
- A variation on this theme is York's progam: a concurrent B.Ed. program with the faculties of Arts, Science and Fine Arts. For admission to this program, however, your first-year university marks will be considered. Thus, you apply to your chosen under-

graduate faculty for first- year studies, hoping also to be accepted into the Faculty of Education in second or even third year. Even if you have a high secondary-school average, you will also need to achieve marks in the range of 70% or higher in first- or second-year university studies to be admitted to Education. In other words, you are staking your future on being admitted to the Faculty of Education based on your performance in university studies. If you are not chosen you can, of course, continue your undergraduate degree and, upon graduation, apply to consecutive programs at several universities (including York) across Ontario.

- Scarborough College has initiated an Early Teacher Option which is integrated with a Physical Sciences program. There is direct placement into Scarborough secondary schools arranged by the College and 30 spaces reserved for high achievers at the U of T's Faculty of Education upon completion of the program.
- Nipissing College in North Bay offers a B.A. Orientation to Teaching Programs which is limited to 40 students but guarantees a place in the one-year B.Ed. consecutive program to successful graduates.

The competition is stiff for admission to one-year consecutive programs. Only those with good undergraduate marks and volunteer teaching skills will be considered. The educational ice cream with the vanilla and chocolate flavours combined is most definitely preferable to the vanilla ice cream that *may* be topped with chocolate sauce in the future. The first option gives you an opportunity to practise educational theory and test your dedication to a teaching career as you proceed with two degrees.

15.7 *ENGINEERING*

So you want to be an engineer? Well, you're in luck, because 13 of the Ontario post-secondary institutions that grant degrees award them in engineering. Only Brock, Laurier, Trent and York do not. According to *Info*, the Guide to Ontario Universities for Professional Counsellors, issue no. 35 (Fall 1988), there are almost 4000 first-year places available in Ontario university engineering programs.

Some universities don't have separate faculties for engineering, but offer it through a faculty of science or faculty of professional studies. In the university profiles, engineering programs are always coded 15.7, regardless of which faculty they come under.

Guelph has a Bachelor of Sciences in Engineering, B.Sc. (Eng.), which has six major areas of study: Agricultural, Biological, Environmental, Engineering Systems and Computing, Food, and Water Resources engineering. All programs can be co-op. This option, however, should be requested on entrance. If the student's grades are appropriate after the first four semesters, co-op studies will be approved.

The other 12 universities span the gamut from Aerospace Engineering (Carleton, Ryerson and Trent) to Systems Design Engineering (Carleton, McMaster, Toronto and Waterloo). Most universities have a first year that is common to all engineering programs, which usually consists of courses in chemistry, mathematics, physics and English plus one elective.

To highlight all the engineering programs, for which there are at least 35 different designations, would require a complete book in itself. Here, instead, are some observations:

- Not all engineering specialties are over-subscribed. Some do not have as many students as could be accommodated. It might be worthwhile to find out what the least popular ones are, if you are not sure of acceptance. Then apply to one of those if it doesn't disturb you to swerve from one area of expertise to another. Some universities admit to a specific area, while others give you first year to decide. Even so, it will be difficult to enrol in aerospace or some other over-subscribed program unless you're a first-class student.
- There is a heavy attrition rate in engineering at some Ontario universities. You might want to ask each one you visit how many fail or drop out from year one to two. Waterloo, for instance, is proud of its very low 10% failure and drop-out rate. Queen's University supports its engineering students, particularly through the Buddy System, which eases the transition of first-year students to university.
- Ryerson is moving towards four-year degree programs. It is possible, however, to still receive a diploma after successful completion of the first three years of most engineering programs, if a three-year diploma is available (it isn't in all programs) and warranted.
- McMaster's Faculty of Engineering eases first-year jitters and provides a fifth-year option. When you enter into first-year studies

you will be welcomed by the Director of Level One Engineering. According to a faculty publication, this position has, as its main responsibility, "maintaining the 'esprit de corps' of the first year class." This means that each engineering student is assigned a faculty adviser, special tutorials are scheduled, career-related counselling is available and a student's academic progress is captured on a data-base to monitor academic performance. McMaster presents an attractive fifth-year option that gives you an engineering degree *and* management skills if you enter the program in second year. For the next four years, engineering and business courses are combined within a specific discipline. This program is conducted in co-operation with the Faculty of Business.

- Toronto, which offers eight engineering programs with several options within each program, has a Professional Experience Year (PEY). The program is a 16-month optional work term that begins in the May after completion of second year and continues until August of the following year. PEY allows students to obtain industrial experience in the midst of their engineering degree.
- Waterloo's president, Douglas Wright, comments that "Waterloo has always done things that needed to be done, that no one else was doing, in the interest of good students." This philosophy led to Waterloo's co-op program in engineering, which admits over 800 students every year to a total of six programs.
- Ottawa, with its co-op program, and Laurentian, with its emphasis on northern Ontario realities, both have bilingual engineering programs. Laurentian provides the first two years only of Chemical, Civil and Mechanical engineering programs, but has four-year programs in Mining and Extractive Metallurgical Engineering. Students enrolled in the former specializations must transfer to another intitution to complete their degrees.
- The greatest number of students enrolled at RMC are in engineering. RMC, too, teaches engineering students in either English or French.

15.8 ENVIRONMENTAL STUDIES, FORESTRY AND RELATED FIELDS

Ontario universities are very good at specializing in environmental issues that are of particular concern to their specific geographical location.

- Windsor's Great Lakes Institute and Department of Biological Science co-operative programs enable students from the university to specialize in environmental concerns that relate directly to the ecology of the Great Lakes. This co-op program is a first in Canada and offers students both theoretical and practical avenues for their environmental concerns.
- Trent, situated on a river in another section of Ontario, has become vitally interested in resource management. The Environmental and Resource Studies program is a co-operative undertaking of 13 departments and programs, and leads to either a B.A. or B.Sc.
- To the north, Lakehead offers a Forestry program that defines forestry in environmental terms as "the education of skilled foresters who have the desire to manage [Canada's] forests for the optimum benefit of man and his environment" – a worthy, if sexist, statement whose purpose is borne out in a four-year Honours Bachelor of Science in Forestry degree.
- Lakehead and Toronto are the only two universities in Ontario to offer forestry programs. At Toronto, after two integrated years of study, students choose between Forest Science or Wood Products Science as their major program area.
- There are several programs at Toronto's St George campus that address the environment and one at Scarborough, Terrain and Environmental Earth Sciences (TEES), which draws on the expertise and facilities of both the St George and Scarborough campuses.

Every Ontario university addresses environmental concerns in a number of faculties and departments. Engineering faculties are as cognizant of the issues as are deparments of geography. If you are interested in this field, research widely. A university may be hiding its ecological light under a bushel of another name, and without careful probing you may not find the course appropriate for you in terms of investment of time and money. Geology or biology, although not strictly environmental departments, may be program areas that will allow you to address the problems in an innovative manner. For instance, McMaster offers as B.Sc. in Honours Geography and Environmental Sciences and a B.A. in Honours Geography and Environmental Studies. Western couples a Geography program with Resources Conservation in the Faculty of Social Science. Guelph offers an Environmental Biology major in its Bachelor of Science in Agriculture program.

There are numerous other possibilities available at universities that address environmental issues. Here are some you should note:

- According to its fact sheet , Ryerson's School of Urban and Regional Planning has, as one of its goals, to "envision and formulate concepts and objectives to improve urban and regional environments, and to develop an understanding of how the process of change can be influenced in the public interest." This four-year program leads to a Bachelor of Applied Arts.
- Brock's Institute of Urban and Environmental Studies offers combined major programs leading to B.A. and B.Sc. degrees, as well as a co-op option that allows practical work experience for four or eight months.
- The newest Faculty of Environmental Studies is at York which offers four honours programs. The 80 students accepted directly from secondary school are expected to complete a 12 week practicum prior to graduation.
- The Faculty of Environmental Studies at Waterloo is the largest of its kind in Canada. It comprises two professional schools, of Architecture and of Urban and Regional Planning, and two academic departments, of Environmental and Resource Studies and of Geography. The Department of Environmental and Resource Studies is the least structured of the four and focuses on individual projects. It attracts independent, highly motivated students who don't need guidance. Co-op studies are available in each program in the faculty.

15.9 DENTAL SURGERY, OPTOMETRY, PHARMACY AND VETERINARY SCIENCE

These four programs are all very prestigious and are only available at one or two universities in the province. All of them require previous studies at the university level.

- Dental Surgery is available at both Toronto and Western. Both universities require at least two years of undergraduate study that includes laboratory courses in biology, chemistry, physics and organic chemistry. Therefore, a student who wants to enter dentistry would apply to a faculty of science (or faculty of arts and science, if appropriate) and register in science courses. The degree granted is a D.D.S. and requires four further years of study at a faculty of dentistry.

- Optometry is a four-year program at Waterloo leading to a Doctor of Optometry degree (O.D.). Waterloo is one of two optometry schools in Canada and is the only one to provide instruction in English. Competition is intense for the 60 places (in 1989, over 500 applications were received) and only excellent students with a minimum of one year of general science will be considered. The subjects that must be taken within the first year of university study for admission consideration are general biology, chemistry, physics, calculus and introductory psychology.
- Pharmacy is taught at the University of Toronto and can be entered directly from secondary school as long as the applicant has an extremely high average, with OAC subjects in English, algebra and geometry, calculus, chemistry, physics and one other subject. Also, results of the Pharmacy College Admission Test (PCAT), which should be written in the spring of the year in which you apply, will be considered in selecting the one candidate in six who will be admitted.
- Pre-Veterinary Medicine applicants to the University of Guelph require six OACs, including calculus, biology, physics, chemistry, and English. Candidates enrol in the Faculty of Science for a qualifying year that requires courses in biology, chemistry, physics and mathematics among others, before being admitted to a further Pre-Veterinary year. One hundred students are chosen to enter Veterinary Medicine each year. The Guelph calendar states that "the best preparation for the Pre-Veterinary year is to fulfill all course requirements while attaining excellence in the preparation for an alternative career" – a warning that not many students gain entry.

That advice is useful in regard to all limited-access university programs. The competition is intense and, while you may be an outstanding secondary-school student, it is within the realm of possibility that you will **not** meet your career objective. That's why preparing for a possible second career option while you are striving for your favoured choice is so important. If all your hopes revolve around one definite career and your expectations of success do not transpire, you will despair. But remember, it's the broader life work within which you can adjust your career goals that is important. So plan your educational life with options that allow you fluidity within desired career areas. And, if you are accepted, then rejoice because you will be one of a chosen few.

15.10 FINE ARTS

Sixteen of the 17 degree-granting institutions in Ontario have some breadth or depth in the area of fine arts, with the exception of RMC. As a result, if you want to take one or two elective courses in music, visual art or history you should be able to do so. Certain programs are highlighted here:

- Ryerson's degree programs in Photography and in Radio and Television both have a "definite career orientation with a good blend of theory, liberal studies and actual practice," states Dr Dennis Mock, vice-president, academic, of Ryerson Polytechnical Institute. Radio and Television, at present, is a three-year degree program.
- Queen's offers a Bachelor of Fine Arts degree in Visual Art, a Bachelor of Arts in Drama, Film Studies, Art History and Music, as well as a Bachelor of Music degree. According to a Queen's publication, the four-year Music degree aims at the "acquisition of sound musicianship and professional competence."
- York's Faculty of Fine Arts awards Bachelor of Arts and Bachelor of Fine Arts degrees in Dance, Film/Video, Fine Arts Studies, Music, Theatre and Visual Arts. Harry Arthurs, president of York, states that York's Faculty of Fine Arts is "the most complete Faculty of its kind in the country. It encompasses all of the fine art disciplines while combining academic and professional work at a very high standard."
- Toronto's Faculty of Music has unique ties to the cultural life of Toronto. The opera stage in MacMillan Hall is used for rehearsals by the Canadian Opera Company. The new music library "will be the best in Canada," according to Alan Hill, director of admissions at Toronto.
- Music, at Laurier, is restricted to approximately 200 undergraduate students – a group large enough to form an orchestra, but small

enough to ensure individual attention. Areas of study range from Baroque and Early Music to Jazz, with an area of specialization in Music Therapy, which combines music, psychology and sociology.

- Toronto has a very select program in medical illustration: Art as Applied to Medicine. The calendar states that medical illustration "involves scholarly research in the creation of graphic art." Some university courses in anatomy, biology, zoology and human physiology, as well as applied-art courses and a portfolio of original work, are recommended before entry to this three-year Bachelor of Science (B.Sc. AAM) degree is considered.
- Waterloo began a co-op program in Arts Administration in 1984. Scarborough College has a similar program, which is also co-op; typically, because of the work placement, co-op programs require up to five years to complete.

There are possibilities for using your talent in ways that might not readily occur to you. Two programs will serve as examples. There is a Dance Program in Human Kinetics and Leisure Studies at Waterloo that balances courses in technique, dance, academics and liberal arts for the student who is interested in dance but wants more than a performance focus. Also, Windsor offers Drama in Education as part of its School of Dramatic Art. This honours course is designed for students interested in careers as elementary teachers, theatre-arts instructors or special-education practitioners. Graduates wishing to teach in public or secondary schools have to enrol in a faculty of education after graduation.

There are many possibilities for fine-art studies at most institutions. The variations necessitate a visit to the campus to talk with faculty. That's the only possible way to find out which university will meet your special needs. This is one area where high marks don't count as much as ability, because each program requests tangible proof of your talent. If applicants lack the talent necessary to become a professional in the artistic field to which they aspire, all the teaching in the world will not inspire them. Faculty, therefore, want to be assured that the successful applicants have imagination and creativity as well as intelligence. That is why portfolios and auditions are so important. Each university will have varying requirements for the evaluation of your genius; it is to your advantage to find out exactly what each university wants. To assemble a portfolio or structure your performance to meet the requirements of all the universities to which you have applied is no easy task. You may want to take your flute; a piano will be provided. Also be sure you know the dates when auditions are available. If you miss the scheduled time, you may be denied a later date. Good fine-arts programs can afford to be choosy.

15.11 JOURNALISM AND TRANSLATION

Journalism is an option at two Ontario degree-granting institutions: Carleton and Ryerson. Ryerson's journalism program is a three-year degree (B.A.A.). After a common first year, students specialize in either newspaper, broadcast or magazine journalism. At Carleton, students are trained "to investigate, interpret and communicate clearly in any mass media." A television studio, radio newsroom and community newspaper are facilities available at Carleton to help students prepare for their career. Journalism students must enrol in courses in disciplines other than their major to ensure a broad educational experience. One first-year course must be the study of a language, usually French.

Translation is available at three universities across Ontario, all of which are bilingual. At Glendon, the Translation program begins in second year, enrolling 50 students with equal numbers of francophones and anglophones being accepted. An entrance exam in the mother tongue of the applicant is held in the spring before entering the Translation program, which is an honours B.A. program requiring three years of study after the qualifying year. Laurentian, too, offers a four-year degree for English- and French-speaking students that confers a B.S.L. (Bachelor of Science in Language) degree upon the graduate. Laurentian requires at least one OAC credit in English and one in French or *français* for admission to the School of Translators and Interpreters. Ottawa's School of Translators and Interpretors offers an honours B.A. program that is entered after one year of university study on the successful completion of an entrance examination. Within this option, there is a co-op possibility that commences after second year and includes three work terms.

A word about bilingual universities. As you will note in the section in the next chapter entitled "Quick Facts about Ontario Universities," there are four bilingual degee-granting institutions in Ontario: Glendon College (York), Laurentian, Ottawa and RMC. At none of these institutions is it necessary to be bilingual to be admitted, except for Ottawa's Occupational Therapy and Physiotherapy programs. You should, however, have some facility in the second language before entering for two reasons. One is that you will be socializing with students who speak French as their first language and it would grease the wheels of communication to be able to converse, even to a limited degree, in French. Secondly, both Ottawa and Glendon require proof of bilingual competency before you can graduate. At Glendon, second-language skills will be tested by the successful completion of a second-year-level course in the second language. At Ottawa, all students must demonstrate a certain level of competence in their second language by enrolling, and passing, a course in that language. Ottawa offers "sheltered" courses through their Centre for Second Language Learning, which pairs a regular introductory subject (psychology, for instance) taught in the second language with second-language instruction. For an additional 90 minutes a week, the introductory-course material is enhanced by a review of the course content and work on second-language skills. If the course is passed successfully, the student receives credit for a language course and for the introductory course in less time than it would require to pass two separate courses.

At RMC, second-language training is mandatory for all students who are not functionally bilingual before entering the college. Engineering and science courses are taught in both languages, arts in English only. Since 75% of the students are in science and engineering, most are fairly competent in French and English by the time they graduate. At Laurentian, the Bachelor of Education degree, which is available only to graduates from a university, is available in French only; the rest of the university's programs are taught in both languages.

You can also enhance your second-language skills at a university that is not bilingual. Several universities have "French Houses": residences designated for students who want to cross cultural boundaries linguistically. Students bring a mixture of French and English backgrounds into a social environment that promotes expanded language facility and informal conversational practice. Sometimes a unilingual university will offer a certificate of competence in the French language to augment university study in other areas. At Western, you may obtain a Certificat de français pratique while pursuing a degree in an area of specialization other than the French language. Five courses in French plus a successfully completed oral examination are required for accreditation.

If you want to practise your expert use of the French language and soak up European ambiance on the French Riviera at the same time, you can enrol in the Universite Canadienne en France after completing one full year of study at any Canadian university. Students admitted to this co-operative venture between Laurentian University and Blyth & Company study at the second-year university level. Laurentian provides the academic component, while Blyth & Company arranges travel and accommodation. Students must choose to take a course in their second language (English or French) after they have taken a placement test to determine their language facility, and can apply to complete the examination for the Certificate of Bilingualism while enrolled in the program.

All universities have special programs available in other countries or cities within Canada to allow an academically qualified student to study in a broader context, and possibly in a foreign language. If this appeals to you, find out what is available before your decide on a specific university. There are distinct variations based on institutional areas of expertise and interest. Sometimes there are even scholarships available. So, as always, check it out!

15.12 LAW

If you want to enrol in an Ontario university to become a lawyer, there are law schools at Ottawa, Queen's, Toronto, Western, Windsor and York. To enter law anywhere you need excellent grades in your university studies as well as a high LSAT (Law School Admission Test) score. You can apply to law school after second-year studies; most applicants, however, complete an undergraduate degree before continuing on to legal studies.

There are no pre-required courses for admission to law school. Some universities have undergraduate programs, such as York's Law and Society, that explore concepts of law and justice and the rights of the individual within society. The rule of thumb is to enrol in a course of study that will allow a viable alternative career option if you are not accepted into law; only about one candidate in fifteen is accepted into a law program. Within the qualifying undergraduate program you should address academic skills that will allow you to score highly on the LSAT. You can take the LSAT more than once, except often the marks are averaged on the completion of subsequent tests. The LSAT is based on language, logic and mathematical skills at a high level. Most libraries carry copies of sample LSATs and, by referring to them, you can assess what undergraduate courses will best help you address deficiencies. (A manual on walking on water might also help.)

If you want to prepare yourself for life after undergraduate study in a faculty of law, you might consider enrolling in degree courses that would allow you to be eligible for specialized programs such as the following:

- Ottawa has both a Civil Law School and a Common Law School. Therefore, it is possible to graduate with a combined LL.L/LL.B. in four years. This unique program allows the successful graduate to practise in both Ontario and Quebec; however the Civil Law program requires a completed undergraduate degree except for students applying from Ontario universities.
- Windsor's Law School allows a restricted number of students to pursue a Bachelor of Law and a Doctor of Jurisprudence simultaneously to obtain a J.D./LL.B. With the implementation of free trade, lawyers will be needed with knowledge of both the U.S. and Canadian legal systems. Taken over three complete calendar years, courses given by the universites of Detroit and Windsor allow the bar exams to be written in either country.
- Combined M.B.A./LL.B. degrees can be undertaken at several law schools in Ontario; these programs usually take one extra year to complete.
- York's Osgoode Hall Law School has a combined M.E.S./LL.B. degree that allows a student to combine the study of law with a masters degree in Environmental Science. Graduates of this program clean up in more ways than one.

Perhaps you may want to include some French-language, administration or American history courses in your undergraduate program. Then, if you wish to become one of the select few who are admitted to these demanding co-ordinated programs, you will be qualified.

15.13 MEDICINE, NURSING, OCCUPATIONAL THERAPY AND PHYSIOTHERAPY

The four professions covered in this section are all in demand. Universities that have a faculty of medicine offer physiotherapy and occupational therapy as well as nursing programs. Nursing programs, however, are sometimes available at universities without medical faculties.

Medicine

McMaster, Queen's, Ottawa, Western and Toronto all have faculties of medicine. With the exception of McMaster, they require a minimum of two years of university study, with courses in biology, chemistry and physics as well as other prerequisites, prior to acceptance. Western requires an A average in the university preparation courses and the other three universities have corresponding requirements. A superior score on the Medical College Admission Test (MCAT), letters of reference and personal interviews all weigh in the admissions decision. Applications are not accepted from applicants who are neither Canadian citizens nor landed immigrants, although Ottawa makes an exception for the children of alumni. All four institutions require four years of medical studies.

McMaster currently has a three-year medical program, although it, too, may be four years long by the time you have the credentials to apply. Three years of university study is usually, but not necessarily, a prerequisite for entry at McMaster. A very limited number of applicants are considered who have attended university on a part-time basis only and who have "made a contribution to the community" for at least seven years. In the profile of initial admission offers to the class of 1991, only one of the 100 successful candidates came from this Special Applicant category. Therefore, don't count on being accepted with less than a full background. McMaster also differs in that it doesn't require the MCAT. Instead, it makes a decision based on academic prowess and personal qualities, as revealed by marks (most successful candidates had A's) and a personal letter supported by references.

Because of the very limited numbers of students accepted for the study of medicine, you should be extremely realistic about your chances. Have another career choice in reserve in case you don't meet the stringent requirements for admission. Perhaps one of the other health sciences could be an option.

Nursing

You don't have to have a university degree to become a nurse. It is possible to become a registered nurse by entering a community-college nursing program for three years, passing college exams and then writing the R.N. qualifying exams. Some years ago, though, the Registered Nurses' Association of Ontario suggested that, by the year 2000, each registered nurse in the province should obtain a university degree. To meet the needs of R.N.'s attempting to upgrade their diplomas to degrees, most university nursing programs have responded with a modified curriculum that gives some advanced credit to registered nurses. There is a great divergence in advanced credits awarded for community-college courses depending on the type of program and the prerequisites for entrance.

If you're considering entering a university nursing program as an R.N., you should contact each university that offers nursing programs. Atkinson College at York and the School of Nursing at Toronto have part-time programs that may be of interest. Ryerson's B.A.A. in nursing can be earned in two years of full-time study, as can McMaster's B.Sc.N. Laurentian offers its B.Sc.N. program for R.N.'s through distance education in ten locations throughout northeastern Ontario. However, if you are an R.N. wanting to improve or enhance your qualifications, check it out with the nearest university. Some run on-site courses at local hospitals.

Nursing courses are still, for the most part, over-subscribed. However, the publicity about poor pay and long working hours in difficult circumstances has begun to dampen the enthusiasm for nursing careers among recent secondary-school graduates. Therefore, there is a better chance now for admission into a nursing degree program than there was previously.

The student who wants to enter a nursing program directly from secondary school should have OACs in English, chemistry, biology and mathematics. There are also variations that should be explored through your guidance office. The programs offered are four years in length and move from a general first year into specific nursing components. The degree usually awarded is a B.Sc.N.

Lakehead and Laurentian both have nursing programs that are addressed to the needs of people in northern Ontario. Laurentian offers a bilingual stream in nursing for those students wishing to take their clinical and theory components in French. Students must be adept at both languages to enrol since some reading material is only available in English. Lakehead has a nine-month Native Nurses Entry Program that is designed to provide the necessary skills and academic preparation for entry into the regular nursing program. The entry program has two 12-week semesters, with two weeks of field experience that can be either in a student's own community or in another native health setting.

Ryerson awards a B.A.A. in nursing. Its program is designed to prepare nurses "to function in a variety of roles and health care services" such as public-health nursing. It offers courses in economics, philosophy and history as electives within the four years of study. This is a divergence from the usual scientific orientation of most nursing programs.

Occupational Therapy and Physiotherapy

Universities that have a medical school often have occupational therapy and physiotherapy programs. What's the difference? Quite a lot. The purpose in both cases is to help people cope with disabilities, but the methods of doing so differ widely. Ottawa states that the goal of occupational therapy is "to guide dysfunctional individuals to use the dynamic and curative qualities of activity and intervene constructively within their environment so as to adapt, develop and grow." In simpler English, that means disabled people will be challenged through activities to cope with their physical and social problems. Physiotherapy, by contrast, centres on "the prevention, assessment and treatment of mobility problems" and is considerably more medical in training, with courses from the general biomedical, motion and clinical sciences. At Ottawa, all courses relating to these professions are given in the French language, but professional courses can be chosen – and assignments and examinations written – in English, if that is preferable.

Both occupational therapy and physiotherapy programs are four years long, the first year having several components common to both rehabilitation programs. Occupational therapy does not require as many science OACs as physiotherapy, which has a heavy science and math component. One math and one science, at a minimum, are required for occupational therapy. At Toronto, for entry into either of these programs, you must designate them as first choice on the Supplementary Application Form required by the university. Toronto, which calls its physiotherapy course Physical Therapy, has paid, mandatory work terms in the summers after years one, two and three. Do not expect to be richly rewarded for this work experience in monetary terms; students are paid at apprenticeship, not professional, rates.

Very few students are admitted into either program. Western requires a general year in the Faculty of Science or Social Science before a student can apply to the Faculty of Applied Health Sciences for Occupational or Physical Therapy. Queen's is raising the number of entrants to both its programs from the 30 admitted in 1989 to 40 by 1991. McMaster has signalled that it will be phasing out its current Bachelor of Health Science program, which currently admits graduates from Mohawk College of Applied Arts and Technology's occupational therapy and physiotherapy programs, in September 1991. Instead McMaster, in co-operation with Lakehead, will offer a two-year program to candidates with a bachelor's degree and a better than average grade-point average. Both the Occupational Therapy and Physiotherapy programs will involve 23 months of study over a two-year period. "It is anticipated that the students will have an option to participate in a 14 week block of northern studies at Lakehead University," states McMaster's 1989/90 undergraduate calendar.

To gain admission to the either program is like crawling through a hedge backwards. Besides the science and math OACs required for admission, all universities ask you to submit a personal background information form. Because of limited space at Toronto, both programs are closed to foreign and some out-of-province applicants. Western gives preference to Canadian and permanent residents, especially in Physiotherapy where only 60 spaces are available. There are 45 admission spaces in Occupational Therapy at Western.

15.14 *PHYSICAL EDUCATION, KINESIOLOGY, RECREATION AND LEISURE STUDIES*

More than two-thirds of Ontario universities have programs that address physical fitness and human movement. Most physical-education programs are of four years' duration.

- Toronto's School of Physical and Health Education admits 120 students per year to its St George campus and requires math and science OACs for admission. The first two years have a common core program, while in the last two years students select an individualized program of study from available options.
- McMaster's School of Physical Education and Athletics also has core subjects in the first two years and more choice in the final two years to allow for personal career preparation.
- Neither Queen's nor Western is as strict about OAC math and science requirements. Western offers both a three- and four-year degree, while Queen's students can choose from a Bachelor of Arts degree or a Bachelor of Physical and Health Education (B.P.H.E.) degree.
- At York, students can enter physical-education courses in the Faculty of Arts, which requires an English OAC, or the Faculty of Science, which has modified its usual math and science requirements for this particular program.
- Both Laurier and Brock have physical-education programs if you want to consider a smaller university campus. The aim of Laurier's Physical Education and Health program is to provide "a course of study which will lead to effective teaching and coaching at the public, senior public, and secondary school levels." Brock has a Physical Education program that awards a B.Ph.Ed. and a Recreation and Leisure Studies degree (B.R.L.S.) at both the general and honours levels.

There has been a broadening of the physical-education area to include programs in recreation and leisure studies and in kinetics.

- Waterloo's Faculty of Human Kinetics and Leisure Studies offers Kinesiology, as well as a Recreation and Leisure Studies (B.A.) program with a co-op option available. Waterloo, the first university to use the term kinesiology (the science of motion), also presents a Health Studies program that emphasizes "both the scientific and behavourial aspects of health, disease and disease prevention."
- There is a Faculty of Human Kinetics at Windsor that offers Honours Applied Kinesiology, Sports Administration, and Teaching and Coaching as three separate majors, all of which have a co-op option. Guelph's Bachelor of Science in Human Kinetics is an eight-semester degree that includes courses in many fields of science, allowing students specifically interested in teaching or health sciences to have qualifications in biology, chemistry or physics.
- The two northern universities again address the challenge of their location by presenting courses that are uniquely appropriate to their regions. As well as a Bachelor of Physical Education degree, which requires an honours thesis in the fourth year of study, Lakehead offers a Bachelor of Outdoor Recreation degree, which is concerned with leisure pursuits as they relate directly to the natural environment. Students are expected to become knowledgeable about issues and trends that might affect outdoor recreation in the future.
- Laurentian's Division of Physical Education presents several options in Physical and Health Education, Health Promotion, Kinesiology and an Adventure Leadership program, designed to foster the personal growth of the individual through direct interaction with the natural environment. If you want outdoor adventure along with academic theory, go north, young man and woman, because it awaits you in Thunder Bay and Sudbury.

Sometimes it's harder to make a choice when the number of options is very wide. It certainly is true where physical education and kinesiology programs are concerned. First decide whether you want to enrol in a science or arts program. Then consider your career goal as it relates to the programs offered at specific institutions. You might also inquire as to which programs are entered directly in first year. If you are assured of admission into a first-year physical education or kinesiology program, then all you have to do is maintain a sufficiently high academic average in first and subsequent years to continue. If there is a general first year, it may mean that you are competing academically to enter the program in second year. If so, you'd be wise to know now so that there are no surprises after deciding on a university. Narrow the possibilities sufficiently so that you won't be run ragged by visiting all universities that offer a physical education or kinesiology program. When you visit the university campuses, ask to see the athletic and lab facilities; their condition and availability could make a difference to the quality of your educational experience.

15.15 SOCIAL-ISSUE PROGRAMS

Universities present many programs that are specifically intended to meet the present, or emerging, needs of society. These social-issue programs, whether early childhood education or gerontology, social work or criminology, food production or restaurant management, are related to specific career options.

Guelph's roots go back to the Ontario College of Agriculture, which was chartered in 1875. Building on its past, Guelph has moved with the times by incorporating an interest in food production into a myriad of courses ranging from agricultural growth and harvesting to hotel management. Brian Segal, president of Guelph, envisions this theme as a continuing one in the university's development. From courses in plant protection to soil science, the Bachelor of Science programs in agriculture meet the needs of the primary production of food. You can, for instance, enrol as a major in food engineering in the Faculty of Science. Continuing the theme, there is a Consumer Studies program available in the Applied Science area that views people primarily as users of products and services and considers how their consumption relates to product development and standards.

Guelph also as an option for those who wish to graduate with a Bachelor of Commerce degree designed for the food and service industries. Institutional Foodservice Management and Hotel and Food Administration are two of the programs available in the commerce area.

There is also the option to enrol in two programs that are service-oriented at Ryerson. One of them, Hospitality and Tourism Management, requires a fourth year spent working with corporate partners on a senior research paper that relates to a managerial issue confronting the industry. The other, Nutrition, Consumer and Family Studies, breaks into the three separate streams of study after an introductory year studying the applied, physical and social sciences.

There are family-studies programs at other degree-granting institutions in Ontario that you will want to look into, as well as programs related to young children and social work. Ryerson's diploma in the School of Early Childhood Education integrates class-room studies and field placements in its two day-care centres. York offers an Early Childhood Education program in psychology in co-operation with Seneca College of Applied Arts and Technology which awards both a B.A. in psychology and an early childhood education diploma. At Brock, there is a B.A. program, Child Studies, designed for students who wish to understand child-development theory and its applications. Exceptionalities in Human Learning, a unique course taught at Erindale College, considers the social, emotional, educational and intellectual implications of different disabilities. Toronto gives priority to qualified graduates of this program who apply to the primary/junior division of its Faculty of Education.

From the cradle to the grave, all people need social services. Ryerson, with its mandate to provide programs that address the requirements of an ever-changing community, is at the forefront of programs that meet societal needs. Social Work at Ryerson requires an admissions test to elicit an applicant's interest and aptitudes for a career in social service. There are social-work programs at several other institutions as well. Both Lakehead and Laurentian have programs in which courses are unique to aboriginal communities. Carleton offers an Honours Social Work program that admits students directly from secondary school. McMaster has a combined B.A./B.S.W. that commences in second year. You are eligible to apply as long as introductory psychology and sociology are part of your first-year studies. It is a limited-access program and above-average marks are required. The same is true at Windsor, although there are two points of admission in its Bachelor of Social Work program. Admission to first-year studies is not particularly restrictive, but to be accepted in the upper two years of the four-year program depends on personal qualities and academic qualifications. The successful candidates to the final two years spend two days a week in community agencies during the fall and winter semesters. At Western, the four-year Social Work program is available only at King's College, which is a co-educational college affiliated with the Roman Catholic church as well as with Western.

DISCOURAGED?

I bet you are. So many programs take only one applicant in fifteen, like law, or one out of nine, like dentistry. Every year the admissions average at most universities rises, even in non-limited programs like arts and science. The sheer number of applicants to professions can make you think, "What's the use? I'll never be the lucky one. Why try so hard?" Well, why not attempt to be one of the chosen few? You'll turn another year older with or without giving your OAC year all your energy, and one year from now you might be delighted by the result.

Once upon a time there was a Mongol war-lord who captured two mercenaries who'd been fighting against him. When they were called before the war-lord for sentencing, he asked the first prisoner if he had anything to say in his defence. When the prisoner kept silent, the war-lord ordered, "Off with his head!" When the second prisoner was asked the same question, he stepped foward and said, "Your exalted majesty, I have one great talent. I can teach horses to fly. I have seen your great white stallion and am convinced that, given a year, I could teach him to lift you to the heavens and back." The war-lord thought for a while and then said, "All right, I grant you your year, but if you have not taught my Tartar to fly by then, your head will fly from your body."

As the two were being dragged off, the one on his way to the executioner said, "What nonsense! You don't know how to teach a horse to fly." The one being led to the stable said, "But in a year, I might escape, the war-lord may be defeated and, who knows, I might even teach the horse to fly."

Which is, of course, a long-winded way of saying that while there's life, there's hope, and with work and imagination people can achieve miracles.

You can expect, even demand, more consideration from a university than a prisoner can from a war-lord. Remember, you're paying for the privilege of going to university. As a consumer it's your right to be given fair consideration. If you think that a university to which you have applied is not treating you with the respect you deserve, then complain.

Sometimes mistakes are made; an admissions file is mislaid or a document doesn't arrive to complete an application. These errors are regrettable but understandable. Sometimes, though, decisions aren't made on limited programs until mid-summer, and non-traditional or community-college transfer applicants are kept waiting for no discernible reason. These internal delays and machinations may benefit the institution, but they don't do much for the student's planning process.

A rule of thumb is that, if you have fulfilled your application commitments and have submitted all the necessary information, you can expect the university to which you have applied to respond. If there is an unwarranted delay or lack of communication, you have the right to complain. First, try to find out the circumstances – courteously – and, if you're still not satisfied ask your guidance office to intercede on your behalf. If it is closed for the summer or you are not a secondary-school student, start at the top of the university – with the president. Presidents get irritable over complaints and will request the appropriate department to deal with the problem.

Remember that the prisoner had more options open to him than just letting them chop off his head. You've worked hard to prepare yourself for university. Exercise your options and, if one university doesn't seem to welcome your application, no doubt another one will.

University profiles

HOW TO READ THE PROFILES

If you've read much of the last chapter ("Using the university profiles"), you'll know that it provides a running commentary on the information presented here. It's important to *take a little time* to read those parts of chapter 3 that relate to the sections of the profiles in which you are most interested (the section numbers in chapter 3 follow those in the profiles). That way you can make the most of the information presented here.

The profiles are the result of a questionnaire completed by the staff of each university; the profile texts were later approved by these same people. The information is for the 1990/91 academic year unless otherwise noted. Three universities – Laurentian, Toronto, York – that have full-time, day undergraduate study available at locations other than the main campus have those colleges listed directly following their profile. For instance, Erindale and Scarborough colleges' profiles continue after Toronto's.

The letters "N/A" are used when information was not available from the institution. The letters "N/R" mean that information would not be relevant to that particular question. In all cases, the information has been arranged to make it as easy as possible for readers to compare university services and programs. All business programs, for instance, whether commerce or administration, are coded 15.3. They may appear as a separate faculty, or as part of a faculty that incorporates several professional programs.

Some common abbreviations occur throughout the profiles:
M, F and C (Male, Female and Co-ed);
FTE (Full-time equivalent - see Glossary);
GPA (Grade Point Average - see Glossary);
OAC (Ontario Academic Credit - see Glossary).

The profiles should point you in the right research direction. If you need more specific information you should call, or write, the contact person listed in section 5. Collect all the information you can before visiting the campus to check it out.

Just to get you warmed up, we'll start with some assorted 'quick facts' about Ontario universities.

QUICK FACTS ABOUT ONTARIO UNIVERSITIES

Size

Largest Ontario universities (ranked by size), based on full-time undergraduate enrolment

1 University of Toronto, Toronto
2 York University, Toronto
3 University of Western Ontario, London

Medium-sized Ontario universities (unranked, under 15,000), based on full-time undergraduate enrolment

Carleton University, Ottawa
University of Guelph, Guelph
McMaster University, Hamilton
Ottawa University, Ottawa
Queen's University, Kingston
Ryerson Polytechnical Institute, Toronto
University of Waterloo, Waterloo
University of Windsor, Windsor

Smallest Ontario universities (unranked, under 5000), based on full-time undergraduate enrolment

Brock University, St Catharines
Lakehead University, Thunder Bay

Laurentian University, Sudbury
Royal Military College, Kingston
Trent University, Peterborough
Wilfrid Laurier University, Waterloo

Some historical facts

Universities founded in the 19th century
McMaster University, 1887
Queen's University, 1841
Royal Military College, 1874
University of Toronto, 1827 (as King's College)
University of Western Ontario, 1878

Universities that began in the 20th century but had roots in the 19th century
University of Guelph (1964), which sprang fom the Ontario Colleges of Agriculture and Veterinary Sciences and MacDonald Hall
University of Ottawa (1965), which was started by the Oblate Fathers in 1848
University of Windsor (1953), which was started as Assumption College in 1857

Universities that were started in the 1940s
Carleton University, 1942
Ryerson Polytechnical Institute, 1948

The Great Building Boom (1957–64)
University of Waterloo, 1957
York University, 1959
Laurentian University, 1960
Lakehead University, 1962
Trent University, 1964
Brock University, 1964

Wilfrid Laurier University's unique history
- began as a Lutheran seminary in 1911
- affiliated with Western in 1925

- spawned the University of Waterloo in 1957
- became Waterloo Lutheran University in 1960, but remained a church-related institution
- in 1973, became Wilfrid Laurier University, fifteenth provincially assisted university

Some other useful facts

Northern universities

Lakehead and Laurentian universities are situated in northern Ontario, which has roughly 10% of the province's total population. However, Lakehead attracts 52% of its student population from southern Ontario. Laurentian has campuses in Sault Ste Marie (Algoma), North Bay (Nipissing College) and Hearst (Collège Hearst). Both universities have a commitment to the social, economic and cultural development of northern Ontario and present programs that address the needs of a diverse population.

Larger colleges attached to existing universities

Algoma College, Sault Ste Marie (Laurentian University)
Erindale College, Mississauga (University of Toronto)
Glendon College, Toronto (York University)
Nipissing College, North Bay (Laurentian University)
Scarborough College, Scarborough (University of Toronto)

Bilingual options at Ontario universities

Laurentian University
University of Ottawa
Royal Military College
York University, Glendon College

The Polytechnical Institute

Ryerson Polytechnical Institute awards Bachelor of Applied Arts (B.A.A.), Bachelor of Technology (B.Tech.) and Bachelor of Business Management (B.B.M.) degrees, as well as three-year diplomas. Its mandate is to combine theory with applied learning to provide a professionally relevant education.

The Military College
Royal Military College (RMC) awards Bachelor of Arts, Science and Engineering degrees to young men and women who wish to serve as commissioned officers in the Canadian Forces. RMC offers a university-level education and develops the qualities of leadership appropriate to its purpose.

Co-operative Education Programs
Co-operative study means alternating university courses with paid work experience that is relevant to the course of study. The University of Waterloo introduced co-op studies in 1957 when it enrolled its first students in a co-op engineering program. By initiating three academic terms a year, Waterloo also became Canada's first year-round university. There are now over 9,000 students taking advantage of the co-op option. Several other universities have limited co-op placements in specified areas of study.

Brock University

1. OVERVIEW
Brock University, founded in 1964, is situated in the southwest part of St Catharines (population 130,000). It offers eight undergraduate degrees plus master's programs for some 6300 full-time and 4400 part-time students. Emphasis is placed on individual participation in small group seminar, laboratory or tutorial settings in addition to the lectures.

2. PRESIDENT
Terrance H. White

3. ENROLMENT
(1990 Fall semester; rounded to nearest 50)

Registration
Undergraduate full-time 6300 (M 2835, F 3465)
Undergraduate part-time 4400 (M 1980, F 2420)
Graduate 980 (M 490, F 490)

Residence
Undergrads in residence 20% (M 50%, F 50%)
Undergrads in off-campus housing 40%
Undergrads commuting 40%

4. ADMISSIONS TO FIRST YEAR

Entry dates

Fall	Full-time
Winter	Part-time
Spring	Part-time

First-year entries

	Fall	Winter	Spring
Applications	10,000	200	600
Admissions	4,600	150	550
Enrolments	1,600	100	300

Other entry dates
Spring evening begins late April and finishes July 1.

Admissions offered to qualified candidates before early admission
Yes

Community-college transfer requirements
Year 1: 80%
Year 2 or 3: 75%

Advanced standing granted with minimum overall average of 75% from 2 or 3 years of CAAT program.

Mature students admission requirements
Age 21, 2 years work experience
Number of courses allowed: 2 credits initially

5. ADMISSIONS CONTACT

Keith Rae
Associate Registrar, Admissions
Brock University
St. Catharines, Ontario L2S 3A1
(416) 688-5550, ext. 3566

6. STRUCTURE AND DEGREES

Board of Trustees
32 members (M 25, F 7; 3 faculty, 3 students; support staff and alumni N/R)

Teaching faculty
Full-time 331 (M 250, F 81)
Part-time N/A

Faculty/Student ratio (FTE basis)
N/A

Undergraduate degrees conferred
Accounting, Arts,

Business Administration, Business Economics, Education, Physical Education, Recreation and Leisure Studies, Science

7. TEACHING FACILITIES

Largest first-year class 390
First-year courses with tutorials 100%
Lab places for first-year students N/A

Research grants and contracts N/A

Graduate programs
Number of programs 7
Enrolment in master's programs 920; doctoral programs 0

Libraries
With open stacks 1
With closed stacks 0
Total holdings 800,000 volumes

8. STUDENTS

Undergraduates
1st year 1650
2nd year N/A
3rd year N/A
4th year N/A

Entering as Ontario Scholars Approx. 13%
Entering with scholarships 10%
Entering with OSAP help N/A

9. ENTRANCE SCHOLARSHIPS

Most prestigious
Founders Scholarship:
No application necessary
Deadline June 1
Requirements: 90%; no supporting documentation

Full-tuition scholarships None

Partial-tuition scholarships (161)
No application necessary
Deadline June 1
Requirements: approx. 83%; no supporting documentation

Scholarships for entering students
Offered 672
Accepted 197
Total budget for undergraduate scholarships N/A

10. INTERNATIONAL STUDENTS

Students from outside Canada 5%
Scholarships awarded None
Services available Adviser; Academic; Foreign Student Officer
Language requirements for admission TOEFL score 550

11. ATHLETIC FACILITIES

Gyms (3)
Playing fields
Squash courts
Swimming pool
Track centre (outdoor)
Weight/workout rooms

Inter-university sports
Basketball M, F
Cross-country running M, F
Curling M, F
Fencing M
Golf M
Hockey M
Rowing M, F
Rugby M
Soccer M, F
Swimming M, F
Tennis M
Volleyball M, F
Waterpolo F
Wrestling M

Intra-mural organized sports
Badminton C
Basketball M, F
Football F, M, C
Hockey (ice, ball) M
Ringette F
Slowpitch C
Soccer (indoor) M, F
Volleyball C

Recreation and fitness programs

12. STUDENT LIFE

Student councils N/A
Student clubs N/A

Pubs 1

Drinking awareness program

First-year orientation
July, opening week in September; parent sessions

13. STUDENT SERVICES

Counselling
Psychological, Career, Peer

Medical
Nurse, Doctors

Special needs
80% of campus wheelchair accessible
Learning disability program

Other
Essay writing/study skills program
Off-campus housing registry

14. RESIDENCES

Residence places 1015
M 455, F 560; Co-ed and apartments/townhouses

First-year students
Places reserved 55%
Application deadline June 30
Places reserved for scholarship winners; 80% minimum required
No eligibility limitations based on student's home location
Allocations announced July

Upper-year students
Places reserved 45%
Allocations announced July

Wheelchair-accessible rooms All

Meal-plan options
All you can eat; various numbers of meals per week

15. PROGRAMS OF UNDERGRADUATE STUDY

15.1 FACULTY OF HUMANITIES

Degree
Bachelor of Arts, B.A.

Level
General, Honours

Programs
Applied Languages
Canadian Studies
Classics
Drama
English
Film
History
Languages*
Liberal Studies
Music
Philosophy

Visual Arts
* French, Italian, Spanish, German and Slavic

First-year entry Yes

Entry requirements
Minimum average: 70%
OAC English

Students accepted 220
Total in faculty N/A

Co-op (work/study) available
No; no correspondence or self-paced study

Graduation requirements
Minimum GPA: 60% on scale of 100%
Full credits/courses: Honours 70%, General 60%

Graduating students N/A

15.1 FACULTY OF SOCIAL SCIENCES

Degree
Bachelor of Arts, B.A.

Level
General, Honours

Programs
Applied Linguistics
Asian Studies
Business Economics
Child Studies
Communication Studies
Economics
Environmental Science
Geography
Health Studies

Labor Studies
Politics
Psychology
Sociology
Urban and Environmental Studies

First-year entry Yes

Entry requirements
Minimum average: 70%
OAC English

Students accepted 520
Total in faculty N/A
Co-op (work/study) available
No; no correspondence or self-paced study

Graduation requirements
Minimum GPA: 60% on scale of 100%
Full credits/courses: Honours 70%, General 60%

Graduating students N/A

15.2 FACULTY OF MATHEMATICS AND SCIENCE

Degree
Bachelor of Science, B.Sc.

Level
General, Honours

Programs
Biochemistry
Biological Sciences
Chemistry
Computer Science
Geology
Mathematics
Neuroscience
Physics
Pre-professional Studies for Health Sciences

First-year entry Yes

Entry requirements
Minimum average: 70%
See Brock calendar for requirements

Students accepted 165
Total in faculty N/A

Co-op (work/study) available
No; no correspondence or self-paced study
Graduation requirements
Minimum GPA: 60% on scale of 100%
Full credits/courses: Honours 70%, General 60%

Graduating students N/A

15.3 FACULTY OF BUSINESS

Degrees
Bachelor of Business Administration, B.Admin.
Bachelor of Business Economics, B.B.E.
Bachelor of Accounting, B.Actg.

Level
Honours, General for B.B.E.

Programs
Accounting Co-op
Accounting Non Co-op
Business Administration
Business Economics

First-year entry Yes

Entry requirements
Minimum average: 72–80%
OAC English, 2 OACs in Mathematics

Students accepted 475
Total in faculty N/A

Co-op (work/study) available
Accounting co-op; no correspondence or self-paced study

Graduation requirements
Minimum GPA: 60% on scale of 100%
Full credits/courses: Honours 70%, General 60% (B.B.E. only)

Graduating students N/A

15.6 FACULTY OF EDUCATION

Degrees
Bachelor of Arts/Bachelor of Education, B.A./B.Ed.
Bachelor of Science/Bachelor of Education, B.Sc./B.Ed.

Level
General

Programs
Child Studies
General Studies in Science
General Studies in Mathematics

First-year entry Yes

Entry requirements
B.A./B.Ed. 80% OAC English 1
B.Sc./B.Ed. - Science - 80% in 2 Science OACs, 1 Math, 1 English OAC - Mathematics 80% in 2 Math OACs, 1 Science, 1 English OAC

Students accepted 80
Total in faculty 200

Co-op (work/study) available
No; no correspondence or self-paced study

Graduation requirements
Minimum GPA: 75% on scale of 100%
Full credits/courses: N/A

Graduating students 80

15.14 FACULTY OF PHYSICAL EDUCATION AND RECREATION

Degrees
Bachelor of Physical Education, B.Phed.
Bachelor of Recreation and Leisure Studies, B.R.L.S.

Level
General, Honours

Programs
Physical Education
Recreation and Leisure Studies

First-year entry Yes

Entry requirements
Minimum average: 70%
OAC English

Students accepted 220
Total in faculty N/A

Co-op (work/study) available
No; no correspondence or self-paced study

Graduation requirements
Minimum GPA: 60% on scale of 100%
Full credits/courses: Honours 70%, General 60%

Graduating students N/A

Carleton University

1. OVERVIEW
Carleton University is just ten minutes from Ottawa's Parliament Hill. Founded in 1942, Carleton offers more than 50 undergraduate specializations plus master's and Ph.D. programs. The university's 20,000 students come from across Canada and some 90 foreign countries. Its programs in architecture, Canadian studies, social sciences and journalism are known world-wide.

2. PRESIDENT
Robin H. Farquhar

3. ENROLMENT
(1988 Fall semester; rounded to nearest 100)

Registration
Undergraduate full-time 12,500 (M 6900, F 5600)
Undergraduate part-time 4900 (M 2300, F 2600)
Graduate 2200 (M 1200, F 1000)

Residence
Undergrads in residence 11% (M 54%, F 46%)
Undergrads in off-campus housing 34%
Undergrads commuting 55%

4. ADMISSIONS TO FIRST YEAR

Entry dates
Fall, Summer

First-year entries

	Fall (July 1)	Summer (March 1)
Applications	18,200	350
Admissions	11,350	250
Enrolments	4,800	190

Admissions offered to qualified candidates before early admission
Yes

Community-college transfer requirements
2- or 3-year program graduates with 2nd-class standing in their last 2 CAAT semesters

Advanced standing granted of a maximum of 5 credits to 3-year CAAT program graduates depending on program/courses taken and Carleton program they are trying to enter.

Mature students admission requirements
Age 21 or over, away from full-time studies for 2 years; allowed to take equivalent of 5 credits.

5. ADMISSIONS CONTACT

Victor J. Chapman
Director of Admissions and Academic Records
Room 405, Administration Building
Carleton University
Ottawa, Ontario K1S 5B6
(613) 788-3663 or 1-800-267-7366

6. STRUCTURE AND DEGREES

Board of Governors
32 members (M N/A, F N/A; 3 faculty, 2 alumni, 2 students)

Teaching faculty
Full-time and part-time 724 (M 582, F 142)

Faculty/Student ratio (FTE basis)
1:26

Undergraduate degrees conferred
Architecture, Arts, Commerce, Computer Science, Engineering,

Industrial Design, Journalism, Music, Public Administration, Science, Social Work

7. TEACHING FACILITIES

Largest first-year class 475
First-year courses with tutorials 75%
Lab places for first-year students
Languages 25

Research grants and contracts
$12 million

Graduate programs
Number of degrees 9
Number of master's programs 34; doctoral programs 14
Enrolment in master's programs 1652; doctoral programs 455

Libraries
Open stack 1,352,667 volumes
Closed stack 50,000 volumes
Total holdings 2,200,000 volumes

8. STUDENTS

Undergraduates

1st year	5300
2nd year	4000
3rd year	3400
4th year	1500

Entering as Ontario Scholars 15%
Entering with scholarships 6%
Entering with OSAP help 35%

9. ENTRANCE SCHOLARSHIPS

Most prestigious
Chancellor's Scholarship (4):
Application necessary by May 14
Requirements: minimum 85%

Full-tuition scholarships (54)
No application necessary
Deadline June 15
Requirements: minimum 85%; no supporting documentation

Partial-tuition scholarships (915)
No application necessary
Deadline June 15
Requirements: percentage varies; no supporting documentation

Scholarships for entering students
Offered 1000 (approx.)
Accepted 350
Total budget for undergraduate scholarships $700,000

10. INTERNATIONAL STUDENTS

Students from outside Canada 9%
Scholarships awarded N/A
Services available Adviser; Academic Counsellor
Language requirements for admission TOEFL score 580; Carleton Assessment of English as a Second Language

11. ATHLETIC FACILITIES

Combatives room
Fitness centre
Gym
Ice rink (outdoor)
Playing fields
Squash courts
Swimming pool
Tennis courts (outdoor)
Weight/workout rooms

Inter-university sports
Basketball M, F
Cross-country skiing M, F
Fencing M, F
Field hockey F
Football M
Rugby M
Soccer M, F
Swimming M, F
Volleyball F
Water polo M

Intra-mural organized sports
Badminton
Basketball
Broom-ball
Cross-country running
Hardball
Hockey
Inner-tube water polo
Softball
Touch football
Volleyball

Recreation and fitness programs

12. STUDENT LIFE

Student councils 1
Student clubs more than 100

Pubs 4
Drinking awareness program

First-year orientation
First 2 weeks of classes; parent sessions

13. STUDENT SERVICES

Counselling
Psychological, Career, Peer

Medical
Nurses 6; Doctors M (4), F (5)

Special needs
Handicapped/special needs centre
100% of campus wheelchair accessible
Learning disability program

Other
Essay writing/study skills program
Mature student association
Off-campus housing registry

14. RESIDENCES

Residence places
503 M, 493 F, 591 C

First-year students
Places reserved 60%; all double
Application deadline prior to lottery date
Places reserved for scholarship winners; 80% guarantees residence
Eligibility limitations based on student's home location: must reside 35 miles or more from Ottawa
Allocations announced in early July

Upper-year students
Places reserved 40%
Allocations announced: varies

Wheelchair-accessible rooms 15

Meal-plan options
Lunch and dinner 7 or 5 days a week; lunch or dinner 5 days a week

15. PROGRAMS OF UNDERGRADUATE STUDY

15.1 FACULTY OF ARTS, FACULTY OF SOCIAL SCIENCES

Degree
Bachelor of Arts, B.A.

Level
Pass, Honours

Programs
Anthropology
Art History
Biology
Canadian Studies
Classics
Criminology and Criminal Justice
Directed Interdisciplinary Study
Economics
English Language and Literature
Film Studies
French
Geography
German
History
Italian
Law
Linguistics
Mass Communications
Music
Philosophy
Political Science
Psychology
Religion
Russian
Sociology
Soviet and Eastern Europe Studies
Spanish
Women's Studies

First-year entry Yes

Entry requirements
Minimum average: 60% Pass, 65% Honours
OAC English recommended
No specific OACs required

Students accepted (both faculties) 3000
Total (both faculties) 9000

Co-op (work/study) available
No; no correspondence or self-paced study

Graduation requirements
Minimum GPA: Pass - 4.0 on scale of 12.0; Honours - 6.0 in 2nd, 3rd year; 6.5 in 4th year
Full credits/courses: Honours B.A. 20, Pass B.A. 15

Graduating students 1492

15.2 FACULTY OF SCIENCE

Degree
Bachelor of Science, B.Sc.

Level
Pass, Honours

Programs
Biochemistry
Biology
Biotechnology
Chemistry
Environmental Sciences
Earth Sciences
Geography
Mathematics and Statistics
Physics
Psychology
Integrated Science Studies

First-year entry Yes

Entry requirements
Minimum average: 60% Pass, 65% Honours
OAC Calculus, Algebra and Geometry, plus one of Algebra and Geometry, Biology, Chemistry, Physics
English recommended

Students accepted 350
Total in faculty 900

Co-op (work/study) available
Yes, Earth Sciences; no correspondence or self-paced study

Graduation requirements
Consult Carleton calendar
Full credits/courses: Honours 20, Pass 15

Graduating students 187

15.3 FACULTY OF SOCIAL SCIENCES

Degree
Bachelor of Commerce, B.Com.
Bachelor of Public Administration, B.P.A.

Level
Honours

Programs
Accounting
Finance
Human Resources
International Business
Management Information Systems
Marketing
Public Administration

First-year entry Yes

Entry requirements
Minimum average: 65% Honours
B.Com OAC Calculus and one of Algebra and Geometry or Finite Mathematics
B.P.A. - no specific OAC's
English recommended
Public Administration no special OACs required.

Students accepted 405
Total in faculty 1125

Co-op (work/study) available
No; no correspondence or self-paced study

Graduation requirements
Minimum GPA: 4.0 overall, 6.0 in Honours courses on scale of 12.0
Public Administration: 6.0 in 2nd, 3rd year, 6.5 in 4th year
Full credits/courses: Honours 20

Graduating students 187

15.4 FACULTY OF ENGINEERING

Degree
Bachelor of Architecture, B.Arch.

Level
5-year program

Program
Architecture

First-year entry Yes

Entry requirements
Minimum average: 65%
OAC Calculus, Algebra and Geometry, Physics

Students accepted 75
Total in faculty 318
Co-op (work/study) available
No; no correspondence or self-paced study

Graduation requirements
Consult Carleton calendar

Graduating students 38

15.4 FACULTY OF ENGINEERING

Degree
Bachelor of Industrial Design

Level
Honours

Program
Industrial Design

First-year entry Yes

Entry requirements
Minimum average: 65%
OAC Calculus, Algebra and Geometry, Chemistry, Physics
Portfolio required

Students accepted 35
Total in program 125

Co-op (work/study) available
No; no correspondence or self-paced study

Graduation requirements
Minimum G.P.A. 3.4 (cumulative)
Consult undergraduate calendar

15.5 FACULTY OF SCIENCE

Degree
Bachelor of Computer Science, B.C.S.

Level
Honours

Programs
Hardware
Management and Business Systems
Scientific Applications
Software
Theory of Computing

First-year entry Yes

Entry requirements
Minimum average: 65%
OAC Calculus, Algebra and Geometry
Physics required for Hardware and Scientific Applications
English recommended

Students accepted 115
Total in program 300

Co-op (work/study) available
Yes; no correspondence or self-paced study

Graduation requirements
Consult Carleton calendar
Full credits/courses 20

Graduating students 40

15.7 FACULTY OF ENGINEERING

Degree
Bachelor of Engineering, B.Eng.

Level
Honours

Programs
Aerospace Eng.
Civil Eng.
Electrical Eng.
Mechanical Eng.
Computer Systems Eng.

First-year entry Yes

Entry requirements
Minimum average: 65%
OAC Calculus, Algebra and Geometry, Chemistry, Physics
English recommended

Students accepted 350
Total in program 950

Co-op (work/study) available
Limited; no correspondence or self-paced study

Graduation requirements
Minimum GPA: 3.4 (cumulative weighted)

Graduating students 158

15.10 FACULTY OF ARTS

Degree
Bachelor of Music, B.Mus.

Level
Honours

Program
Music

First-year entry Yes

Entry requirements
Minimum average: 65%
No special OACs required

Students accepted 25
Total in program 37

Co-op (work/study) available
No; no correspondence or self-paced study

Graduation requirements
6.0 in 2nd, 3rd year; 6.5 in 4th year
Minimum GPA: N/A
Full credits/courses: Honours 20

Graduating students 7

15.11 FACULTY OF ARTS

Degree
Bachelor of Journalism, B.J.
Level
Honours

Program
Journalism

First-year entry Yes

Entry requirements
Minimum average: 65%
No special OACs required
English recommended

Students accepted 225
Total in program 550

Co-op (work/study) available
No; no correspondence or self-paced study

Graduation requirements
Minimum GPA: 6.0 in 2nd, 3rd year; 6.5 in 4th year
Full credits/courses: Honours 20.5
Consult Carleton calendar for other special requirements

Graduating students 83

15.12 FACULTY OF SOCIAL SCIENCES

Degree
Bachelor of Social Work, B.S.W.

Level
Honours

Program
Social Work

First-year entry
Yes

Entry requirements
Minimum average: 65%
No specific OACs required

Students accepted N/A
Total in program N/A

Co-op (work/study) available?
No: no correspondence or self-paced study

Graduation requirements
Consult undergraduate calendar

Graduating students N/A

16. FUTURE PLANS

Buildings
New buildings on campus by 1992 include fine arts, centre for advanced studies in engineering

University of Guelph

1. OVERVIEW

On a scenic 479-hectare (1200-acre) campus one hour's drive from Toronto, the University of Guelph continues a tradition that reaches back over 100 years. The friendly environment, high-calibre instruction in a wide range of academic areas, and the third most research-intensive program in the country make Guelph an outstanding choice.

2. PRESIDENT

Brian Segal

3. ENROLMENT

(1990 Fall semester; undergraduate totals rounded to nearest 100)

Registration

Undergraduate full-time 10,900 (M 4500, F 6400)
Undergraduate part-time 2500 (M 900, F 1600)
Graduate 1457 (M 873, F 584)

Residence

Undergrads in residence 39% (M 37%, F 63%)
Undergrads in off-campus housing 46%
Undergrads commuting 15%

4. ADMISSIONS TO FIRST YEAR

Entry dates

Fall, Winter, Spring

First-year entries (full-time only)

	Fall (Sept)	Winter (Jan)	Spring (May)
Applications	16,193	1,022	856
Admissions	7,500	568	706
Enrolments	3,620	462	147

Admissions offered to qualified candidates before early admission

Yes

Community-college transfer requirements

2-year CAAT program graduates, or students with 2 years of 3-year program

Advanced standing granted

3-year CAAT program graduates with a high average over 3 years may be granted a maximum of 10 semester courses.

Mature students admission requirements

Age 21, away from secondary school for at least 2 years; 3 courses allowed. Consult Guelph calendar for specific details.

5. ADMISSIONS CONTACT

Trish Walker
Associate Registrar, Admissions
Admissions Office, University Centre
University of Guelph
Guelph, Ontario N1G 2W1
(519) 824-4120, ext. 8721

6. STRUCTURE AND DEGREES

Board of Governors

23 members (M 17, F 6; 3 senate, 1 support staff, 4 alumni, 2 students)

Teaching faculty

Full-time 738 (M 626, F 112)
Part-time 40 (M 25, F 15)

Faculty/Student ratio (FTE basis)

1:16

Undergraduate degrees conferred

Agricultural Science, Applied Science, Arts, Commerce, Engineering Science, Human Kinetics Science, Landscape

Architecture, Science, Veterinary Medicine

7. TEACHING FACILITIES

Largest first-year class 300
First-year courses with tutorials 50%
Lab places for first-year students
Biology 900, Chemistry 1440, Computers 750, Languages 600, Physics 1050

Research grants and contracts
$54 million

Graduate programs
Number of programs 45
Enrolment in master's programs 997; doctoral programs 448

Libraries
With open stacks 2
With closed stacks N/A
Total holdings 2.5 million volumes

8. STUDENTS

Undergraduates

1st year	4665
2nd year	3814
3rd year	2950
4th year	1872

Entering as Ontario Scholars 33%
Entering with scholarships 10%
Entering with OSAP help 45%

9. ENTRANCE SCHOLARSHIPS

Most prestigious
President's Scholarships (10):
Application necessary
Deadline April 1
Requirements: 80%; principal's or head of guidance's nomination; references

Full-tuition scholarships (300 or more) $1500 or more each
No application necessary
No deadline
Requirements: 80% or more; no supporting documentation

Partial-tuition scholarships (numerous)
No application necessary
No deadline
Requirements: 80% or more; no supporting documentation

Scholarships for entering students
Offered 1085
Accepted 475
Total budget for undergraduate scholarships $1,200,000

10. INTERNATIONAL STUDENTS

Students from outside Canada 4%
Scholarships awarded None
Services available Adviser; Academic Counsellor; International Student Advisory Council
Language requirements for admission TOEFL score 575; minimum B final standing in OAC English 1 may also satisfy requirement

11. ATHLETIC FACILITIES

Athletic complex
Gyms
Ice rinks
Jogging trails
Playing fields
Squash courts
Stadium
Swimming pool
Tennis courts (outdoor)
Track centre (outdoor)
Weight/workout rooms

Inter-university sports
Basketball M, F
Cheerleading M, F
Cross-country running M, F
Curling M, F
Football M
Figure skating F
Golf M
Hockey, field F
Hockey, ice M, F
Rugby M
Skiing (Nordic) M, F
Soccer M, F
Squash M
Swimming M, F
Tennis F

Track M, F
Volleyball M, F
Wrestling M

Intra-mural organized sports
Basketball M, F, C
Broom-ball C
Hockey M, F
Inner-tube water polo C
Lob ball M
Slow pitch C
Soccer M, F
Softball M
Touch football M, C
Volleyball M, F, C

Recreation and fitness programs

12. STUDENT LIFE

Student councils 8
Student clubs 50

Pubs 3
Drinking awareness program

First-year orientation
Start of each semester; 2-day orientation held 3 times each summer; parent sessions

13. STUDENT SERVICES

Counselling
Psychological, Career, Peer

Medical
Nurses 10; Doctors M (6) F (3)

Special needs
Handicapped/special needs centre
70% of campus wheelchair accessible

Other
Learning disability adviser
Essay writing/study skills program
Mature student association
Off-campus housing registry

14. RESIDENCES

Residence places 4100
160 M, 570 F, 3370 C
139 townhouses for married students

First-year students
Places reserved 2500 (if deadline is met)
Application deadline: late June for fall semester
1st-year students given priority
No places reserved for scholarship winners
No eligibility limitations based on student's home location
Allocations announced 2nd to 3rd week of August

Upper-year students
Places reserved: approx. 1600
Allocations announced 1st week of June

Wheelchair-accessible rooms 8

Meal-plan options
Various plans ranging in cost from $790 to $1000 per semester

15. PROGRAMS OF UNDERGRADUATE STUDY

15.1 COLLEGE OF ARTS, COLLEGE OF SOCIAL SCIENCE

Degree
Bachelor of Arts, B.A.

Level
General, Honours

Programs
Agricultural Economics
Canadian Studies
Classical Studies
Drama
Economics
English
Fine Art
French
Geography
German
History
Information Systems and Human Behaviour
International Development
Italian
Management Economics
Mathematics/Computer Science
Music
Philosophy
Political Science
Psychology

Settlement Studies
Sociology/Anthropology
Spanish
Statistics
Women's Studies

First-year entry Yes

Entry requirements
Minimum average: low 70%
6 OACs including English 1; 1 credit in Mathematics or French or another language recommended

Students accepted 910
Total in program 4740

Co-op (work/study) available
Yes; Computing and Information Science, Psychology; correspondence and self-paced study available

Graduation requirements
Full credits/courses: Honours, 40 courses, including at least 14 at 300 level or above, with cumulative average of 70% for all course attempts in Honours subjects
General, 30 courses, including at least 8 at 300 level or above; minimum C grade in at least 60% of all course attempts

Graduating students 817

15.2 ONTARIO AGRICULTURAL COLLEGE

Degree
Bachelor of Science, Agriculture, B.Sc.Agr.

Level
Honours

Majors
Agricultural Economics
Agronomy
Animal Science
Environmental Biology
Horticultural Science and Business
Plant Protection
Resources Management

First-year entry Yes

Entry requirements
Minimum average: low 60% to low 70%
6 OACs including English 1, Calculus, Chemistry or Biology, Mathematics or Science

Students accepted 215
Total in program 799

Co-op (work/study) available
Yes; Agricultural Economics, Agronomy, Animal Science, Horticultural Science and Business, Resources Management; correspondence and self-paced study available

Graduation requirements
Full credits/courses: Honours, 40, with minimum C grade in at least 60% of all course attempts, excluding diploma courses

Graduating students 208

15.2 COLLEGES OF BIOLOGICAL AND PHYSICAL SCIENCES

Degree
Bachelor of Science, B.Sc.

Level
General, Honours

Majors
Animal Biology
Applicable Mathematics
Applied Biochemistry
Applied Chemistry
Biochemistry
Biological Science
Biomedical and Health Science
Biophysics
Chemical Physics
Chemistry
Computing and Information Science
Earth Science
Ecology
Entomology
Entomology with Apiculture
Environmental Protection
Environmental Soil Science

Fisheries Biology
Food and Dairy Science
Food Science
Human Biology
Marine Biology
Mathematics
Microbiology
Molecular Biology and Genetics
Nutritional Sciences
Physical Geography
Physical Science
Physics
Plant Biology
Plant Science and Plant Biotechnology
Psychology
Statistics
Theoretical Physics
Toxicology
Wildlife Biology
Zoology

First-year entry Yes

Entry requirements
Minimum average: high 60% to low 70%
6 OACs including Calculus, Chemistry, 2 of Algebra and Geometry, Biology, Physics
Biology recommended for Biological Science
Chemistry and Algebra and Geometry or Relations and Functions recommended for Physical Science

Students accepted 860
Total in program 3260

Co-op (work/study) available
Yes; Applied Biochemistry, Applied Chemistry, Biochemistry, Biophysics, Chemistry, Computing and Information Science, Food Science, Microbiology, Physics, Plant Biology, Toxicology; correspondence and self-paced study available

Graduation requirements
Full credits/courses: Honours, 40 courses, with minimum C grade in at least 60% of all course attempts excluding diploma courses
General, 30 acceptable courses; minimum C grade in at least 60% of all course attempts

Graduating students 510

15.3 COLLEGE OF SOCIAL SCIENCE, ONTARIO AGRICULTURAL COLLEGE, COLLEGE OF FAMILY AND CONSUMER STUDIES, SCHOOL OF HOTEL AND FOOD ADMINISTRATION

Degree
Bachelor of Commerce, B.Comm.

Level
Honours

Majors
Agricultural Business
Hotel and Food Administration
Institutional Foodservice Management
Management Economics (Industry and Finance)
Marketing

First-year entry Yes

Entry requirements
Minimum average: mid 60% to low 70%
6 OACs including English 1, Mathematics,
Background Information Sheet required for majors in Hotel and Food Administration and Institutional Foodservice Management

Students accepted 310
Total in program 929

Co-op (work/study) available
Yes; Agricultural Business, Hotel and Food Administration; correspondence and self-paced study available

Graduation requirements
Full credits/courses: Honours, 40, with minimum C grade in at least 60% of all course attempts, excluding diploma courses

Graduating students
116 from Hotel and Food Administration and Institutional Foodservice Management; other majors new, no graduates yet

15.4 ONTARIO AGRICULTURAL COLLEGE, SCHOOL OF LANDSCAPE ARCHITECTURE

Degree
Bachelor of Landscape Architecture, B.L.A.

Level
Honours

Programs
Landscape Architecture

First-year entry Yes

Entry requirements
Minimum average: low 70%
6 OACs including Biology, Mathematics, English; 1 credit in Geography, Visual Arts, French or *Français* or another language
Portfolio and Background Information Sheet required, an interview may be required

Students accepted 33
Total in program 164

Co-op (work/study) available
No; work placement in upper years; correspondence and self-paced study available

Graduation requirements
Full credits/courses: Honours 42, with minimum C grade in at least 60% of all course attempts, excluding diploma courses

Graduating students 33

15.7 COLLEGE OF PHYSICAL SCIENCE, COLLEGE OF ENGINEERING

Degree
Bachelor of Science, Engineering, B.Sc.Eng.

Level
Honours

Majors
Agricultural Eng.
Biological Eng.
Engineering Systems and Computing
Environmental Eng.
Food Eng.
Water Resources Eng.

First-year entry Yes

Entry requirements
Minimum average: low 70%
6 OACs including English 1, Calculus, Algebra and Geometry, 3 of Chemistry, Physics, Biology, Computer Studies

Students accepted 95
Total in program 310

Co-op (work/study) available
Yes; correspondence and self-paced study available

Graduation requirements
Full credits/courses: Honours 43, with pass standing in each course and minimum C grade in at least 60% of all course attempts

Graduating students 32

15.9 ONTARIO VETERINARY COLLEGE

Degree
Doctor of Veterinary Medicine, D.V.M.

Level
Honours

Majors
Veterinary Medicine

First-year entry No

Entry requirements
Minimum average: high 70% to low 80%
1st-year university science program with minimum of 10 semester courses or equivalent required to enter Pre-Veterinary Year; successful completion of 2 semesters of Pre-Veterinary allows

entry to Doctor of Veterinary Science degree program
OACs recommended in Calculus, Algebra and Geometry or Relations and Functions, Biology, Chemistry and Physics
Background Information Sheet, personal interview

Students accepted 100
Total in program 406

Co-op (work/study) available
No; no correspondence or self-paced study

Graduation requirements
Full credits/courses: Honours 50, minimum C grade in at least 60% of all course attempts in Doctor of Veterinary Medicine program

Graduating students 98

15.14 COLLEGE OF BIOLOGICAL SCIENCE, COLLEGE OF HUMAN BIOLOGY

Degree
Bachelor of Science, Human Kinetics, B.Sc. (H.K.)

Level
Honours

Majors
Human Kinetics

First-year entry Yes

Entry requirements
Minimum average: mid 60% to low 70%
6 OACs including English 1, Calculus, Chemistry; 2 credits from Algebra and Geometry or Relations and Functions, Biology or Physics
Biology recommended

Students accepted 120
Total in program 452

Co-op (work/study) available
No; correspondence and self-paced study available

Graduation requirements
Full credits/courses: Honours 40, with minimum C grade in at least 60% of all course attempts, excluding diploma courses

Graduating students 70

15.15 COLLEGE OF FAMILY AND CONSUMER STUDIES

Degree
Bachelor of Applied Science, B.A.Sc.

Level
Honours

Majors
Applied Human Nutrition
Child Studies
Consumer Studies
Family and Social Relations
Gerontology

First-year entry Yes

Entry requirements
Minimum average: mid 60% to high 70% for Co-op
6 OACs including English 1, Mathematics (Calculus strongly recommended), Chemistry or Biology

Students accepted 240
Total in program 1228

Co-op (work/study) available
Yes; Child Studies, Family and Social Relations, Gerontology; correspondence and self-paced study available

Graduation requirements
Full credits/courses: Honours 40, with minimum C grade in at least 60% of all course attempts, excluding diploma courses

Graduating students 257

16. FUTURE PLANS

Buildings
Environmental Biology / Horticultural Science greenhouse complex, 1991

Thornborough Building, 300 seat lecture theatre, 1991

Programs

A new 1st-year program, AKADEMIA, allows students interested in arts and science to take courses in both. Specially designed, interdisciplinary courses are also available. Selection of study program leading to either a B.A. AKADEMIA or B.Sc. AKADEMIA occurs in the 3rd semester. Students live in a special residence area. Admission requirements include 6 OACs with a minimum 75% average. B.A. AKADEMIA requires OAC English 1, Mathematics (Calculus recommended) and 1 of Science (Biology, Physics or Chemistry), 1 Arts or Social Studies. B.Sc. AKADEMIA requires OAC English 1, Calculus, 3 credits from Algebra and Geometry, Biology, Chemistry or Physics and 1 Arts or Social Science.

Students with exceptional talents in the sciences may apply to a new enriched 1st-year program, MPC2 (Mathematics, Physics, Chemistry and Computing and Information Science). MPC2 requires OAC English 1, Calculus, Chemistry, Physics, Algebra and Chemistry or Relations and Functions, Computer Science recommended

Lakehead University

1. OVERVIEW

Dynamic, modern and set in beautiful Thunder Bay, a northwestern Ontario city of 120,000, Lakehead University offers a wide range of personal educational opportunities to its 6100 students. Established in 1965, Lakehead is one of the few Canadian universities that offers both degree and diploma programs at the undergraduate level, as well as master's programs.

2. PRESIDENT

R.G. Rosehart

3. ENROLMENT

(1990 Fall semester; undergraduate totals rounded to nearest 50)

Registration
Undergraduate full-time 4100 (M 2090, F 2010)
Undergraduate part-time 2000 (M 580, F 1420)
Graduate 274 (M 122, F 152)

Residence
Undergrads in residence 19% (M 57%, F 43%)
Undergrads in off-campus housing N/A
Undergrads commuting 30%

4. ADMISSIONS TO FIRST YEAR

Entry dates
Fall, Winter, February, Spring, Summer

First-year entries (full-time)

	Fall
Applications	5194
Admissions	2835
Enrolments	1441

Admissions offered to qualified candidates before early admission
Yes

Community-college transfer requirements
Depends on CAAT program and level attained

Advanced standing granted
Based on past academic performance and CAAT course content

Mature students admission requirements
Age 21, resident of Canada; 2 years away from high school; number of courses allowed varies

5. ADMISSIONS CONTACT

Assistant Registrar, Admissions
Office of the Registrar
Lakehead University
955 Oliver Road
Thunder Bay, Ontario P7B 5E1
(807) 343-8500

6. STRUCTURE AND DEGREES

Board of Governors
30 members (M 18, F 12)

Teaching faculty
Full-time 261 (M N/A, F N/A)
Part-time 260

Faculty/Student ratio (FTE basis)
N/A

Undergraduate degrees conferred
Administration, Arts, Commerce, Education, Engineering, Forestry Science, Outdoor Recreation, Nursing Science, Physical Education, Science, Social Work

7. TEACHING FACILITIES

Largest first-year class 360
First-year courses with tutorials
N/A

Lab places for first-year students
Biology 150, Chemistry 100, Computers 175, Drafting 50, Languages 75, Physics 100
Research grants and contracts N/A

Graduate programs
Number of programs N/A
Enrolment in master's programs 274; doctoral programs None

Libraries
With open stacks 2
With closed stacks 0
Total holdings 600,000 volumes

8. STUDENTS

Undergraduates

1st year	1739*
2nd year	1025
3rd year	763
4th year	467

*includes B.Ed. students

Entering as Ontario Scholars 12%
Entering with scholarships 12%
Entering with OSAP help N/A

9. ENTRANCE SCHOLARSHIPS

Most prestigious
Lakehead University Presidential Scholarship (2):
$10,000 each
Application necessary
Deadline May 15
Requirements: 90% minimum; interview may be necessary

Full-tuition scholarships
Lakehead University Northwestern Ontario Leader's Scholarship (number varies):
$8000 each
No application necessary
No deadline
Requirements: 80% minimum
Each Northwestern Ontario high school recommends highest ranking graduate

Partial-tuition scholarships
Lakehead University Entrance Award of Academic Excellence (unlimited):
No application necessary
No deadline
95% or more: $2000 per year X 4 yrs
90% to 94.5%: $1500 per year X 4 yrs
85% to 89.9%: $1000 per year X 4 yrs

Scholarships for entering students
Offered: approx. 352
Accepted 169
Total budget for undergraduate scholarships: approx. $250,000

10. INTERNATIONAL STUDENTS

Students from outside Canada 4%
Scholarships awarded 2
Services available Adviser; Academic Counsellor; Host Family Program; International Student clubs; Interim accommodation service
Language requirements for admission TOEFL score 550; MELAB score 90

11. ATHLETIC FACILITIES

Gym
Ice rink
Playing fields
Saunas
Sports-medicine clinic
Squash courts
Stadium
Swimming pool
Tennis courts (indoor/outdoor)
Weight/workout rooms
Wrestling area

Inter-university sports
Basketball M, F
Running (cross-country) M, F
Skiing (Alpine) M, F
Skiing (Nordic) M, F
Track and field (indoor) M, F
Volleyball F
Wrestling M

Intra-mural organized sports
Aerobics
Aquabics
Basketball

Biathalon
Bowling
Broom-ball
Curling
Golf
Hockey, ice M, C
Inner-tube water polo
Soccer
Squash
Slow-pitch
Swimming
Touch football C
Volleyball
Weightlifting

Recreation and fitness programs

12. STUDENT LIFE

Student council 1
Student clubs approx. 30

Pubs 1
Drinking awareness program

First-year orientation
Week after Labour Day

13. STUDENT SERVICES

Counselling
Psychological, Career

Medical
Nurse 1; Doctors M (3), F (3)

Special needs
Handicapped/special needs centre
100% of campus wheelchair accessible

Other
Learning disability program
Essay writing/study skills program
Mature student association
Off-campus housing registry

14. RESIDENCES

Residence places 879
208 M, 112 F, 308 C
238 apartments/townhouses

First-year students
Places reserved 350
Applications accepted as received up to start of term
No places reserved for scholarship winners
No eligibility limitations based on student's home location
Allocations announced June 14 or date of acceptance

Upper-year students
Places reserved N/A
Allocations announced commencing April

Wheelchair-accessible rooms 50

Meal-plan options
Residences 15 to 21 meals per week
Townhouses optional meal plan

15. PROGRAMS OF UNDERGRADUATE STUDY

15.1 FACULTY OF ARTS AND SCIENCE

Degree
Bachelor of Arts, B.A.

Level
General, Honours

Programs
Anthropology
Anthropology and Boreal Studies
Anthropology and Native Studies
Economics
Economics and Geography
Economics and Mathematical Sciences
English
English, general concentration in Canadian Studies
English and French
French*
General Arts Program
Geography
Geography and Economics
Geography and H.B.O.R.† (4-yr program)
History
History and English
History and Philosophy
History and Political Studies
Library and Information Studies
Mathematical Sciences
Mathematics, Actuarial Option

Mathematics and Economics
Music
Philosophy
Philosophy and Religious Studies
Political Studies
Psychology
Psychology and Philosophy
Psychology and Sociology
Religious Studies
Religious Studies and Philosophy
Sociology
Sociology and Political Studies
* Minors in Classics, Cree, Finnish, French, German, Ojibwa, Spanish, Women Studies
† Hon. Bach. of Outdoor Recreation

First-year entry Yes

Entry requirements
Minimum average: 60%
OAC English
Mathematical Sciences: OAC English, Calculus, Algebra and Geometry or Finite Mathematics
French: OAC English, French or equivalent recommended

Students accepted 1276
Total in faculty 1714

Co-op (work/study) available
No; no correspondence or self-paced study

Graduation requirements
Minimum GPA: General 60%, Honours 70% average in major subjects
Full credits/courses: Honours 20, General 15; see special requirements in Lakehead calendar

Graduating students 452

15.2 FACULTY OF ARTS AND SCIENCE

Degree
Bachelor of Science, B.Sc.

Level
General, Honours

Programs
Biology
Biology and Chemistry
Biology and Geography
Biology (Natural Science)
Chemistry
Chemistry with Energy and Fuel Science
Chemistry Industrial Experience Option
Computer Science Co-operative Program
Energy and Fuel Science (minor)
General Science Program
Geo-Archaelogy
Geography
Geography and Biology
Geography with Geology minor
Geology
Mathematics
Mathematical Physics
Mathematics and Physics
Medical Lab Sciences
Natural Science and H.B.O.R.* (4-yr program)
Physics
Physics and Energy and Fuel Science
Physics and Mathematics
Psychology
* Hon. Bach. of Outdoor Recreation

First-year entry Yes

Entry requirements
Minimum average: 60%
OAC English; plus for Science programs: OAC Calculus and 3 of Algebra and Geometry, Finite Mathematics, Chemistry, Physics and Biology
Mathematics and Computer Science programs: OAC Calculus, 1 of Algebra and Geometry, Finite Mathematics, 2 of Algebra and Geometry, Finite Mathematics, Chemistry, Physics, Biology

Students accepted 234
Total in faculty 310

Co-op (work/study) available
Yes, Computer Science and Chemistry; no self-paced study available

Graduation requirements
Minimum GPA: General 60%, Honours 70% average in major subject
Full credits/courses: Honours 20, General 15; see special requirements in Lakehead calendar

Graduating students 115

15.3, 15.6, 15.7, 15.8, 15.13, 15.14
FACULTY OF PROFESSIONAL STUDIES

Degree
Bachelor of Administration, B.Admin.
Bachelor of Applied Science (1st year only)
Bachelor of Education (Concurrent), B.Ed.
Bachelor of Engineering, B.Eng.
Honours Bachelor of Commerce, H.B.Comm.
Honours Bachelor of Outdoor Recreation, H.B.O.R.
Honours Bachelor of Physical Education, H.B.P.E.
Honours Bachelor of Science (Forestry), H.B.Sc.F.
Honours Bachelor of Science (Nursing), H.B.Sc.N.

Level N/R

Programs
See Degree list

First-year entry Yes

Entry requirements
Minimum average: 60%
Subjects required:
Honours Bachelor of Commerce: 6 OACs including English, 2 Mathematics
Concurrent Bachelor of Education, Bachelor of Arts / Bachelor of Science: 6 OACs with same requirements for either Arts B.A. or Science B.Sc.; Grade 12 advanced-level Mathematics recommended
Bachelor of Engineering: See Lakehead calendar
Honours Bachelor of Science (Forestry): 6 OACs including Biology, Calculus, Chemistry, English and either Finite Mathematics or Algebra and Geometry
Honours Bachelor of Science (Nursing): 6 OACs including English, Biology and Chemistry; Mathematics strongly recommended
Honours Bachelor of Outdoor Recreation: 6 OACs including English
Honours Bachelor of Physical Education: 6 OACs including English, Chemistry

Students accepted 1319
Total in faculty 2373

Co-op (work/study) available
Yes, Forestry; no correspondence or self-paced study

Graduation requirements
Minimum GPA: varies; see Lakehead calendar
Full credits/courses: varies; see calendar

Graduating students 797

15.10 FACULTY OF FINE ARTS

Degree
Honours Bachelor of Fine Arts, H.B.F.A.

Level
Honours

Programs
Visual Arts

First-year entry Yes

Entry requirements
Minimum average: 60%
6 OACs, including English
Portfolio of work required

Students accepted 32
Total in faculty N/A

Co-op (work/study) available
No; no correspondence or self-paced study

Graduation requirements
Minimum GPA: 70%
Full credits/courses: Honours 20

Graduating students 8

15.15 FACULTY OF ARTS AND SCIENCE

Degree
Honours Bachelor of Social Work, H.B.S.W.
Level
Honours

Programs
Social Work

First-year entry
Yes; admission to years 3 and 4 on formal application, with documentation to Admissions Committee of Social Work (personal and academic suitability)

Entry requirements
Minimum average: 60%
6 OACs including English

Students accepted
Year 1: 86
Year 3: 26
Total in faculty 155

Co-op (work/study) available
No; no correspondence or self-paced study

Graduation requirements
Minimum GPA: 70% average in major
Full credits/courses: Honours 20

Graduating students 51

Laurentian University

1. OVERVIEW

Laurentian University of Sudbury provides a strong focus on outdoor activities and recreation. "Accessible" aptly describes this northern bilingual university, which provides a full complement of Arts and Science offerings in concert with a series of professional schools. Algoma and Nipissing University Colleges, situated in Sault Ste Marie and North Bay respectively, are affiliated with Laurentian University.

2. PRESIDENT

Dr. R. Paul

3. ENROLMENT

(1990 Fall semester; undergraduate totals rounded to nearest 50)

Registration

Undergraduate full-time 4400 (M 1950, F 2450)
Undergraduate part-time 2700 (M 600, F 2100)
Graduate 176 (M 105, F 71)

Residence

Undergrads in residence 16.6% (M 45%, F 55%)
Undergrads in off-campus housing N/A
Undergrads commuting 83.4%

4. ADMISSIONS TO FIRST YEAR

Entry dates

Fall

First-year entries

	Fall
Applications	6779
Admissions	4270
Enrolments	1711

Other entry dates

April (spring session), July (summer session); January enrolment limited

Admissions offered to qualified candidates before early admission

Yes

Community-college transfer requirements

3.2 GPA for 1-year CAAT studies; 2.5 GPA for 2- and 3-year CAAT graduates

Advanced standing granted

See Laurentian calendar.

Mature students admission requirements

Age 21; success in work field; 2 years or more out of school; 5 courses allowed

5. ADMISSIONS CONTACT

Mr Matthew Brennan
or Ms Anne Hodges
Admissions Officers
Laurentian University
Ramsey Lake Road
Sudbury, Ontario P3C 2C6
(705) 675-1151

6. STRUCTURE AND DEGREES

Board of Governors

35 members (M 29, F 6; 4 faculty, 2 students, 3 support staff, 1 alumni)

Teaching faculty

Full-time 263 (M 205, F 58)
Part-time 290 (M 129, F 161)

Faculty/Student ratio (FTE basis)

1:15

Undergraduate degrees conferred

Arts, Commerce, Education, Engineering, Nursing, Physical

Health and Education, Science, Science of Language, Social Work

7. TEACHING FACILITIES

Largest first-year class 211
First-year courses with tutorials
Mathematics, Nursing and English only
Lab places for first-year students
Varies

Research grants and contracts
$2,220,583 (1989–90)

Graduate programs
Number of programs 8
Enrolment in master's programs 176; doctoral programs None

Libraries
With open stacks 4
With closed stacks None
Total holdings 800,000 volumes

8. STUDENTS

Undergraduates

1st year	1549
2nd year	1219
3rd year	1026
4th year	580

Entering as Ontario Scholars 7.3%
Entering with scholarships 4.7%
Entering with OSAP help 40%

9. ENTRANCE SCHOLARSHIPS

Most prestigious
Inco Bilingual Scholarship:
Renewable
Application necessary
Deadline June 1
Requirements: 85% or more; secondary-school principal's recommendation

Full-tuition scholarships (40)
No application necessary
No deadline
Requirements: 80% or more

Partial-tuition scholarships (21)
Application required for 6 of 21
Deadline June 1
Requirements: 80%; bursary application

Scholarships for entering students
Offered 64
Accepted 64
Total budget for undergraduate scholarships $192,000

10. INTERNATIONAL STUDENTS

Students from outside Canada 1.1% of year 1
Scholarships awarded None
Services available Student Services; Language training in English; Laurentian Christian Fellowship
Language requirements for admission TOEFL score 550 for clear admission, 530–49 for conditional admission; MELAB score 95 for clear admission, 90 for cond. adm. to Arts, 85 for cond. adm. to Sciences

11. ATHLETIC FACILITIES

Cross-country trails
Gym
Playing fields
Stadium
Swimming pool
Tennis courts (outdoor)
Track centre (outdoor)
Vita parcour trail
Warm-up track
Weight/workout rooms

Inter-university sports
Basketball M, F
Cross-country running M, F
Curling F
Hockey, field F
Hockey, ice M
Indoor track and field M, F
Skiing (Alpine/Nordic) M, F
Soccer M
Swimming M, F
Volleyball M

Intra-mural organized sports
available in most areas

Recreation and fitness programs

12. STUDENT LIFE

Student councils 3
Student clubs Varies

Pub 1
Drinking awareness program

First-year orientation
Yes; Frosh week and Labour Day weekend; parent sessions

13. STUDENT SERVICES

Counselling
Psychological, Career, Peer

Medical
Nurses 3; Doctors M (1), F (1)

Special needs
Handicapped/special needs centre
85% of campus wheelchair accessible

Other
Essay writing/study skills program
Mature student association
Off-campus housing registry

14. RESIDENCES

Residence places
M 540, F 540 (Co-ed)
128 apartments/townhouses

First-year students
Places reserved 400 plus
Application deadline: first-come basis
5 places reserved for scholarship winners
No eligibility limitations based on student's home location
Allocations announced mid-May to mid-June

Upper-year students
Places reserved: up to 700
Allocations announced mid-June

Wheelchair-accessible rooms Varies

Meal-plan options
Meal tickets; access to kitchen facilities in all buildings

15. PROGRAMS OF UNDERGRADUATE STUDY

15.1 FACULTY OF ARTS

Degree
Bachelor of Arts, B.A.

Level
General, Honours

Programs
Anthropology*
Canadian Studies*
Classical Studies*
Computer Science
Earth Science†
Economics
Education in French*
English
Ethics*
French
French Language and Civilization* (for anglophones)
Geography
German*
History
Italian*
Law and Justice
Linguistics*
Mathematics*
Music
Native Studies*
Philosophy
Political Science
Psychology
Religious Studies
Russian*
Sociology
Spanish*
Theatre Arts*
* General only
† Honours only

First-year entry Yes

Entry requirements
Minimum average: 60%, 70% to continue in Honours
OAC English or *Français*
Music: Grade 12 Theory, Grade 8 Performance; auditioning may be substituted

Students accepted 737
Total in faculty 2154
Co-op (work/study) available
No; correspondence and self-paced study

Graduation requirements
Minimum GPA: General, 60% on scale of 100%; Honours, 70% on subject major
Full credits/courses: General, 15 full courses (90 credits); Honours, 20 full courses (120 credits)
Successful completion of English-language competency test

Graduating students 494

15.2 FACULTY OF SCIENCE AND ENGINEERING, SCIENCE

Degree
Bachelor of Science, B.Sc.

Level
General, Honours

Programs
Applied Physics
Behavioral Neuroscience†
Biochemistry†
Biology
Chemistry
Computer Science
Geology
Kinesiology†
Mathematics*
Mining Geology†
* General only
† Honours only

First-year entry Yes

Entry requirements
Minimum average: 60% for entrance, 70% to continue in Honours
OAC Calculus, Chemistry; 2 others from Mathematics or Sciences
OAC Physics, Biology recommended

Students accepted 136
Total in faculty 458

Co-op (work/study) available
No; no correspondence or self-paced study

Graduation requirements
Minimum GPA: General, 60% on scale of 100%; Honours, 70% on scale of 100%
Full credits/courses: General, 15 full courses (90 credits); Honours, 20 full courses (120 credits)

Graduating students 76

15.3 FACULTY OF PROFESSIONAL SCHOOLS, COMMERCE

Degree
Bachelor of Commerce, B.Comm.

Level
Honours

Programs
Accounting
Marketing
Sports Administration (S.P.A.D.)

First-year entry Yes

Entry requirements
Minimum average: 60%
OAC English or *Français*, 2 Mathematics
Sports Administration: 3 letters of reference and personal statement

Students accepted 168
Total in faculty 556

Co-op (work/study) available
Yes, internship after year 3 in some areas of Sports Administration; correspondence or self-paced study available for some electives

Graduation requirements
Minimum GPA: 60% on scale of 100%
Full credits/courses: Honours, 20 full courses

Graduating students 81

15.7 FACULTY OF SCIENCE AND ENGINEERING, ENGINEERING

Degree
Bachelor of Engineering, B.Eng.

Level
4-year specialized

Programs
Mining Eng.
Extractive Metallurgical Eng.
Civil, Chemical and Mechanical Eng. (1st 2 years only)

First-year entry Yes

Entry requirements
Minimum average: 60%
2 of OAC Mathematics, Physics, Chemistry

Students accepted 37
Total in faculty 101

Co-op (work/study) available
No; no correspondence or self-paced study

Graduation requirements
Minimum GPA: 60% on scale of 100%
Full credits/courses:
Mining Eng. and Extractive Metallurgical Eng. - 4 years
Civil, Chemical and Mechanical Eng. - after 2 years students proceed to other institutions for years 3 and 4

Graduating students 11

15.11 FACULTY OF PROFESSIONAL SCHOOLS, SCHOOL OF TRANSLATORS AND INTERPRETERS

Degree
Bachelor of Science of Language, B.Sc.L.

Level
Honours

Programs
Translation

First-year entry Yes

Entry requirements
Minimum average: 60%
OAC English, French (minimum 66% in each)

Students accepted 10
Total in faculty 42

Co-op (work/study) available
No; no correspondence or self-paced study

Graduation requirements
Minimum GPA: N/R
70% on Translation courses, 60% overall
Full credits/courses: Honours, 21 full courses

Graduating students 16

15.13 FACULTY OF PROFESSIONAL SCHOOLS, SCHOOL OF NURSING

Degree
Bachelor of Science, Nursing, B.Sc.N.

Level
Specialized Program

Programs
Nursing

First-year entry Yes

Entry requirements
Minimum average: approx. 67%
OAC English or *Français*, Chemistry, Biology

Students accepted 59
Total in faculty 220

Co-op (work/study) available
Clinical work/study required; correspondence and self-paced study in some courses

Graduation requirements
Minimum GPA: 60% on scale of 100%
Full credits/courses: Honours 23 full courses

Graduating students 73

15.14 FACULTY OF PROFESSIONAL SCHOOLS

Degree
Bachelor of Physical Health and Education, B.P.H.E.

Level
Honours, Specialized

Programs
General B.P.H.E.
Health Promotion
Adventure Leadership
Kinesiology as a Science program

First-year entry
No; in year 2

Entry requirements
Minimum average: 69%
OAC English or *Français*, plus 1 Mathematics or Science

Students accepted 130
Total in faculty 350

Co-op (work/study) available
No; no correspondence or self-paced study

Graduation requirements
Minimum GPA: N/R
Honours 70%, Specialized 60%
Full credits/courses: 20 full courses (120 credits)

Graduating students 35

15.15 FACULTY OF PROFESSIONAL SCHOOLS, SCHOOL OF SOCIAL WORK

Degree
Bachelor of Social Work, B.S.W.

Level
Honours

Programs
Social Work

First-year entry Yes

Entry requirements
Minimum average: 60%
Open enrolment year 1; years 3 and 4 limited to 45 students

Students accepted 72
Total in faculty 206

Co-op (work/study) available
Volunteer placement; optional in years 1 and 2, mandatory in years 3 and 4
Correspondence and self-paced study for some courses

Graduation requirements
Minimum GPA: 70% minimum on 8 social-work courses; 60% on others
Full credits/courses: 20 full courses (120 credits)

Graduating students 38

16. FUTURE PLANS

Buildings
New Student Centre
Major renovations providing more class rooms

Algoma University College, Laurentian University

1. OVERVIEW
Algoma University College was founded in 1965 as a liberal arts institutions. Three- and four-year degree programs in the humanities, social sciences and sciences are available in addition to a Bachelor of Business Administration. Co-op learning programs in Accounting, Business Administration, Computer Science, Economics, Liberal Science, Mathematics and Psychology are also available.

2. PRESIDENT
J. Douglas Lawson

3. ENROLMENT
(1988 Fall semester)

Registration
Undergraduate full-time 380
(M 160, F 220)
Undergraduate part-time 850
(M 350, F 500)
Graduate N/R

Residence
Undergrads in residence 0%
Undergrads in off-campus housing 20%
Undergrads commuting 80%

4. ADMISSIONS TO FIRST YEAR

Entry dates
Fall, Winter, Summer

First-year entries

	Fall	Winter	Summer
Applications	280	75	125
Admissions	200	70	118
Enrolments	180	65	10

Admissions offered to qualified candidates before early admission
Yes

Community-college transfer requirements
3.2 GPA on 2 CAAT years
2.5 GPA on 3 CAAT years

Advanced standing granted if conditions of Senate met.

Mature students admission requirements
Usually age 21; out of formal education 2 years; 5 courses allowed

5. ADMISSIONS CONTACT

Liaison Officer, Registrar's Office
Algoma University College
1520 Queen Street East
Sault Ste Marie, Ontario P6A 2G4
(705) 949-2301 (collect calls accepted)

6. STRUCTURE AND DEGREES

Board of Governors
18 members (M 15, F 3; 2 faculty, 1 student, 1 support staff, 1 alumnus)

Teaching faculty
Full-time 30 (M 25, F 5)
Part-time 27 (M 17, F 9)

Faculty/Student ratio (FTE basis) 1:13

Undergraduate degrees conferred
Arts, Liberal Science

7. TEACHING FACILITIES

Largest first-year class 65
First-year courses with tutorials
34%
Lab places for first-year students
Biology 48, Chemistry 24, Computers 200, Languages 60, Physics 24

Libraries
With open stacks 1
With closed stacks 0
Total holdings 120,000 volumes

8. STUDENTS

Undergraduates

1st year	187
2nd year	101
3rd year	81
4th year	11

Entering as Ontario Scholars 5%
Entering with scholarships 5%
Entering with OSAP help 60%

9. ENTRANCE SCHOLARSHIPS

Most prestigious
John Rhodes Scholarship (1)
Application necessary
Deadline May 15
85% required

Full-tuition scholarships (up to 12)
No application necessary
No deadline
80% required

Partial-tuition scholarships (12)
No application necessary
No deadline
80% required

Scholarships for entering students
Offered 16
Accepted 11
Total budget for undergraduate scholarships $35,000

10. INTERNATIONAL STUDENTS

Students from outside Canada 1%
Scholarships awarded None
Services available Adviser; Academic Counsellor
Language requirements for admission TOEFL score 550

11. ATHLETIC FACILITIES

Fitness trails
Ice rink
Playing fields
Weight/workout rooms

Inter-university sports supported
Skiing (Nordic) M, F

Intra-mural organized sports
Badminton
Hockey, ball
Baseball
Basketball
Volleyball

Recreation and fitness programs

12. STUDENT LIFE

Student councils 1
Student clubs 8

Pubs 1
Drinking awareness program

First-year orientation
August to November; parent sessions

13. STUDENT SERVICES

Counselling
Psychological, Career, Peer

Medical
Nurses No; Doctors M, F, on call only

Special needs
Handicapped/special needs centre
100% of campus wheelchair accessible

Other
Essay writing/study skills program
Off-campus housing registry

14. RESIDENCES

N/A

15. PROGRAMS OF UNDERGRADUATE STUDY

15.1, 15.2, 15.3, 15.5, 15.15 FACULTY OF ARTS AND SCIENCE

Degree
Bachelor of Arts, B.A.
Bachelor of Science, B.Sc. (Liberal)

Level
General
15.1 B.A.
15.2 B.Sc. (Liberal), 3 years
15.3 B.Com., Years 1 and 2 only
15.3 B.B.A., 4 years
15.5 B.Sc. Computer Science, 3 years
15.15 B.S.W., Years 1 and 2 only

Programs
Arts and Science:
Accounting
Anthropolgy*
Computer Science
Economics
English (Honours)
French
Geography
History
Italian
Law and Justice
Mathematics
Music*
Philosophy
Political Science
Psychology (Honours)
Sociology
Spanish*
* Courses are limited; students may complete some by correspondence or by transferring to another institution.

First-year entry Yes

Entry requirements
Minimum average: 60%
B.A./B.B.A.: OAC English
Computer Science or Mathematics: 2 OAC Mathematics, including Calculus
B.Com./B.B.A.: 2 OAC Mathematics

Students accepted 320
Total in faculty 875

Co-op (work/study) available
In Accounting, Business Administration, Computer Science, Economics, Liberal Science, Mathematics, Psychology
Correspondence and self-paced study available through Laurentian University

Graduation requirements
Minimum GPA: 60% on scale of 100%
Full credits/courses: Honours 20, General 15
Language Competency Test for all B.A. and B.Sc. students

Graduating students 80

16. FUTURE PLANS

Programs
Expansion of Co-op program

Nipissing University College, Laurentian University

1. OVERVIEW

Nipissing University College in North Bay is a young, progressive university offering Arts, Education, Science, Administrative Studies, Business Administration, Environmental Geography, Liberal Science, Social Work and a B.A. / Orientation to Teaching program. Situated on a 720-acre campus, Nipissing's small class size creates a comfortable atmosphere for learning.

2. PRESIDENT

D. Marshall

3. ENROLMENT

(1990 Fall semester; rounded to nearest 100)

Registration

Undergraduate full-time 1000 (M 300, F 700)
Undergraduate part-time 2700 (M 1000, F 1700)
Graduate N/R

Residence

Undergrads in residence 20% (M 10%, F 10%)
Undergrads in off-campus housing 30%
Undergrads commuting 50%

4. ADMISSIONS TO FIRST YEAR

Entry dates

Fall, Winter, Summer

First-year entries

	Fall	Winter	Summer
Applications	800	50	40
Admissions	600	40	30
Enrolments	320	20	20

Admissions offered to qualified candidates before early admission
Yes

Community-college transfer requirements
See Nipissing University calendar

Advanced standing granted
3-year CAAT diploma 5 credits maximum (2.5 G.P.A.); 2-year CAAT diploma 3 credits maximum (3.2 G.P.A.)

Mature students admission requirements
Written and oral test; 3 courses allowed

5. ADMISSIONS CONTACT

Maureen Knight
Admissions Officer
Nipissing University College
100 College Drive, Box 5002
North Bay, Ontario P1B 8L7
(705) 474-3450

6. STRUCTURE AND DEGREES

Board of Governors
24 members (M 14, F 10; 3 faculty, 3 students, 1 alumnus)

Teaching faculty
Full-time 62 (M 47, F 15)
Part-time 172 (M N/A, F N/A)

Faculty/Student ratio (FTE basis)
1:12

Undergraduate degrees conferred
Arts, Business, Science

7. TEACHING FACILITIES

Largest first-year class N/A
First-year courses with tutorials 50%
Lab places for first-year students
Biology 40, Chemistry 40, Computers 80, Languages 150, Physics 40

Research grants and contracts
$73,000

Graduate programs N/R

Libraries
With open stacks 1
With closed stacks None
Total holdings 110,000 volumes

8. STUDENTS
(rounded to nearest 50)

Undergraduates

1st year	300
2nd year	200
3rd year	150
4th year	50

Entering as Ontario Scholars 12%
Entering with scholarships 12%
Entering with OSAP help 75%

9. ENTRANCE SCHOLARSHIPS

Most prestigious
President's Scholarship (3):
No application necessary
No deadline
Requirements: 88%; supporting documentation

Full-tuition scholarships
No limit
No application necessary
No deadline
Requirements: 80%; no supporting documentation

Partial-tuition scholarships None

Scholarships for entering students
N/A; total budget for undergraduate scholarships $120,000

10. INTERNATIONAL STUDENTS

Students from outside Canada 1%
Scholarships awarded None
Services available Advisers; Academic Counsellor; other
Language requirements for admission TOEFL score 550

11. ATHLETIC FACILITIES

Playing fields
Tennis courts (outdoor)
Weight/workout rooms

Inter-university sports N/R

Intra-mural organized sports
Badminton M, F
Basketball M, F
Curling M, F
Hockey M
Skiing (cross-country) M, F
Table tennis M, F
Volleyball M, F
Weight-lifting M, F

Recreation and fitness programs

12. STUDENT LIFE

Student councils 1
Student clubs 6

Pubs 1
Drinking awareness program

First-year orientation
At registration

13. STUDENT SERVICES

Counselling
Psychological, Career, Peer

Medical
Nurses, Doctors

Special needs
Handicapped/special needs centre
100% of campus wheelchair accessible

Other
Learning disability program
Essay writing/study skills program
Mature student association
Off-campus housing registry

14. RESIDENCES

Residence places 200
M 80, F 120
Apartments/townhouses

First-year students
Places reserved: 100 single
Application deadline June 15
Places reserved for scholarship winners; 80% minimum required
No eligibility limitations based on student's home location
Allocations announced July 15

Upper-year students
Places reserved 100
Allocations announced June 15–July 15

Wheelchair-accessible rooms 8

Meal-plan options available

15. PROGRAMS OF UNDERGRADUATE STUDY

15.1, 15.2, 15.3, 15.15 FACULTY OF ARTS AND SCIENCE

Degree
Bachelor of Arts, B.A.
Bachelor of Science, B.Sc.
Bachelor of Science (Liberal), B.Sc.(Lib.)
Bachelor of Business Administration, B.B.A.

Level
General, Honours
15.1 B.A. - Arts
15.2 B.Sc. - 1st year only or 3-year Liberal Science program
15.3 B.B.A. - 4 years
15.15 B.S.W. - 1st 2 years only

Programs
Arts and Science:
Administrative Studies
Economics
English
Environmental Geography
History
Orientation to Teaching
Psychology
Social Welfare

First-year entry Yes

Entry requirements
Minimum average: 60% and O.S.S.D.
B.A.: OAC English or French
B.Sc.: OAC Calculus, Chemistry, 2 of Biology, Geology or Physics or Mathematics not already credited
B.B.A.: OAC English or French, 2 OAC Mathematics
B.S.W.: OAC English or French

Students accepted N/A
Total in faculty 1200

Co-op (work/study) available
No; correspondence and self-paced study available

Graduation requirements
Minimum GPA: 60% on scale of 100%, 70% for Honours
Full credits/courses: Honours 20, General 15

Graduating students 100

16. FUTURE PLANS

Buildings
Expansion to library, class-room and laboratory facilities in progress
Daycare Centre, 1991

McMaster University

1. OVERVIEW
McMaster University provides an exciting and attractive intellectual, social and physical environment in which students can realize their full potential in learning, critical inquiry and training. Committed to maintaining high standards, it offers a wide selection of high-quality undergraduate programs emphasizing excellence in teaching, research and scholarship.

2. PRESIDENT
Geraldine Kenney-Wallace

3. ENROLMENT
(1990 Fall semester; rounded to nearest 100)

Registration
Undergraduate full-time 10,900 (M 5100, F 5800)
Undergraduate part-time 3500 (M 1100, F 2400)
Graduate 2200 (M 1400, F 800)

Residence
Undergrads in residence 22% (M 20%, F 23%)
Undergrads in off-campus housing N/A
Undergrads commuting N/A

4. ADMISSIONS TO FIRST YEAR

Entry dates
Fall, Winter, Summer

First-year entries

	Fall	Winter	Spring
Applications	18,220	54	493
Admissions	9,973	13	349
Enrolments	3,122	N/A	N/A

Admissions offered to qualified candidates before early admission
Yes

Community-college transfer requirements
1 year CAAT with GPA 3.2: entrance to 1st year in Humanities or Social Sciences faculty
2 years CAAT with GPA 2.5: entrance to Humanities or Social Sciences faculty with 6 to 18 units of advanced credit
3 years CAAT with GPA 2.5: entrance to Humanities or Social Sciences faculty with up to 24 units of advanced credit
See McMaster calendar for business and engineering transfer requirements

Mature students admission requirements
Age 21 or more and must have been away from secondary education for 2 years; applicant for full-time studies must pass scholastic aptitude test.

5. ADMISSIONS CONTACT

Elizabeth McCallum
Assistant Registrar, Admissions
McMaster University
Hamilton, Ontario L8S 4L8
(416) 525-9140, ext. 4542

6. STRUCTURE AND DEGREES

Board of Governors
37 members (M 31, F 6; 3 faculty, 2 students, 2 support staff, 5 alumni)

Teaching faculty
Full-time 1046 (M 840, F 206)
Part-time 23 (M 9, F 14)

Faculty/Student ratio (FTE basis)
1:21

Undergraduate degrees conferred
Arts, Arts and Science, Arts/Social Work, Commerce, Engineering, Engineering Management, Health Sciences, Medicine, Music, Nursing, Physical Education, Science

7. TEACHING FACILITIES

Largest first-year class 400
First-year courses with tutorials 88%
Lab places for first-year students
Languages 370, Biology 1008, Chemistry 808, Physics 1567

Research grants and contracts
$63 million

Graduate programs
Number of programs 36
Enrolment in master's programs 1486; doctoral programs 688

Libraries
With open stacks 5
With closed stacks 0
Total holdings exceed 2.9 million items.

8. STUDENTS

Undergraduates

1st year	4493
2nd year	3771
3rd year	3493
4th year	1800
5th year	66

Entering as Ontario Scholars 57%
Entering with scholarships 12.4%
Entering with OSAP help 28%

9. ENTRANCE SCHOLARSHIPS

Most prestigious
McMaster Scholars:
Application necessary
Deadline end of February
Requirements: 90%; essay and 2 letters of recommendation

Full-tuition scholarships (250)
No application necessary
Deadline May 30
Requirements: 87%; no supporting documentation

Partial-tuition scholarships (43)
Application necessary for McMaster Merit Awards
Deadline mid-April
Requirements: 80%; documentation of extracurricular and community activities

Scholarships for entering students
Offered 338
Accepted 338
Total budget for undergraduate scholarships $980,405 (includes in-course and graduate funds)

10. INTERNATIONAL STUDENTS

Students from outside Canada 4.2%
Scholarships awarded 5
Services available Adviser; Academic; McMaster International
Language requirements for admission TOEFL score 580; MELAB score 90% for Arts, 85% for Engineering

11. ATHLETIC FACILITIES

Combative gym
Cross-country trails
Dance studio
Gym
Gymnastics centre
Playing fields
Squash courts
Stadium
Swimming pool
Tennis courts (outdoor)
Track centre (outdoor)
Weight/workout rooms

Inter-university sports
Badminton M, F
Basketball M, F
Curling M, F
Fencing M, F
Football M
Gymnastics M, F
Hockey, ice F
Rugby M
Skiing: cross-country M, F; Alpine M; Nordic M, F
Soccer M, F

Squash M, F
Swimming M, F
Synchronized swimming F
Tennis M, F
Track and Field M, F
Volleyball M, F
Water polo M, F
Wrestling M

Intra-mural organized sports
Badminton M, F, C
Basketball M, F
Football M, F
Golf M, F
Hockey, floor M, F
Hockey, ice M
Hockey, street M, F
Inner-tube water polo C
Lacrosse M, F
Soccer (outdoor) M
Soccer (indoor) M, F
Team squash M, F, C
Tennis M, F, C
Three pitch C
Volleyball M, F, C

Other sports
Slow pitch, Snow pitch, Three-on-three ball, Walley ball

Recreation and fitness program

12. STUDENT LIFE

Student councils 3
Student clubs more than 100

Pubs 3
Drinking awareness program

First-year orientation
1st week of September

13. STUDENT SERVICES

Counselling
Psychological, Career, Peer

Medical
Nurses 5; Doctors M (1), F (4)

Special needs
Handicapped/special needs centre
75% of campus wheelchair accessible

Other
Essay writing/study skills program
Mature student association
Off-campus housing registry

14. RESIDENCES

Residence places 2765
1220 M, 1545 F
1901 of the places are co-ed

First-year students
Places reserved 1360 double
Application deadline: 1st week of July
Places reserved for scholarship winners; 78% minimum required
No eligibility limitations based on home location within Ontario
Allocations announced mid-August, before early registration

Upper-year students
Places reserved 1405
Allocations announced mid-August

Wheelchair-accessible rooms 27

Meal-plan options
12, 14 or 19 meals per week
mandatory in traditional residence; optional in off-campus or non-traditional residence

15. PROGRAMS OF UNDERGRADUATE STUDY

Units are the amount of credit for a course and are used to calculate averages. 1 unit generally equals 1 lecture-hour per week for 1 term or 2 hours of labs/seminars per week for 1 term. Most courses are 3 or 6 units (half- or full-year credit).

15.1 ARTS AND SCIENCE PROGRAM

Degree
Bachelor of Arts and Science, B.Arts Sc.

Level
Honours B.Arts Sc. (4 or 5 years)
B.Arts Sc. (3 years)

Programs
Arts and Science and:
Anthropology
Biochemistry
Biology*
Computer Science
Drama
Economics
English
French
Geography
German
Gerontology
History
Mathematics
Philosophy
Physics*
Political Science
Psychology
Religious Studies
Sociology
Social Work (B.Arts Sc./B.S.W)
* 5-year program

First-year entry Yes

Entry requirements
Minimum average: high 80%
6 OACs including English, Calculus plus 3 OACs from broad academic category
Supplementary application form required

Students accepted 50
Total in faculty 205

Co-op (work/study) available
No; no correspondence or self-paced study

Graduation requirements
Minimum GPA: 4.0 on scale of 12.0
Full credits/courses: Honours B.Arts Sc. 120 units, B.Arts Sc. 90 units

Graduating students 33

15.1 FACULTY OF HUMANITIES

Degrees
Bachelor of Arts, B.A.
Bachelor of Music, B.Mus.

Level
Honours B.A. (4 years)
Honours B.Mus. (4 years)
B.A. (3 years)

Programs
Honours Bachelor of Arts:
Art
Art History
Classical Studies
Classics
Comparative Literature
Drama
English
French
German and another subject
Hispanic and another subject
History
Italian and another subject
Modern Languages and Linguistics
Philosophy
Philosophy and Biology
Russian and another subject

Honours Bachelor of Music:
Music Education
Music History and Education

Bachelor of Arts:
Art History
Classical Studies
Drama
English
French
History
Music
Philosophy

First-year entry
Yes, for Music and Art programs; others begin after general Humanities 1 year.

Entry requirements
Minimum average: mid 70%
6 OACs including English 1; for other requirements contact Faculty of Humanities.

Students accepted 470
Total in faculty 2725

Co-op (work/study) available
No; no correspondence or self-paced study

Graduation requirements
Minimum GPA: 4.0 on scale of 12.0
Full credits/courses: Honours B.A. 120 units, Honours B.Mus. 120 units, B.A. 90 units

Graduating students 487

15.1 FACULTY OF SOCIAL SCIENCES

Degree
Bachelor of Arts, B.A.
Bachelor of Arts/Bachelor of Social Work, B.A./B.S.W.
Bachelor of Physical Education, B.P.E.

Level
Honours B.A. (4 years)
Major B.A. (4 years)
B.A. (3 years)

Programs
Honours Bachelor of Arts:
Anthropology
Economics
Combined Economics and another subject
Geography
Geography and Environmental Studies
Geography and Geology
Combined Gerontology and another subject
Labour Studies
Labour Studies and another subject
Physical Education
Political Science
Combined Political Science and another subject
Psychology
Religious Studies
Combined Religious Studies and another subject
Combined Bachelor of Arts and Social Work
Sociology
Sociology and another subject

Major Bachelor of Arts:
Psychology

Bachelor of Arts:
Anthropology
Economics
Gerontology and another subject
Labour Studies
Political Science
Psychology
Religious Studies
Sociology

First-year entry
No; except for Physical Education, enter in year 2 after general Social Sciences 1.

Entry requirements
Minimum average: low to mid 70%
6 OACs, including English and Mathematics

Students accepted 750 Social Science, 235 Physical Education
Total in faculty 5441

Co-op (work/study) available
No; no correspondence or self-paced study

Graduation requirements
Minimum GPA: 4.0 on scale of 12.0
Full credits/courses: Honours B.A. and Major B.A. 120 units, B.A. 90 units

Graduating students 944

15.2 FACULTY OF SCIENCE

Degree
Bachelor of Science, B.Sc.

Level
Honours B.Sc. (4 years)
Major B.Sc. (4 years)
B.Sc. (3 years)

Programs
Honours Bachelor of Science:
Applied Chemistry
Applied Physics
Biochemistry
Biochemistry and Chemistry
Biology

Biology and Geology
Biology and Pharmacology*
Biology and Philosophy
Biology and Psychology
Chemistry
Chemistry and Geology
Chemistry and Physics
Computer Science
Computer Science and Mathematics
Computer Science and Psychology
Computer Science and Statistics
Geography
Geography and Environmental Sciences
Geography and Geology
Geology
Geology and Physics
Material Science and Engineering
Mathematical Sciences
Mathematics
Mathematics and Physics
Molecular Biology and Biotechnology
Physics
Psychology
Statistics
Theoretical Physics and Applied Mathematics
* 5-year co-op

Major Bachelor of Science:
Biochemistry
Biology
Chemistry
Computer Science
Computer Science and Mathematics
Geology
Geology and Physics
Materials Science and Engineering
Mathematical Sciences
Physics
Psychology
Statistics

Bachelor of Science:
Biology
Chemistry
Computer Science
Geography
Geology
Mathematics
Physics
Psychology
Science

First-year entry
No; specific programs are usually entered in year 2.

Entry requirements
Minimum average: 75%
6 OACs; including 1 of English 1 or *Anglais* 1 or 2; Calculus; 1 of Algebra and Geometry or Finite Mathematics, 2 of Biology, Chemistry or Physics

Students accepted 760
Total in faculty 2384

Co-op (work/study) available
Yes; Honours combined degree in Biology and Pharmacology; no correspondence or self-paced study

Graduation requirements
Minimum GPA: 4.0 on scale of 12.0
Full credits/courses: Honours B.Sc., Major B.Sc. 120 units, B.Sc. 90 units

Graduating students 413

15.3 FACULTY OF BUSINESS

Degree
Bachelor of Commerce, B.Com.
Honours Bachelor of Commerce, Hon.B.Com.
Honours Bachelor of Commerce, and Arts, Hon.B.Com. & Arts

Level
Honours Com. (4 years)
Honours Com. and Arts (Economics) (4 years)
B.Com. (4 years)

Areas of specialization
Accounting
Finance
Human Resources and Labour Relations
Information Systems
Marketing
Operations Management
Organizational Behaviour
Quantitative Methods

First-year entry
Yes; but selection for year 2

Entry requirements
Minimum average: high 70%
6 OACs; including English 1, Mathematics, plus 3 OACs from broad academic category, 1 additional OAC (under review)
For year 2, students must have taken full course load with no failures on 1st attempt.

Students accepted
450 in Business 1; 300 enter year 2
Total in faculty 1421

Co-op (work/study) available
No; no correspondence or self-paced study

Graduation requirements
Minimum GPA: 4.0 on scale of 12.0
Full credits/courses: Honours Com., Honours Com. and Arts, B.Com. 120 units

Graduating students 242

15.7 FACULTY OF ENGINEERING

Degree
Bachelor of Engineering, B.Eng.
Bachelor of Engineering and Management, B.Eng. & Mgt.

Level
B.Eng. (4 years)
B.Eng. and Mgmt (5 years)

Programs
Bachelor of Engineering:
Ceramic Eng.
Chemical Eng.
Civil Eng.
Computer Eng.
Electrical Eng.
Engineering Physics
Manufacturing Eng.
Materials Eng.
Mechanical Eng.
Metallurgical Eng.
Bachelor of Engineering and Management:
Ceramic Eng. and Mgmt
Chemical Eng. and Mgmt
Civil Eng. and Computer Systems
Civil Eng. and Mgmt
Computer Eng. and Mgmt
Electrical Eng. and Mgmt
Engineering Physics and Mgmt
Materials Eng. and Mgmt
Mechanical Eng. and Mgmt
Metallurgical Eng. and Mgmt

First-year entry
No; common year 1; specific program begins year 2.

Entry requirements
Minimum average: mid to high 70%
6 OACs including English 1, Calculus, Algebra and Geometry, Chemistry, Physics
Supplementary application required

Students accepted 450
Total in faculty 1365

Co-op (work/study) available
No; no correspondence or self-paced study

Graduation requirements
Minimum GPA: 4.0 on scale of 12.0
Full credits/courses: B.Eng. 137–150 units, B.Eng. and Mgmt 175–189 units

Graduating students 202

15.13 FACULTY OF HEALTH SCIENCES, SCHOOL OF MEDICINE

Degree
Doctor of Medicine, M.D.

Level
Professional

Programs
Medicine

First-year entry
No; enter after year 3 of undergraduate study.

Entry requirements
Minimum average: 2.5 on scale of 4.0
No prerequisite subjects or courses; contact Faculty of Health Sciences for special requirements.

Students accepted 100
Total in school 300

Co-op (work/study) available
No; self-paced and self-directed study available

Graduation requirements N/R

Graduating students 100

15.13 FACULTY OF HEALTH SCIENCES, SCHOOL OF NURSING

Degree
Bachelor of Science in Nursing, B.Sc.N.

Level
B.Sc.N. Honours (4 years)
Honours Diploma for Registered Nurses only (2 years)

Programs
Nursing

First-year entry Yes

Entry requirements
Minimum average: high 70%
6 OACs, including 1 of English 1 or *Anglais* 1 or 2; 1 of Calculus, Algebra and Geometry or Finite Mathematics; Chemistry; 1 of Biology or Physics

Students accepted
105 (55 from high school, 50 from post-RN and non-high school)
Total in school 421

Co-op (work/study) available
No; clinical placements for some courses; self-directed learning available

Graduation requirements
Minimum GPA: 4.0 on scale of 12.0
Full credits/courses: B.Sc.N. 135

Graduating students
76 (includes 2-year diploma)

15.14 FACULTY OF SOCIAL SCIENCES, SCHOOL OF PHYSICAL EDUCATION

Degree
Bachelor of Physical Education, B.P.E.

Level
B.P.E. (4 years)

Areas of specialization
Adapted Physical Activity for Special Populations
Biomechanics
Coaching
Education
Fitness Appraisal
Movement Arts
Physical Rehabilitation
Sports Administration
Sports Sciences

First-year entry Yes

Entry requirements
Minimum average: mid to high 70%
6 OACs including English 1 and 1 of Calculus, Algebra and Geometry or Finite Mathematics; 1 OAC Biology, Chemistry or Physics recommended

Students accepted 235
Total in school 730

Co-op (work/study) available
No; no correspondence or self-paced study

Graduation requirements
Minimum GPA: 4.0 on scale of 12.0
Full credits/courses: B.P.E. 133 units

Graduating students 137

16. FUTURE PLANS

Buildings
Science and Engineering faculty research wing, July 1991
385-bed undergraduate residence, January 1991
New Business Faculty building, fall 1991
Library expansion, spring 1992
New Art Gallery, fall 1991
Addition to Engineering building, September 1991

Services for disabled

10 rooms for disabled in new residence

Purchase of computer access and other technical devices for disabled

Development of services (e.g., volunteer bureau, tutorial assistance)

Increased information services through office of co-ordinator for disabled

University of Ottawa

1. OVERVIEW
Located in the national capital, the University of Ottawa is the largest bilingual university in the country. With its 24,000 students, the University of Ottawa remains close to its constituents and preserves high standards in its teaching and services. It is composed of nine faculties and offers 150 different programs of study that cover the complete spectrum of professional sectors.

2. RECTOR
Marcel Hamelin

3. ENROLMENT
(1990 Fall semester; totals rounded to nearest 100)

Registration
Undergraduate full-time 13,000 (M 5700, F 7600)
Undergraduate part-time 7400 (M 2500, F 4900)
Graduate 3635 (M 1381, F 1804)

Residence
Undergrads in residence 16%
Undergrads in off-campus housing 18%
Undergrads commuting 66%

4. ADMISSIONS TO FIRST YEAR

Entry dates
Fall, Winter, Summer

First-year entries

	Fall	Winter	Summer
Applications	25,519	1269	726
Admissions	12,370	620	496
Enrolments	4,938	388	329

Admissions offered to qualified candidates before early admission
Yes

Community-college transfer requirements
2 complete CAAT years

Advanced standing granted with more than 2 complete CAAT years.

Mature students admission requirements
2 years away from full-time studies; promise of academic success; must satisfy chosen faculty's requirements; 5 courses allowed

5. ADMISSIONS CONTACT

M André Pierre Lepage
Director of Admissions and Associate Registrar or
Michèle Dextras
Senior Adminissions Officer
Admissions Office
University of Ottawa
550 Cumberland Street
Ottawa, Ontario K1N 6N5
(613) 564-2262

6. STRUCTURE AND DEGREES

Board of Governors
40 members (M 26, F 6; 2 faculty, 2 students, 2 support staff, 2 alumni)

Teaching faculty
Full-time 1120 (M 868, F 252)
Part-time 405 (M 242, F 163)

Faculty/Student ratio (FTE basis)
1:24

Undergraduate degrees conferred
Administration, Arts, Education, Engineering, Health Sciences, Law, Medicine, Science, Social Sciences

7. TEACHING FACILITIES

Largest first-year class 150
First-year courses with tutorials
12%

Lab places for first-year students
Biology 375, Chemistry 784, Computers 150, Physics 720, Languages 30/course/section

Research grants and contracts
$36 million

Graduate programs
Number of programs 75
Enrolment in master's programs 3060; doctoral programs 580

Libraries
With open stacks 6
With closed stacks 2
Total holdings 3,286,354 volumes

8. STUDENTS

Undergraduates
1st year 4228
2nd year 3558
3rd year 3424
4th year 1670

Entering as Ontario Scholars 34.9%
Entering with scholarships 11%
Entering with OSAP help N/A

9. ENTRANCE SCHOLARSHIPS

Most prestigious
Rector's Scholarship (2):
No application necessary; complete questionnaire after preliminary selection
Deadline mid July
Highest possible average required

Full-tuition scholarships
Rodrigue Normandin (5):
No application necessary
No deadline
Offered to 5 winners of francophone academic game show, *Génie en herbe*

Partial-tuition scholarships
English Debating Society (no. varies)
Bourse pour talents particuliers (20)
Concours de français (varies)
Admission Bursary (varies)
No application necessary
85% required for Admission Bursary

Scholarships for entering students
Offered 1339
Accepted 460
Total budget for undergraduate scholarships $510,500

10. INTERNATIONAL STUDENTS

Students from outside Canada 3%
Scholarships awarded N/R
Services available Adviser; Academic Counsellor; Club International
Language requirements for admission TOEFL score: Sciences and Engineering 550, Administration, Arts and Social Sciences 580; MELAB score 85; average of 4.5 on Cantest

11. ATHLETIC FACILITIES

Gym
Ice rink
Playing fields
Racketball
Squash courts
Stadium
Swimming pool
Weight/workout rooms

Inter-university sports
Basketball M, F
Cross-country skiing M, F
Football M
Hockey M
Swimming M, F
Volleyball F

Intra-mural organized sports
Broom-ball
Hockey
Soccer
Volleyball
Water polo

Recreation and fitness programs

12. STUDENT LIFE

Student councils 5
Student clubs approx. 50

Pubs 2
Drinking awareness program

First-year orientation
First 2 weeks of September

13. STUDENT SERVICES

Counselling
Psychological, Career

Medical
Nurses 5; Doctors M (10), F (4)

Special needs
Handicapped/special needs centre
70% of campus wheelchair accessible

Other
Learning disability program
Essay writing/study skills program
Off-campus housing registry

14. RESIDENCES

Residence places 1284 (Co-ed)
858 apartments/townhouses

First-year students
Places reserved 80%
Application deadline June 30 for 1st draw, July 31 for 2nd
Places reserved for scholarship winners 250; 85% minimum required
No eligibility limitations based on student's home location
Allocations announced 2 weeks after 2 draw dates

Upper-year students
Places reserved 20% of residence places and 100% of apartments/townhouses
Allocations announced approx. 1 month before April exams

Wheelchair-accessible rooms 18

Meal-plan options
3 plans based on number of meals per day

15. PROGRAMS OF UNDERGRADUATE STUDY

Note: As a bilingual university, Ottawa requires a passive knowledge of French prior to graduation from all undergraduate programs except Law and Medicine.

15.1 FACULTY OF ARTS

Degree
Bachelor of Arts, B.A.
Bachelor of Fine Arts, B.F.A.
Bachelor of Music, B.Mus.

Level
Concentration, General, Honours

Programs
A general program has no concentration. List designates Cn - Concentration; H - Honours

Canadian Studies Cn
Classical Art and Archaeology Cn
Classical Studies Cn, H
Communication Cn, H
Economics* Cn
English Cn, H
French as a Second Language* Cn
Geography Cn, H
German Cn
History Cn, H
Italian Cn
Langue et Littérature françaises pour non-francophones Cn
Langue française Cn
Latin and Classical English Cn, H
Lettres françaises Cn, H
Linguistics Cn, H
Mathematics Cn, H
Medieval Studies Cn
Music Cn, H
Philosophy Cn, H
Political Science* Cn
Religious Studies Cn, H
Slavic Studies Cn, H
Sociology* Cn
Spanish Cn, H
Theatre Cn, H
Theory and History of Art H
Translation H
Visual Arts H
Women's Studies Cn
* with double Concentration only

First-year entry
Yes; Communication, Theatre and Translation entry in year 2

Entry requirements
Minimum average: 65%
1 OAC in English or *Français*
Lettres françaises (Cn, H): *Français*
B.F.A., Studio and Photography: portfolio and interview required
B.Mus.: written exam and audition required
Mathematics: Algebra and Geometry, Calculus

Students accepted 3398
Total in faculty 5942

Co-op (work/study) available
Co-op study in Geography, History and Translation; no correspondence course

Graduation requirements
Minimum GPA: 3.5 Concentration, 4.5 Honours on scale of 10
Full credits/courses: Honours 120 credits/20 courses; Concentration and General 90 credits/15 courses

Graduating students 805

15.1 FACULTY OF SOCIAL SCIENCES

Degree
Bachelor of Social Sciences, B.Soc.Sc.
Bachelor of Arts, B.A.

Level
Concentration, Honours

Programs
A general program has no concentration. List designates Cn - Concentration; H - Honours

Canadian Studies* Cn
Criminology Cn, H
Economics Cn, H
Leisure Studies Cn, H
Political Science Cn, H in French only
Psychology Cn, H
Public Policy and Public Management* Cn
Sociology Cn, H in French only
Women's Studies* Cn
* with double Concentration only

First-year entry Yes

Entry requirements
Minimum average: 68-70%
B.A. in Psychology: OAC English or *Français*
B.A. in Economics: OAC Calculus

Students accepted 2908
Total in faculty 4504

Co-op (work/study) available
Yes, Leisure Studies only; no correspondence or self-paced study

Graduation requirements
Minimum GPA: 3.5 Concentration, 4.5 Honours on scale of 10
Full credits/courses: Honours 120 credits/20 courses; Concentration 90 credits/15 courses

Graduating students 747

15.2 FACULTY OF SCIENCE

Degree
Bachelor of Science, B.Sc.

Level
Concentration, General, Honours

Programs
A General program has no concentration. List designates Cn - Concentration; H - Honours

Biochemistry Cn, H
Biochemistry (Nutrition) Cn, H
Biology Cn, H
Chemistry Cn, H
Computer Science Cn, H
Geology Cn, H
Mathematics Cn, H
Physics Cn, H
Physics-Mathematics Cn, H

First-year entry Yes

Entry requirements
Minimum average: 70%
OACs in Chemistry, Physics, Calculus, Algebra and Geometry
(English or Français as of 1992)

Students accepted 1415
Total in faculty 1982

Co-op (work/study) available
Yes, Computer Science, Mathematics (Science); no correspondence or self-paced study

Graduation requirements
Minimum GPA: 3.5 Concentration, 4.5 Honours on scale of 10
Full credits/courses: from 105 to 145 credits

Graduating students 354

15.3 FACULTY OF ADMINISTRATION

Degree
Bachelor of Administration, B.Adm.
Bachelor of Commerce, B.Comm.

Level
General, Minor, Major, Honours

Programs
Bachelor of Administration (General)

Bachelor of Commerce:
Accounting (Honours, Minor)
Finance (Major, Minor)
Computer Science (Minor)
Human Resources Management (Major, Minor)
International Business (Minor)
Law (Minor)
Management (Minor)
Management Science (Major, Minor)
Management and Information Systems (Honours, Minor)
Marketing (Major, Minor)
Public Policy and Public Management (Major, Minor)
Mathematics (Minor)

First-year entry Yes

Entry requirements
Minimum average: 75%
1 OAC English or *Français*, Calculus and Algebra and Geometry or Finite Mathematics

Students accepted 1130
Total in faculty 3596

Co-op (work/study) available
Yes, Accounting, Management and Information Systems; no correspondence or self-paced study

Graduation requirements
Minimum GPA: 3.5 General, 4.5 Honours on scale of 10
Full credits/courses: Honours 120 credits/20 courses; General 90 credits/15 courses

Graduating students 714

15.7 FACULTY OF ENGINEERING

Degree
Bachelor of Applied Science, B.A.Sc.

Level
Professional

Programs
Chemical Eng.
Civil Eng.
Combined Biochemistry / Chemical Eng. in Biotechnology
Computer Eng.
Electrical Eng.
Mechanical Eng.

First-year entry Yes

Entry requirements
Minimum average: 70%
2 OAC Mathematics (Calculus and Algebra and Geometry), Chemistry, Physics

Students accepted 867
Total in faculty 1451

Co-op (work/study) available
Yes, Chemical, Civil, Electrical, Mechanical and Computer Eng.; no correspondence or self-paced study

Graduation requirements
Minimum GPA: 3.5 on scale of 10
Full credits/courses: 155 credits

Graduating students 236

15.12 FACULTY OF LAW

Degree
Bachelor of Law, LL.B.

Level
Professional

Programs
Common Law

First-year entry No

Entry requirements
Minimum average: at least B+ in year 1 and 2 of university study
Law School Admission Test (LSAT)

Students accepted 180
Total in faculty 483

Co-op (work/study) available
No; no correspondence or self-paced study

Graduation requirements
Minimum GPA: 3.5 on scale of 10
Full credits/courses: 100–110 credits

Graduating students 170

15.13, 15.14 FACULTY OF HEALTH SCIENCES

Degree
Bachelor of Science (Human Kinetics), B.Sc. (H.K.)
Bachelor of Science (Nursing), B.Sc.N.
Bachelor of Science (Occupational Therapy), B.Sc. (O.T.)
Bachelor of Science (Physiotherapy), B.Sc. (P.T.)

Level
Honours

Programs
Kinetics
Nursing
Occupational Therapy
Physiotherapy

First-year entry Yes

Entry requirements
School of Human Kinetics:
Minimum average: 68%
1 OAC English or *Français*, 1 of Biology, Chemistry, Physics; 1 of Calculus, Algebra and Geometry or Finite Mathematics

School of Nursing:
Minimum average: 70%
1 OAC English or *Français*, Biology, Chemistry; advanced Grade 12 Mathematics; CPR certification

Physiotherapy and Occupational Therapy:
Minimum average: 75%
1 OAC English or *Français*, Physics, Chemistry, Biology, Mathematics; 2nd-language proficiency test; CPR certification (Physiotherapy only)

Students accepted 884
Total in faculty 1,686

Co-op (work/study) available
No; no correspondence or self-paced study

Graduation requirements
Minimum GPA: 4.5 on scale of 10
Full credits/courses: 133–150 credits

Graduating students 293

15.13 FACULTY OF MEDICINE

Degree
Doctor of Medicine, M.D.

Level
Professional

Programs
Medicine

First-year entry No

Entry requirements (B, B+)
Good academic standing B.A. or B.Sc. course in year 1 and 2 of university B.A. or B.Sc. course
Minimum 1 year of Physics, General or Inorganic Chemistry, General Biology or Zoology, Organic Chemistry
Medical College Admission Test (MCAT)
Personal Interview

Students accepted 84
Total in faculty 975 (includes graduate students)

Co-op (work/study) available
No; no correspondence or self-paced study

Graduation requirements
See Ottawa calendar

Graduating students 101

16. FUTURE PLANS

Programs
Within 5 years, Ottawa hopes to offer a bilingual Pharmacy program

Queen's University

1. OVERVIEW

Granted a charter in 1841, Queen's University is one of Canada's oldest schools. Located in Kingston, Queen's offers 67 undergraduate specializations. The university attracts a large percentage of its 11,200 undergraduate students from outside Ontario; 90% of all students come from outside Kingston, which accounts for the high degree of school spirit and student activities.

2. PRINCIPAL

David Chadwick Smith

3. ENROLMENT

(1988 Fall semester; rounded to nearest 50)

Registration

Undergraduate full-time 11,200 (M 5200, F 6000)
Undergraduate part-time 3500 (M 1100, F 2400)
Graduate 2500

Residence

Undergrads in residence 25%
Undergrads in off-campus housing 65%
Undergrads commuting 10%

4. ADMISSIONS TO FIRST YEAR

Entry dates

Fall

First-year entries

	Fall
Applications	26,000
Admissions	9,000
Enrolments	2,719

Other entry dates N/R

Admissions offered to qualified candidates before early admission

Yes

Community-college transfer requirements

1 year CAAT plus final academic secondary-school standing
2 years CAAT

Advanced standing granted

Up to 5 credits with 3-year CAAT program

Mature students admission requirements

Age 21, out of school 3 years; admission to part-time studies degree program on completion of Arts and Science course

5. ADMISSIONS CONTACT

Shelagh Deeley
Assistant Registrar
(Admissions/Liaison)
Queen's University
131 Union Street
Kingston, Ontario K7L 3N6
(613) 545-2218

6. STRUCTURE AND DEGREES

Board of Governors

38 members (M 26, F 12; faculty, support staff, alumni N/R, 1 student)

Teaching faculty

Full-time 1021 (M 849, F 172)
Part-time N/A

Faculty/Student ratio (FTE basis)

1:16

Undergraduate degrees conferred

Applied Science (Engineering), Arts, Commerce, Education, Fine Art, Law, Medicine, Music, Nursing, Occupational and Physical Therapy, Physical and Health Education, Science

7. TEACHING FACILITIES

Largest first-year class 400
First-year courses with tutorials N/R
Lab places for first-year students Biology 800, Chemistry 1100, Computers 475, Graphics 450

Research grants and contracts $48 million

Graduate programs
Number of programs 47
Enrolment in master's and doctoral programs 2500

Libraries 18
Total holdings 4 million volumes

8. STUDENTS

Undergraduates

1st year	2719
2nd year	2714
3rd year	2702
4th year	1567

Entering as Ontario Scholars 76%
Entering with scholarships 14%
Entering with OSAP help N/A

9. ENTRANCE SCHOLARSHIPS

Most prestigious
Chancellor's Scholarships (9):
Nomination necessary
Deadline March 1
See Guidance Office

Full-tuition scholarships (179)
No application necessary
No deadline
About 93.8% required

Partial-tuition scholarships (111)
No application necessary
No deadline
92% required

Scholarships for entering students
Offered N/A
Accepted 288
Total budget for undergraduate scholarships $537,000

10. INTERNATIONAL STUDENTS

Students from outside Canada 4%
Scholarships awarded N/A
Services available Adviser; Academic Counselling (varies by faculty); English-as-second-language program; LINK program joins Canadian and international students; CBIE (international bursaries) members; Queen's International Centre

Language requirements for admission TOEFL score 580; MELAB score 90

11. ATHLETIC FACILITIES

Combatives room
Dance studios
Gyms
Handball
Ice rink
Playing fields
Projectiles range (indoor)
Racquet-ball
Squash courts
Stadium
Swimming pool
Tennis courts (outdoor)
Track centre (indoor/outdoor)
Trampoline facility
Weight/workout rooms

Inter-university sports
Every CIAU- and OUAA-sanctioned sport is represented; total of 44 teams

Intra-mural organized sports
Every sport available except monster ball

Recreation and fitness programs

12. STUDENT LIFE

Student councils Alma Mater Society plus councils for every individual faculty/school

Student clubs 80

Pubs 3 licensed, 1 non-alcoholic
Drinking awareness program

First-year orientation
1st week after Labour Day; parent sessions

13. STUDENT SERVICES

Counselling
Psychological, Career, Peer

Medical
Nurses 5; Doctors 6

Special needs
Handicapped/special needs centre
% of campus wheelchair accessible N/A

Other
Learning disability program
Essay writing/study skills program
Mature student association
Off-campus housing registry

14. RESIDENCES

Residence places
617 M, 703 F, 1751 C
383 apartments/townhouses

First-year students
Places reserved 362 single, all doubles
Application deadline late June
Places reserved for scholarship winners; minimum average varies
No eligibility limitations based on student's home location
Allocations announced last week in August

Upper-year students
Places reserved 30%
Allocations announced during winter term

Wheelchair-accessible rooms 10

Meal-plan options
7 days a week; 3 meals a day
Monday to Friday, Saturday brunch and dinner, Sunday brunch

15. PROGRAMS OF UNDERGRADUATE STUDY

Note: The minimum average required to enter all Queen's programs is 10% above the passing grade in the applicant's school system. All degree programs have limited enrolment, so admission is competitive and offers depend on the number of qualified applicants.

The minimum average in brackets in "Entry Requirements" for each faculty represents the lowest average awarded early admission in 1990, based on combined academic and non-academic data.

15.1, 15.2 FACULTY OF ARTS AND SCIENCE

Degree
Bachelor of Arts, B.A., B.A.H.
Bachelor of Science, B.Sc.

Level
General, Honours

Programs
Honours:
Art History
Biochemistry
Biology
Chemistry
Classical Studies
Computing and Information Science
Drama
Economics
English
Film
French
Geography
Geological Sciences
German
Greek
History
Latin
Mathematics
Music
Philosophy
Physics
Political Studies
Psychology
Religion
Russian
Sociology
Spanish and Italian
Statistics

General (same as Honours plus):
Health
Modern Literature
Italian
Life Sciences
Music
Women's Studies

Special Field Concentrations:
Astrophysics
Biochemistry
Biology
Canadian Studies
Chemical Physics
Chemistry
Classical Studies
Cognitive Science
Commonwealth Studies
Geography
Geological Sciences
Language and Linguistics
Latin Language and Civilization
Life Sciences
Mathematical Physics
Mathematics
Medieval Studies
Physics
Theoretical Physics
Social Behaviour
Spanish and Latin American Studies
Statistics
Studies in Communications, Culture and Society
Translation
Women's Studies

First-year entry Yes

Entry requirements
Minimum average: 60% (high 70%)
Arts: OAC English
Sciences: OAC English, 3 of Algebra and Geometry, Calculus, Physics or Chemistry
Personal Information Form

Students accepted 1476
Total in faculty 5133

Co-op (work/study) available
No; correspondence and self-paced study available

Graduation requirements N/A

Graduating students 964

15.3 SCHOOL OF BUSINESS

Degree
Bachelor of Commerce, B.Com.

Level
Honours

Programs
Commerce

First-year entry Yes
Entry requirements
Minimum average: 60% (mid 80%)
OAC English, 2 of Calculus, Algebra and Geometry, Finite Mathematics
Personal Information Form

Students accepted 213
Total in school 825

Co-op (work/study) available
No; no correspondence or self-paced study

Graduation requirements
Minimum GPA: 65%
Full credits/courses: Honours 22

Graduating students 186

15.6 FACULTY OF EDUCATION

Degree
Bachelor of Arts / Bachelor of Education, B.A./B.Ed.
Bachelor of Science / Bachelor of Education, B.Sc./B.Ed.

Level
General, Honours

Programs
Primary-Junior
Junior-Intermediate
Intermediate-Senior

First-year entry Yes

Entry requirements
Minimum average: 60% (Arts/Ed. low 80s%, Science/Ed. mid 80%)
Arts/Ed.: OAC English
Science/Ed.: OAC English, 3 of

Algebra and Geometry, Physics, Chemistry or Calculus
Personal Information Form

Students accepted 117
Total in faculty 440

Co-op (work/study) available
No; correspondence and self-paced study

Graduation requirements N/A

Graduating students 68

15.7 FACULTY OF APPLIED SCIENCE

Degree
Bachelor of Science in Engineering, B.Sc.

Level
Honours

Programs
Chemical Eng.
Civil Eng.
Electrical Eng.
Engineering Chemistry
Engineering Physics
Geological Eng.
Mechanical Eng.
Metallurgical Eng.
Mathematics and Engineering
Mining Eng.

First-year entry Yes

Entry requirements
Minimum average: 60% (high 70%)
OAC English, Calculus, Algebra and Geometry, Chemistry, Physics
Personal Information Form

Students accepted 510
Total in faculty 1789

Co-op (work/study) available
No; no correspondence or self-paced study

Graduation requirements N/A

Graduating students 382

15.10 DEPARTMENT OF ART

Degree
Bachelor of Fine Art, B.F.A.

Level
Honours

Programs
Drawing
Painting
Printmaking
Sculpture

First-year entry Yes

Entry requirements
Minimum average: 60% (low 70%s)
OAC English; OAC Art recommended
Portfolio

Students accepted 26
Total in department 102

Co-op (work/study) available
No; no correspondence or self-paced study

Graduation requirements
Minimum GPA: 60%
Full credits/courses: Honours 20

Graduating students 26

15.10 SCHOOL OF MUSIC

Degree
Bachelor of Music, B.Mus.
Licentiate of Music, L.Mus.

Level
Honours

Programs
Applied Study (Performance)
History/Literature
Music Education
Theory/Composition

First-year entry Yes

Entry requirements
Minimum average: 60% (high 60%)
OAC English
Audition, aural discrimination test, certain level of proficiency

Students accepted 46
Total in school 154

Co-op (work/study) available
No; no correspondence or self-paced study

Graduation requirements
Minimum GPA: 60%
Full credits/courses: Honours 20

Graduating students 26

15.12 FACULTY OF LAW

Degree
Bachelor of Law, LL.B.

Level
Professional

Programs
Law

First-year entry
No; after 2 years of undergraduate study

Entry requirements
77% or more in university courses
Must score in top third of LSAT

Students accepted 150
Total in faculty 473

Co-op (work/study) available
No; no correspondence or self-paced study

Graduation requirements N/R

Graduating students 152

15.13 FACULTY OF MEDICINE

Degree
Doctor of Medicine, M.D.

Level
Professional

Programs
Medicine

First-year entry
No; after at least 2 years' undergraduate study

Entry requirements
Minimum average: OACs necessary for entrance into a faculty of science
University-level courses in General and Organic Chemistry, Biology and General Physics, with minimum B+ average
MCAT with 40% weighting to Personal Information Form

Students accepted 76
Total in faculty 303

Co-op (work/study) available
No; no correspondence or self-paced study

Graduation requirements N/R

Graduating students 76

15.13 SCHOOL OF NURSING

Degree
Bachelor of Nursing Science, B.N.Sc.

Level
Honours

Programs
Nursing

First-year entry Yes

Entry requirements
Minimum average: 60% (mid 70%)
OAC English, Mathematics, Biology and Chemistry
Personal Information Form

Students accepted 68
Total in school 286

Co-op (work/study) available
No; no correspondence or self-paced study

Graduation requirements
Minimum GPA: 65%
Full credits/courses: N/A

Graduating students 48

15.13 SCHOOL OF REHABILITATION THERAPY

Degree
Bachelor of Science, Occupational Therapy, B.Sc.O.T.

Bachelor of Science, Physical Therapy, B.Sc.P.T.

Level
Honours

Programs
Occupational Therapy
Physical Therapy

First-year entry Yes

Entry requirements
Minimum average: 60% (P.T. low 90%, O.T. mid 80%)
OAC Biology, Chemistry; 1 Mathematics; OAC Physics, English recommended
Personal Background Form

Students accepted 65
Total in school 219

Co-op (work/study) available
No; no correspondence or self-paced study

Graduation requirements
Minimum GPA: 60%
Full credits/courses: N/A

Graduating students 28

15.14 SCHOOL OF PHYSICAL AND HEALTH EDUCATION

Degree
Bachelor of Arts / Bachelor of Physical and Health Education, B.A./B.P.H.E

Level
Honours

Programs
Physical and Health Education

First-year entry Yes

Entry requirements
Minimum average: 60% (low 80%)
OAC English, Chemistry; OAC Physical and Health Education recommended
Personal Information Form

Students accepted 71
Total in school 305

Co-op (work/study) available
No; no correspondence or self-paced study

Graduation requirements
Minimum GPA: 60%
Full credits/courses: Honours N/A

Graduating students 80

16. FUTURE PLANS

Buildings
New library to open in 1994

Programs
Enrolment will remain stable at about 10,000 undergraduates.

Royal Military College

1. OVERVIEW

The Royal Military College of Canada, a "university with a difference," has been serving Canada, and Canadians, since its beginnings in 1876 as an institution dedicated to the education and training of military officers. RMC's graduates can be found not only in military service but in government, industry, business and the professions, in positions of leadership and responsibility.

2. PRESIDENT

Marcel Masse, Minister of National Defence

3. ENROLMENT

(1990 Fall semester)

Registration
Undergraduate full-time 731
(M 635, F 96)
Undergraduate part-time 14
(M 10, F 4)
Graduate 94 (M 92, F 2)

Residence*
Undergrads in residence 88.5%
(M 87.9%, F 92.7%)
Undergrads in off-campus housing
N/A
Undergrads commuting 11.5%
* All ROTP/RETP cadets must live in residence.

4. ADMISSIONS TO FIRST YEAR

Entry dates
Fall (Sept.)

Note: All candidates apply through Canadian Forces Recruiting Centres. Successful applicants are enrolled in the Canadian Forces, Regular or Reserve. Conditions and standards, usually not required at other universities, must be met such as citizenship and physical fitness. For these reasons, applicant statistics are not comparable and would be misleading. Admission to RMC is limited. Eligible candidates compete for places available.

Admissions offered to qualified candidates before early admission
No

Community-college transfer requirements N/R

Mature students admission requirements N/R

5. ADMISSIONS CONTACT

Barbara Leslie
Assistant Registrar
Royal Military College
Kingston, Ontario K7K 5L0
(613) 541-6212

6. STRUCTURE AND DEGREES

RMC grants degrees under Ontario charter but is funded and directed by the federal government through the Department of National Defence. The minister of national defence serves as both chancellor and president. Apart from departmental officials, RMC has an appointed body, the Canadian Military College Advisory Board, to assist in governance. This board has 21 members, with regional and alumni representation.

Teaching faculty
Full-time 153 (M 146, F 7)
Part-time 24 (M 19, F 5)

Faculty/Student ratio (FTE basis) 1:5

Undergraduate degrees conferred
Arts, Engineering, Science

7. TEACHING FACILITIES

Largest first-year class N/R
First-year courses with tutorials
N/R
Lab places for first-year students
N/R

Research grants and contracts
$4,116,572

Graduate programs
Number of programs 15
Enrolment in master's programs 101; doctoral programs 1

Libraries
With open stacks N/R
With closed stacks N/R
Total holdings 302,000 volumes

8. STUDENTS

Undergraduates

1st year	159
2nd year	122
3rd year	230
4th year	220

Entering as Ontario Scholars 69.4%
Entering with scholarships 4%
Entering with OSAP help None

9. ENTRANCE SCHOLARSHIPS

All RMC students are enrolled in the Canadian Forces Regular or Reserve component. In exchange for service following graduation, they receive tuition without cost and are paid a salary from which room and board are deducted. RMC applicants compete for renewable entrance scholarships awarded by the alumni association, the RMC Club of Canada.

10. INTERNATIONAL STUDENTS

Candidates must be Canadian citizens.

11. ATHLETIC FACILITIES

Gym
Ice rink
Playing fields
Sailing facilities
Squash courts
Swimming pool
Tennis (outdoor)
Track centre (indoor/outdoor)
Weight/workout rooms

Inter-university sports
Curling
Fencing
Hockey
Rugby
Skiing (cross-country)
Soccer
Track (indoor)
Water polo
Wrestling
Volleyball

Intra-mural organized sports
Various

Recreation and fitness programs

12. STUDENT LIFE

Student councils 1
Student clubs approx. 25

Pubs 2
Drinking awareness program

First-year orientation
Yes; week prior to start of classes

13. STUDENT SERVICES

Counselling
Psychological, Career, Peer

Medical
Clinic facilities

14. RESIDENCES

All ROTP/RETP cadets must live in residence.

15. PROGRAMS OF UNDERGRADUATE STUDY

15.1 DIVISION OF ARTS

Degree
Bachelor of Arts, B.A

Level
General, Honours (both 4 years)

Programs
Economics and Commerce
English
History
History and Political Science
Military and Strategic Studies
Political and Economic Science

First-year entry
Yes, years 1 and 2 common; enter program in year 3.

Entry requirements
Minimum average: N/R
OAC English, Mathematics
Calculus recommended

Students accepted N/A
Total in division 189

Co-op (work/study) available
No; no correspondence or self-paced study

Graduation requirements
Minimum GPA: N/R
Full credits/courses: N/R

Graduating students 52

15.2 DIVISION OF SCIENCE

Degree
Bachelor of Science, B.Sc.

Level
General, Honours

Programs
Mathematics and Physics (General, Honours)
Science (Applied)
Space Science

First-year entry
Yes, years 1 and 2 common; students enter Science or Engineering in year 3; Science (Applied) begins year 2.

Entry requirements
Minimum average: N/R
OAC English or French, Calculus, Algebra and Geometry, Chemistry, Physics; 1 other OAC

Students accepted N/R
Total in division: 207 in years 1 and 2 of general program, 36 in upper years of program

Co-op (work/study) available
No; no correspondence or self-paced study

Graduation requirements
Minimum GPA: N/R
Full credits/courses: N/A

Graduating students 18

15.7 DIVISION OF ENGINEERING

Degree
Bachelor of Engineering, B.Eng.

Level
N/R

Programs
Civil Eng.
Computer Eng.
Electrical Eng.
Engineering Physics
Engineering and Management
Fuels and Materials Eng.
Mechanical Eng.

First-year entry
Yes, years 1 and 2 are common; students enter Science or Engineering in year 3; Science (Applied) begins year 2.

Entry requirements
Minimum average: N/R
OAC English or French, Calculus, Algebra and Geometry, Chemistry, Physics; 1 other OAC

Students accepted N/A
Total in division 506 including 207 in years 1 and 2 of general program

Co-op (work/study) available
No; no correspondence or self-paced study

Graduation requirements
Minimum GPA: N/R
Full credits/courses: N/A

Graduating students 150

Ryerson Polytechnical Institute

1. OVERVIEW
A degree-granting member of the Council of Ontario Universities, Ryerson is a leading centre of undergraduate applied professional education for some 12,000 full-time students. Established in 1948 and located in downtown Toronto, Ryerson offers 33 career-oriented programs through its Faculties of Arts, Applied Arts, Business, Community Services and Technology.

2. PRESIDENT
Terence W. Grier

3. ENROLMENT
(1989 Fall semester; totals rounded to nearest 100)

Registration
Undergraduate full-time 12,000 (M 5500, F 6500)
Undergraduate part-time 1000 (M 450, F 550)
Graduate N/R

Residence
Undergrads in residence 5%
This will increase as new Residence (which will accommodate approximately 550) opens Fall 1991
Undergrads in off-campus housing approx. 40%
Undergrads commuting approx. 55%

4. ADMISSIONS TO FIRST YEAR

Entry dates
Fall

First-year entries

	Fall (Sept)
Applications	22,469
Admissions	7,946
Enrolments	4,331

Admissions offered to qualified candidates before early admission
Yes

Community-college transfer requirements
On individual basis

Advanced standing granted
On individual basis

Mature students admission requirements
Age 21, out of school at least 2 years; admitted to full- or part-time degree

5. ADMISSIONS CONTACT

Mr Eugene Logel
Ryerson Polytechnical Institute
350 Victoria Street
Toronto, Ontario M5B 2K3
(416) 979-5028

6. STRUCTURE AND DEGREES

Board of Governors
23 members (M 15 F 8); 3 faculty, 3 students, 2 support staff, 3 alumni)

Teaching faculty
Full-time 597 (M 407, F 190)
Part-time 298 (M 152, F 146)

Faculty/Student ratio (FTE basis)
N/A

Undergraduate degrees conferred
Applied Arts, Business Management, Technology, Engineering, Social Work

7. TEACHING FACILITIES

Largest first-year class 100
First-year courses with tutorials 25%
Lab places for first-year students
Biology 20, Chemistry 20, Computers 32, Graphics 16, Languages 15–18, Physics 20

Research grants and contracts N/A

Graduate programs N/R

Libraries
With open stacks 1
With closed stacks 0
Total holdings approx. 301,158 volumes

8. STUDENTS

Undergraduates

1st year	4300
2nd year	2900
3rd year	2800
4th year	2500

Entering as Ontario Scholars 18%
Entering with scholarships approx. 8%
Entering with OSAP help N/A

9. ENTRANCE SCHOLARSHIPS

Limited number of entrance scholarships ranging in value from $750–$2000 donated by business and industry in the following programs: Applied Computer Science, Applied Geography, Fashion, Hospitality and Tourism Management, Journalism, Radio and Television Arts, Survey Engineering

10. INTERNATIONAL STUDENTS

Students from outside Canada approx. 3%
Scholarships awarded None
Services available Adviser; International Student Service
Language requirements for admission TOEFL score 550–580, depending on program; MELAB score 85–90, depending on program; Ryerson Test of English Proficiency

11. ATHLETIC FACILITIES

Athletic therapy room
Combatives room
Dance studio
Gym
Sauna
Squash courts
Swimming pool
Tennis courts (outdoor)
Track centre (indoor)
Weight/workout rooms

Inter-university sports
Badminton M, F
Basketball M, F
Fencing M, F
Hockey M
Skiing M, F
Soccer M, F
Swimming M, F
Volleyball M, F

Intra-mural organized sports
Badminton M, F, C
Basketball, M, C
Broomball C
Curling C
Hockey, ball M
Hockey, ice M, C
Inner-tube water polo C
Soccer (indoor) M
Soccer (outdoor) C
Softball C
Squash M, F, C
Tennis M, F, C
Volleyball M, F, C
Football M, F
Table Tennis M, W

Recreation and fitness programs

12. STUDENT LIFE

Student councils 1
Student clubs 20

Pubs 1
Drinking awareness program

First-year orientation
Registration week each year; parent sessions, 'Preview Days'

13. STUDENT SERVICES

Counselling
Psychological, Career

Medical
Nurses 1; Doctors M (2), F (2)

Special needs
Handicapped/special needs centre
Most of campus wheelchair accessible

Other
Essay writing/study skills program
Mature student association
Off-campus housing registry

14. RESIDENCES

Residence places
38 M, 0 F
Apartments/townhouses: large house
More than 700 Ryerson students live in co-ed apartments, as well as other residences affiliated with Ryerson; obtain information from Housing Office
New 556 bed residence will open September 1991

First-year students
Places reserved 24 double
Application deadline August 15
No places reserved for scholarship winners
No eligibility limitations based on student's home location
Allocations announced beginning mid-June

Upper-year students
Places reserved 12
Allocations announced N/A

Wheelchair-accessible rooms N/R

Meal-plan options
Communal kitchen

15. PROGRAMS OF UNDERGRADUATE STUDY

15.1 FACULTY OF ARTS

Degree
Bachelor of Applied Arts, B.A.A.

Level
4 years (3-yr 'Diploma in Arts' also available)

Programs
Applied Geography with specialization in:
Environment Resource Management
Public Administration
Recreation Studies
Retail/Industrial Location Analysis
Urban Analysis

First-year entry Yes

Entry requirements
Minimum average: 60%
OAC English, Mathematics, Geography recommended
Interview

Students accepted 66
Total in faculty 124

Co-op (work/study) available
Internships; no correspondence or self-paced study

Graduation requirements
Minimum GPA: 2.00 on 4-point scale
Full credits/courses: N/R

Graduating students 30

15.2 FACULTY OF ENGINEERING AND APPLIED SCIENCE

Degree
Bachelor of Technology, B.Tech.

Level
4 years (optional 5-yr cooperative program in Applied Chemistry and Biology)

Programs
Applied Chemistry and Biology (formerly Laboratory Science; students may graduate with diploma after 3 years)
Applied Computer Science (in the final years of Applied Computer Science, students select options from the Computer Stream, Systems, Mathematical Analysis, Computer Hardware and Management Science)

First-year entry Yes

Entry requirements
Minimum average: 60%
OAC Mathematics; other requirements vary for each program

Students accepted 190
Total in faculty 413

Co-op (work/study) available
Yes, in Applied Chemistry and Biology; no correspondence or self-paced study

Graduation requirements
Minimum GPA: 2.00 on 4-point scale
Full credits/courses: N/R

Graduating students 72

15.3 FACULTY OF BUSINESS

Degree
Bachelor of Business Management, B.B.M.

Level
4 years

Programs*
Administration and Information Management
Business Management
Hospitality and Tourism Management

In year 2, Business Management students may choose to specialize in 1 of:
Accounting/Finance
Business and Economics Decision Support Systems
Business and Enterprise Development
Computer Business Information Systems
Human Resources
Marketing Management
* Students may graduate after 3 years with a diploma.

First-year entry Yes

Entry requirements
Minimum average: 60%
OAC English, OAC or Grade 12 Advanced Mathematics (depending on program)
Administration and Information Management: keyboard skills
Hospitality and Tourism Management: interview and résumé may be required

Students accepted 1041
Total in faculty 3549

Co-op (work/study) available
No; no correspondence or self-paced study

Graduation requirements
Minimum GPA: 2.00 on 4-point scale
Full credits/courses: N/R
Students in Hospitality and Tourism Management must complete 1 academic year of acceptable cumulative work experience

Graduating students 973

15.4 FACULTY OF ENGINEERING AND APPLIED SCIENCE

Degree
Bachelor of Technology, B.Tech.

Level
4 years

Programs
Architectural Science:
In year 3 Architectural Science students choose 1 of Architecture, Building Science or Project Management
3-yr diploma program in Landscape Architecture also offered

First-year entry Yes

Entry requirements
Minimum average: 60%
OAC English, Physics; Grade 12 Advanced Mathematics
Portfolio; interview may be required

Students accepted 133
Total in faculty 317

Co-op (work/study) available
No; no correspondence or self-paced study

Graduation requirements
Minimum GPA: 2.00 on 4-point scale
Full credits/courses: N/R

Graduating students 78

15.7 FACULTY OF ENGINEERING AND APPLIED SCIENCE

Degree
Bachelor of Technology, B.Tech.
Bachelor of Engineering, B.Eng. (Electrical Engineering)

Level
4 years
5 year co-operative program in Chemical Engineering

Programs
Engineering:
Aerospace Eng.
Chemical Eng.
Civil Eng.
Electrical Eng.
Industrial Eng.
Mechanical Eng.
Survey Eng.

First-year entry Yes

Entry requirements
Minimum average: 60%
1 or more OAC Mathematics, Physics, Chemistry
Survey Engineering: OAC or Grade 12 Advanced English

Students accepted 578
Total in faculty 1652

Co-op (work/study) available
In Chemical Eng.; no correspondence or self-paced study

Graduation requirements
Minimum GPA: 2.00 on 4-point scale
Full credits/courses: N/R

Graduating students 318

15.10 FACULTY OF APPLIED ARTS

Degree
Bachelor of Applied Arts, B.A.A.

Level
4 years, 3 years

Programs*
Fashion
Graphic Communications Management
Interior Design
Photographic Arts
Radio and Television Arts

* Fashion students may graduate after 3 years with a diploma; 3-yr diploma programs also offered in Theatre, including Dance, Acting and Technical Production; Radio and Television Arts is a 3-yr degree program.

First-year entry Yes

Entry requirements
Minimum average: 60%; Radio and Television Arts 70%
OAC English; other requirements depend on program; interview, portfolio or essay depending on program

Students accepted 625
Total in faculty 1584

Co-op (work/study) available
No; no correspondence or self-paced study

Graduation requirements
Minimum GPA: 2.00 on 4-point scale
Full credits/courses: N/R

Graduating students 383

15.11 FACULTY OF APPLIED ARTS

Degree
Bachelor of Applied Arts, B.A.A.

Level
4 years

Programs
Journalism

Specialization: Students select 1 of Newspaper, Broadcast or Magazine journalism in 2nd year.

First-year entry Yes

Entry requirements
Minimum average: 70%
OAC English
Test, keyboard skills

Students accepted 141
Total in faculty 345

Co-op (work/study) available
No; no correspondence or self-paced study

Graduation requirements
Minimum GPA: 2.00 on 4-point scale
Full credits/courses: N/R

Graduating students 122

15.13 FACULTY OF COMMUNITY SERVICES

Degree
Bachelor of Applied Arts, B.A.A.

Level
4 years (3-yr diploma also offered)

Programs
Nursing

First-year entry Yes

Entry requirements
Minimum average: 60%
OAC English, Chemistry; 1 of Physics, Biology; Grade 11 or higher Advanced Mathematics

Students accepted 139
Total in faculty 678

Co-op (work/study) available
No; no correspondence or self-paced study

Graduation requirements
Minimum GPA: 2.00 on 4-point scale
Full credits/courses: N/R

Graduating students 109

15.15 FACULTY OF COMMUNITY SERVICES

Degree
Bachelor of Applied Arts, B.A.A.
Bachelor of Social Work, B.SW.

Level
4 years, full-time and part-time

Programs*
Child and Youth Care
Early Childhood Education
Environmental Health
Food, Nutrition, Consumer and Family Services
Social Work
Urban and Regional Planning
* Students may graduate after 3 years with a diploma in Environmental Health and Social Work.

First-year entry Yes

Entry requirements
Minimum average: 60%
Criteria may vary for each program
Interview and/or essay required for Urban and Regional Planning and Early Childhood Education
Social Work: age 18; written test prior to admission

Students accepted 505
Total in faculty 2582

Co-op (work/study) available
No; no correspondence or self-paced study

Graduation requirements
Minimum GPA: 2.00 on 4-point scale
Full credits/courses: N/R

Graduating students 324

16. FUTURE PLANS

Programs
Proposals for B.Eng. degrees in Aerospace, Chemical and Civil Engineering have already gone forward to the government and similar proposals for Mechanical and Industrial Engineering will be presented later this year. In October, a team from the Canadian Engineering Accreditation Board will make a formal visit to Ryerson to assess all six engineering programs for the purpose of professional accreditation by the C.E.A.B.

Buildings
New home for Schools of Radio and Television Arts, Journalism and Applied Computer Science in Rogers Communication Centre; to open Fall 1991
556-bed, co-ed residence opening in Fall 1991; priority given to 1st-year students

University of Toronto
St George Campus

1. OVERVIEW
Chartered in 1827, the University of Toronto is a large, but highly decentralized and diverse community. Its downtown campus consists of seven Arts and Science colleges, a Faculty of Arts and Science, and 14 professional faculties. Several affiliated institutions and the School of Continuing Studies extend the university's programs into other communities.

2. PRESIDENT
J. Robert S. Prichard

3. ENROLMENT
(1990 Fall semester)

Registration
Undergraduate full-time 32,932 (M 49%, F 51%)
Undergraduate part-time 13,533 (M 39%, F 61%)
Graduate 9623 (M 49%, F 51%)

Residence
Undergrads in residence 16% (M 50%, F 50%)
Undergrads in off-campus housing 18%
Undergrads commuting 66%

4. ADMISSIONS TO FIRST YEAR

Entry dates
Fall, Winter, Summer; see Erindale College for February Admissions program.

First-year entries

	Fall (Sept)	Summer (part-time)
Applications	23,134*	841
Admissions	16,669	611
Enrolments	9,011	400

* Applications represent secondary-school 1st-choice applications only; but offers of admission are also made to 2nd- and 3rd-choice applicants.

Admissions offered to qualified candidates before early admission
Yes

Community-college transfer requirements
3-year CAAT graduates eligible for 1 to 5 credits

Mature students admission requirements
Age 21; high standing on a pre-university course

5. ADMISSIONS CONTACT

Office of Admissions
315 Bloor Street West
Toronto, Ontario M5S 1A3
(416) 978-2771

6. STRUCTURE AND DEGREES

Governing Council
50 members (M 34, F 16; 12 faculty, 8 students, 2 support staff, 8 alumni)

Teaching faculty
Full-time 3091 (M 2339, F 752)
Part-time 561 (M 393, F 168)

Faculty/Student ratio, excluding Medicine and Dentistry (FTE basis)
1:17

Undergraduate degrees conferred
Applied Science (Engineering), Architecture, Arts, Commerce, Dental Surgery, Landscape Architecture, Law, Medicine, Music, Music in Performance, Physical and Health Education,

Science, Science degrees in Biomedical Communications, Forestry, Nursing, Pharmacy, Occupational Therapy, Physical Therapy

7. TEACHING FACILITIES

Largest first-year class 1500, but average 75
First-year courses with tutorials more than 50%
Lab places for first-year students All 1st-year students assured lab places

Research grants and contracts
$125 million (1987/88)

Graduate programs
Number of programs 163
Enrolment in master's programs 5606; doctoral programs 3505

Libraries
With open and closed stacks 40
Total holdings 7 million volumes

8. STUDENTS

Undergraduates

1st year	9915
2nd year	8076
3rd year	6753
4th year	4481

Entering as Ontario Scholars 49%
Entering with scholarships 8%
Entering with OSAP help 30%
(except for Ontario Scholars, figures combined for 3 campuses)

9. ENTRANCE SCHOLARSHIPS

Most prestigious
National Admission Scholarship (5–7):
Application necessary
Deadline December 1
Requirements: Nomination by secondary school, references; % N/R

Full-tuition scholarships
Open Scholarships (approx. 350):
Application necessary
Deadline April 30
Requirements: 90% minimum; secondary-school appraisal

Partial-tuition scholarships (340)
Application necessary
Deadline April 30
Requirments: 85% minimum; secondary-school appraisal

Scholarships for entering students
Offered N/A
Accepted approx. 690
Total budget for undergraduate entrance scholarships $1,043,000

10. INTERNATIONAL STUDENTS

Students from outside Canada 7%
Scholarships awarded approx. 40
Services available International Student Centre provides wide range of services.
Language requirements for admission TOEFL score 580; MELAB score 90

11. ATHLETIC FACILITIES

Archery range
Dance studio
Golf cages
Gym
Ice rink
Playing fields
Rifle range
Squash courts
Stadium
Swimming pool
Tennis courts (indoor/outdoor)
Track centre (indoor/outdoor)
Weight/workout rooms

Inter-university sports
42 sports including:
Badminton
Basketball
Cross-country running
Curling
Diving
Fencing
Figure skating
Football
Golf
Gymnastics
Hockey, field

Hockey, ice
Rowing
Rugby
Skiing
Soccer
Squash
Swimming
Tennis
Track and field
Volleyball
Water polo
Wrestling

Intra-mural organized sports
more than 20 sports

Recreation and fitness programs

12. STUDENT LIFE

Student councils 24
Student clubs 138

Pubs 2
Drinking awareness program

First-year orientation
Organized by each college or faculty

13. STUDENT SERVICES

Counselling
Psychological, Career, Peer

Medical
Nurses, Doctors (F and M) several on staff

Special needs
Handicapped/special needs centre
46% of campus wheelchair accessible

Other
Learning Disability Program
Essay writing/study skills program
Off-campus housing registry

14. RESIDENCES

Residence places
1191 M, 1226 F, 558 C

First-year students
Places reserved: approx. 40%, moving towards 50%
Application deadline: None
Places reserved for scholarships winners
Eligibility limitations based on student's home location
Allocations announced after June 15

Upper-year students
Places reserved: 60%, moving towards 50%
Allocations announced after June 15

Wheelchair-accessible rooms
1 women's residence of 186 units; small number in other residences

Meal-plan options
Meal plans, 12–21 meals/week

15. PROGRAMS OF UNDERGRADUATE STUDY
All 1st-year applicants must fill out a Student Profile questionnaire, which enables the university to better assess academic and personal strengths. 70% is the minimum average for admission but it rises for high-demand programs. Criteria considered include Grade 13 or OACs, distribution of subjects, performance in subjects relevant to university program selected, results in senior division prerequisite courses, and information from questionnaires, portfolios or auditions.

15.1, 15.2, 15.3 FACULTY OF ARTS AND SCIENCE

Degree
Bachelor of Arts, B.A.
Bachelor of Science, B.Sc.
Bachelor of Commerce, B.Com.

Level
B.A., B.Sc. 3 and 4 years
B.Com. 4 years

Programs
Approx. 400 programs offered by these departments:
Anthropology
Astronomy
Botany
Chemistry
Classics

Commerce
Computer Science
East Asian Studies
Economics
English
Fine Art
French
Geography
Geology
German
History
Italian Studies
Mathematics
Middle East and Islamic Studies
Near Eastern Studies
Philosophy
Physics
Political Science
Psychology
Religious Studies
Slavic Languages and Literature
Sociology
South Asian Studies
Spanish and Portuguese
Statistics
Zoology

First-year entry
Yes; enter Commerce in year 2

Entry requirements
St. George Campus:
Minimum average: N/A
Sciences: OAC English 1/*Anglais*, OACs depending on program, OAC Algebra and Geometry, Calculus and Physics
B.Com.: OAC English 1/*Anglais*, OAC Algebra and Geometry, Calculus
Arts (Humanities): OAC English 1/*Anglais*, language credits recommended for some language programs
B.Sc.: OAC English 1/*Anglais*, OAC Biology recommended
Note: Scarborough Campus/Erindale Campus:
Arts and Sciences: OAC English 1/*Anglais*, five other OACs which satisfy the prerequisites of specific courses or programs in which applicant intends to enrol.

Students accepted 3885
Total in faculty 20,342

Co-op (work/study) available
Yes, only at Scarborough College; no correspondence or self-paced study

Graduation requirements
Minimum GPA: 1.5 on scale of 4.3

Full credits/courses: Honours 20, General 15
See faculty calendar for special requirements.

Graduating students 4455

15.4 FACULTY OF ARCHITECTURE AND LANDSCAPE ARCHITECTURE

Degree
Bachelor of Architecture, B.Arch.
Bachelor of Landscape Architecture, B.L.A.

Level
5 years

Programs
Architecture
Landscape Architecture

First-year entry Yes

Entry requirements
Minimum average: N/R
Architecture: OAC English 1/*Anglais*, Algebra and Geometry, one credit in Physics or other Mathematics course, three additional credits. Portfolio; questionaire
Landscape Architecture: OAC English/*Anglais*, Algebra and Geometry, one credit in Physics or other Mathematics course, three additional credits. Portfolio; questionnaire

Students accepted
Architecture 66, Landscape Architecture 14
Total in faculty 347

Co-op (work/study) available
No; no correspondence or self-paced study

Graduation requirements
Minimum GPA: N/A
Full credits/courses: N/A

Graduating students
Architecture 54, Landscape Architecture 14

15.7 FACULTY OF APPLIED SCIENCE AND ENGINEERING

Degree
Bachelor of Applied Science, B.A.Sc.

Level
4 years

Programs
Chemical Eng.
Civil Eng.
Computer Science
Electrical Eng.
Engineering Science
Geological and Mineral Engineering
Industrial Eng.
Mechanical Eng.
Metallurgical Eng. and Materials Science

First-year entry Yes

Entry requirements
Minimum average: N/A
OAC English 1/*Anglais*, Calculus, Algebra and Geometry, Chemistry, Physics
Portfolio; questionnaire

Students accepted 903
Total in faculty 2684

Co-op (work/study) available
Optional, Professional Experience Year of 16-month work period after year 2; no correspondence or self-paced study

Graduation requirements
Minimum GPA: N/A
Full credits/courses: N/A

Graduating students 577

15.8 FACULTY OF FORESTRY

Degree
Bachelor of Science in Forestry, B.Sc.F.

Level
4 years

Programs
Students choose Forest Science or Wood Products Science in year 3

First-year entry Yes

Entry requirements
Minimum average: N/A
OAC English 1/*Anglais*, Calculus, Chemistry, Finite Mathematics or Algebra and Geometry, Biology
OAC Physics recommended

Students accepted 13
Total in faculty 86

Co-op (work/study) available
No; no correspondence or self-paced study

Graduation requirements
Minimum GPA: N/A
Full credits/courses: N/A

Graduating students 24

15.9 FACULTY OF DENTISTRY

Degree
Doctor of Dental Surgery, D.D.S.

Level
Professional

Programs
Dentistry

First-year entry
No, enter year 3

Entry requirements
Minimum average: N/A
OACs same as for Faculty of Arts and Science; 2 years of university study with acceptable first year courses in Biology, Chemistry, Organic Chemistry, Physics
Contact faculty admissions office for special requirements.

Students accepted 64
Total in faculty 320

Co-op (work/study) available
No; no correspondence or self-paced study

Graduation requirements
Minimum GPA: N/A
Full credits/courses: N/A

Graduating students 100

15.9 FACULTY OF PHARMACY

Degree
Bachelor of Science, Pharmacy, B.Sc.Phm.

Level
4 years

Programs
Pharmacy

First-year entry Yes

Entry requirements
Minimum average: N/A
OAC English 1/*Anglais*, Biology, Calculus, Chemistry, Physics, Social Science credit
Open only to Ontario students unless sponsored by Canadian government agency
Must be 1st choice on Toronto's Supplementary Information Form

Students accepted 168
Total in faculty 646

Co-op (work/study) available
No; no correspondence or self-paced study

Graduation requirements
Minimum GPA: N/A
Full credits/courses: N/A

Graduating students 156

15.10 FACULTY OF MUSIC

Degree
Bachelor of Music, Mus.Bac.
Bachelor of Music (Performance), Mus.Bac.(Perf.)

Level
4 years

Programs
Music
Music (Performance)

First-year entry Yes

Entry requirements
Minimum average: N/A
Mus.Bac.: English 1/*Anglais*, 5 OACs, one of which may be Music
Mus.Bac.(Perf.): 30 credits for OSSD (5 at grade 12 advanced level)
Audition and musical requirements
Music must be 1st choice on Toronto's Supplementary Information Form.

Students accepted 105
Total in faculty 360

Co-op (work/study) available
No; no correspondence or self-paced study

Graduation requirements
Minimum GPA: N/A
Full credits/courses: N/A

Graduating students 105

15.12 FACULTY OF LAW

Degree
Bachelor of Laws, LL.B.

Level
Professional

Programs
Law

First-year entry
No; enter year 3

Entry requirements
Minimum average: N/A
OACs to enter undergraduate program
Minimum of 10 undergraduate courses (2 year's university study)
LSAT, high undergraduate GPA
Most entrants have completed 4 year degree and possibly some graduate work.
Contact faculty for more information.

Students accepted 174
Total in faculty 532

Co-op (work/study) available
No; no correspondence or self-paced study

Graduation requirements
Minimum GPA: N/A
Full credits/courses: N/A

Graduating students 185

15.13 FACULTY OF MEDICINE

Degree
Doctor of Medicine, M.D.

Level
Professional

Programs
Medicine
First-year entry
No; enter year 3

Entry requirements
Minimum average: N/A
OAC requirements for Faculty of Arts and Science; a minimum of 2 year's undergradaute study
Contact faculty admissions office for more information.

Students accepted 252
Total in faculty 1008

Co-op (work/study) available
No; no correspondence or self-paced study

Graduation requirements
Minimum GPA: N/A
Full credits/courses: N/A

Graduating students 252

15.13 FACULTY OF MEDICINE – PROGRAM IN REHABILITATION MEDICINE

Degree
Bachelor of Science (Occupational Therapy), B.Sc.(O.T.)
Bachelor of Science (Physical Therapy), B.Sc.(P.T.)

Level
4 years

Programs
Professional

First-year entry Yes

Entry requirements
Minimum average: N/A
OAC English 1/*Anglais*; 1 of Algebra and Geometry, Calculus, Finite Mathematics
B.Sc.(O.T.): Biology
B.Sc.(P.T.): Biology, Chemistry and Physics
Closed to international students and students from some provinces

Students accepted
O.T. 60, P.T. 69
Total in faculty: O.T. 225, P.T. 268

Co-op (work/study) available
No; no correspondence or self-paced study

Graduation requirements
Minimum GPA: N/A
Full credits/courses: N/A

Graduating students
O.T. 63, P.T. 63

15.13 FACULTY OF NURSING

Degree
Bachelor of Science, Nursing, B.Sc.N.

Level
4 years

Programs
Nursing

First-year entry Yes

Entry requirements
Minimum average: N/A
OAC English 1/*Anglais*, Chemistry Biology, Mathematics recommended
Only 10% of places available to international students

Students accepted 107
Total in faculty 443

Co-op (work/study) available
No; no correspondence or self-paced study

Graduation requirements
Minimum GPA: N/A
Full credits/courses: N/A

Graduating students 138

15.14 FACULTY OF PHYSICAL AND HEALTH EDUCATION

Degree
Bachelor of Physical and Health Education, B.P.H.E.
Level
4 years

Programs
Physical and Health Education

First-year entry Yes
Entry requirements
Minimum average: N/A
OAC English 1/*Anglais*, Biology, Physical Education; 1 credit in Mathematics; 1 of Chemistry or Physics

Students accepted 113
Total in faculty 493

Co-op (work/study) available
No; no correspondence or self-paced study

Graduation requirements
Minimum GPA: N/A
Full credits/courses: N/A

Graduating students 99

16. FUTURE PLANS

Buildings
A 1224-bed residence with space for graduate students and students in professional faculties

Programs
New undergraduate program, primarily part-time, in Health Administration, leading to B.H.Sc.; directed to health professionals wanting administrative skills

Erindale College, University of Toronto

1. OVERVIEW
Erindale College is part of the University of Toronto's Faculty of Arts and Science, offering degrees in Arts, Science and Commerce. Located 32 km west of downtown Toronto in the City of Mississauga, Erindale is a thriving educational presence in a prime location.

2. PRINCIPAL
Desmond Morton

3. ENROLMENT
(1990 Fall semester; undergraduate totals rounded to nearest 100)

Registration
Undergraduate full-time 4800
(M 47%, F 53%)
Undergraduate part-time 1400
(M 40%, F 60%)
Graduate N/R

Residence
Undergrads in residence 21%
(M 50%, F 50%)
Undergrads in off-campus housing 10%
Undergrads commuting 69%

4. ADMISSIONS TO FIRST YEAR

Entry dates
Fall, Winter

First-year entries

	Fall (Sept)	Winter* (Feb)
Applications†	2100	1200
Admissions	2400	275
Enrolments	1211	177

* Erindale offers February admission to students who complete secondary school in January.

† Applications represent secondary-school 1st choice only, but offers of admission also made to 2nd- and 3rd-choice applicants.

Admissions offered to qualified candidates before early admission
Yes

Community-college transfer requirements
With no OACs, minimum 2 CAAT years

Advanced standing granted
Minimum 3 years in suitable CAAT program with high academic standing

Mature students admission requirements
Same as for St George campus

5. ADMISSIONS CONTACT

Doug Leeies
Assistant Registrar, Recruiting
Erindale Campus
University of Toronto
Mississauga, Ontario L5L 1C6
(416) 828-5217

6. STRUCTURE AND DEGREES

Governing Council
See St George section.

Teaching faculty
Full-time 204 (M 161, F 43)
Part-time 30 (M 23, F 7)

Faculty/Student ratio (FTE basis)
1:19

Undergraduate degrees conferred
Arts, Commerce, Science

7. TEACHING FACILITIES

Largest first-year class 256
First-year courses with tutorials 75%
Lab places for first-year students
Biology 260, Chemistry 384, Computers 834, Graphics - Sheridan College, Languages 240, Physics 385

Research grants and contracts
$3.75 million

Graduate programs
See St George section.

Libraries
With open stacks 1
With closed stacks 0
Total holdings 250,000 volumes

8. STUDENTS

Undergraduates

1st year	2395
2nd year	1774
3rd year	1164
4th year	911

Entering as Ontario Scholars 27%
Entering with scholarships approx. 6%
Entering with OSAP help approx. 30%
(except for Ontario Scholars, figures combined for 3 campuses)

9. ENTRANCE SCHOLARSHIPS

Erindale students may receive National and Open scholarships; refer to St George section.

Most prestigious
1. Chancellor's (2):
No application necessary
No deadline
Requirements: 87% or more; Student Profile and/or references

2. Dean's (4):
No application necessary
No deadline
Requirements: 87% or more; Student Profile and/or references

Partial-tuition scholarships (48)
No application necessary
No deadline
Requirements: 87% or more (varies); Student Profile

Scholarships for entering students
Offered N/A
Accepted N/A
Total budget for undergraduate scholarships varies

10. INTERNATIONAL STUDENTS

Students from outside Canada 4%
Scholarships awarded N/A
Services available International Students Centre; Personal Counsellor; Teaching and Learning Centre
Language requirements for admission TOEFL score 580; MELAB score 95; COPE score 6

11. ATHLETIC FACILITIES

All Erindale students also have access to the St George campus facilities.

Cross-country skiing
Gym
Playing fields
Rowing course
Squash courts
Swimming pool (outdoor)
Tennis courts (outdoor)
Weight/workout rooms

Inter-university sports
See St George section.

Intra-mural organized sports
Badminton M, F
Basketball M, F
Football M
Football, flag M, F
Hockey, ball M
Hockey, field F
Hockey, ice M, F
Indoor soccer M, F
Inner-tube water polo M, F
Soccer M, F
Volleyball M, F

Recreation and fitness programs

12. STUDENT LIFE

Student councils 1
Student clubs 32

Pubs 1
Drinking awareness program

First-year orientation
Symposium on Success, last 2 weeks of June; every day and some evenings July and August

Parent sessions the Sunday before classes start

13. STUDENT SERVICES

Counselling
Psychological, Career, Peer

Medical
Nurses 2; Doctors M (3), F (1)

Special needs
90% of campus wheelchair accessible

Other
Essay writing/study skills program
Mature student association
Off-campus housing registry

14. RESIDENCES

Residence places
407 M, 408 F, 0 C
231 apartments/townhouses

First-year students
Places reserved 240; single 146, double 84
Application deadline N/A
Places reserved for all Ontario Scholars who list Toronto and Erindale as 1st choice on applications
Eligibility limitations based on student's home location
Allocations announced August 1

Upper-year students
Places reserved 575
Allocations announced May 8

Wheelchair-accessible rooms 11

Meal-plan options
No commercial meal plans; each townhouse has its own kitchen.

15. PROGRAMS OF UNDERGRADUATE STUDY

15.1 FACULTY OF ARTS AND SCIENCE

Degree
Bachelor of Arts, B.A.

Level
3-year Major, 4-year Specialist

Programs
Anthropology
Art and Art History
Canadian Studies
Classics
Crime and Deviance
Drama
Economics
English
Exceptionality in Human Learning
Fine Art
French
Geography
German
History
Industrial Relations
Italian
Latin America
Linguistics
Logic
Native Studies
Peace and Conflict
Philosophy
Political Science
Religious Studies
Sociology
Spanish
Theatre and Drama Studies
Urban Studies

First-year entry
No; enter year 2

Entry requirements
Minimum average: 70%
OAC English 1

Students accepted 1600
Total in college 6500

Co-op (work/study) available
No; no correspondence or self-paced study

Graduation requirements
Minimum GPA: 1.5 on scale of 4.3
Full credits/courses: Specialist 20, Major 15
Students must complete 1 course in each of Humanities, Sciences and Social Sciences.

Graduating students 419

15.2 FACULTY OF ARTS AND SCIENCE

Degree
Bachelor of Science, B.Sc.

Level
3-year Major, 4-year Specialist

Programs
Astronomy
Biochemistry
Biology
Chemistry
Computer Science
Environmental Science
Exceptionality in Human Learning
Mathematics
Physics
Psychology
Statistics
Surveying Science

First-year entry
No; enter in year 2

Entry requirements
Minimum average: 70% plus discretionary range
OAC English 1, Calculus and at least 1 OAC science

Students accepted 1600
Total in college 6500

Co-op (work/study) available
No; no correspondence or self-paced study

Graduation requirements
Minimum GPA: 1.5 on scale of 4.3
Full credits/courses: Specialist 20, Major 15

Graduating students 377

15.3 FACULTY OF ARTS AND SCIENCE

Degree
Bachelor of Commerce, B.Com.

Level
4-year Specialist

Programs
Commerce
Economics

First-year entry
No; enter year 2 with 2.14 GPA minimum

Entry requirements
Minimum average: N/A
OAC English 1, Calculus
2nd OAC Mathematics recommended

Students accepted 1600
Total in college 6500

Co-op (work/study) available
No; no correspondence or self-paced study

Graduation requirements
Minimum GPA: 1.5 on scale of 4.3
Full credits/courses: Specialist 20

Graduating students 97

16. FUTURE PLANS

Buildings
New Centre for Management and Social Sciences started in 1990. The centre includes community auditorium, art gallery, study space, classrooms, laboratories and offices.

Scarborough College, University of Toronto

1. OVERVIEW
Situated just inside the eastern boundaries of Metropolitan Toronto, Scarborough College has an excellent reputation for its innovative programs leading to University of Toronto degrees in the arts and sciences. Scarborough's lovely campus, outstanding faculty and helpful services ensure a rewarding and welcoming environment for all students.

2. PRINCIPAL
Paul Thompson

3. ENROLMENT
(1990 Fall semester; undergraduate totals rounded to nearest 50)

Registration
Undergraduate full-time 3700
(M 1650, F 2050)
Undergraduate part-time 1500
(M 600, F 900)
Graduate N/R

Residence
Undergrads in residence 11%
(M 40%, F 60%)
Undergrads in off-campus housing
N/A
Undergrads commuting 89%

4. ADMISSIONS TO FIRST YEAR

Entry dates
Fall, Summer

First-year entries

	Fall (Sept)	Summer (part-time)
Applications*	2700	100
Admissions	2800	70
Enrolments	1100	50

* Applications represent secondary-school 1st choice only, but offers of admission also made to 2nd- and 3rd-choice applicants.

Admissions offered to qualified candidates before early admission
Yes

Community-college transfer requirements
No OACs, 2 years CAAT; graduates of 3 year CAAT program with high academic standing, 1-5 credits considered.

Mature students admission requirements
Age 21, high standing on a pre-university course

5. ADMISSIONS CONTACT

Ms Susan Martin
Assistant Registrar - Admissions
Scarborough Campus
University of Toronto
1265 Military Trail
Scarborough, Ontario M1C 1A4
(416) 287-7529

6. STRUCTURE AND DEGREES

Governing Council
See St George section.

Teaching faculty
Full-time 215 (M 152, F 63)
Part-time 11 (M 5, F 6)

Faculty/Student ratio (FTE basis)
1:19

Undergraduate degrees conferred
Arts, Science

7. TEACHING FACILITIES

Largest first-year class 200
First-year courses with tutorials
N/R
Lab places for first-year students
All 1st-year students assured lab places

Research grants and contracts
Graduate programs
See St George section.

Libraries
With open stacks 1

With closed stacks 0
Total holdings 225,000 volumes

8. STUDENTS

Undergraduates

1st year	1792
2nd year	1030
3rd year	1132
4th year	685

Entering as Ontario Scholars 28%
Entering with scholarships approx. 8%
Entering with OSAP help 30%
(except for Ontario Scholars, figures combined for 3 campuses)

9. ENTRANCE SCHOLARSHIPS

Students are eligible for all Toronto scholarships and bursaries.
Scarborough offers many admission scholarships; Plumptre Admission Scholarship $2000; F.A. Urquhart Admission Scholarship (8) $1500 each;
Alumni Admission Award (tuition).
Other awards (approximately 60, $500-$1000)

Scholarships for entering students
Offered N/A
Accepted N/A
Total budget for undergraduate scholarships N/A

10. INTERNATIONAL STUDENTS

Students from outside Canada 5%
Scholarships awarded N/R
Services available International Student Centre
Language requirements for admission TOEFL score 580; MELAB score 90

11. ATHLETIC FACILITIES

Dance studio
Gym
Playing fields
Pool tables
Squash courts
Tennis courts (outdoor)
Weight/workout rooms

Inter-university sports
See St George section

Intra-mural organized sports
Badminton tournements
Baseball C
Basketball M, F
Football (flag) F
Football (tackle) M
Football (touch) C
Hockey (ball) C
Hockey (field) F
Hockey (floor) M, C
Hockey (ice) M, F
Rugby M
Skiing C
Soccer (indoor) M, C
Soccer (outdoor) M
Squash M
Tennis M, F, C
Volleyball M, F, C
Water-polo C

Recreation and fitness programs

12. STUDENT LIFE

Student councils 1
Student clubs several

Pubs 1
Drinking awareness program

First-year orientation
Organized by each college or faculty; parent sessions

13. STUDENT SERVICES

Counselling
Career, Peer, Personal

Medical
College Health Centre

Special needs
Handicapped/special needs centre
90% of campus wheelchair accessible

Other
Essay writing/study skills program
Off-campus housing registry

14. RESIDENCES

Residence places
536
Townhouse accommodation

First-year students
Places reserved: see St George section
No application deadline
Places reserved for Ontario Scholars
Eligibility limitations based on student's home location
Allocations announced after June 15

Upper-year students
See St George section.
Allocations announced after June 15

Wheelchair-accessible rooms 10

Meal-plan options
College cafeterias; townhouses have fully equipped kitchens.

15. PROGRAMS OF UNDERGRADUATE STUDY
All 1st-year applicants must fill out Student Profile questionnaire, which enables the university to better assess academic and personal strengths. 70% is the minimum average for admission but it rises for high-demand programs. Criteria considered include Grade 13 or OACs, distribution of subjects, performance in subjects relevant to university program selected, results in senior-division prerequisite courses, and information from questionnaires, portfolios or auditions.

15.1, 15.2, 15.3 FACULTY OF ARTS AND SCIENCE

Degree
Bachelor of Arts, B.A.
Bachelor of Science, B.Sc.

Level
3 and 4 years

Programs
Administration Co-op
Anthropology
Arts Administration Co-op
Biochemistry
Biological Sciences
Canadian Studies
Chemistry
Classics
Cognitive Science
Commerce*
Computer Science
Computer Science and Physical Science Co-op
Development Studies
Drama
Ecology and Environmental Studies
Economics
English
Fine Art
French
Geography
German
History
Humanities
International Development Studies Co-op
Italian
Linguistics
Mathematics
Music
Neuroscience
Philosophy
Physics
Political Science
Psychology
Sociology
Spanish
Statistics
Terrain and Environmental Earth Sciences
Women's Studies

First-year entry Yes

Entry requirements
Minimum average: N/A
6 OACs; English 1 plus OACs required for specific programs

Students accepted 1100
Total in colleges 5200

Co-op (work/study) available
Yes, Administration (B.A.), Arts Administration (B.A.), International Development Studies (B.A., B.Sc.),

Computer Science and Physical Science (B.Sc.); no correspondence or self-paced study

Graduation requirements
Minimum GPA: 1.6 on scale of 4.3
Full credits/courses: 4 years 20 courses, 3 years 15 courses
For other special requirements see faculty calendar.

Graduating students 754

16. FUTURE PLANS

Programs
Management (Commerce) programs to permit direct entry (1992)
Physical Sciences programs will include Early Teaching option (1991)

Trent University

1. OVERVIEW
Situated in Peterborough, Trent University is Canada's outstanding small university. It offers traditional arts and sciences programs complemented by interdisciplinary programs in business, Third World development, culture, the environment, Canadian studies and Native studies. Trent's size and methods encourage close discussion between teachers and students.

2. PRESIDENT
John O. Stubbs

3. ENROLMENT
(1990 Fall semester; undergraduate totals rounded to nearest 100)

Registration
Undergraduate full-time 3700 (M 1480, F 2220)
Undergraduate part-time 1800 (M 780, F 1080)
Graduate 90 (M 52, F 38)

Residence
Undergrads in residence 33%
Undergrads in off-campus housing N/A
Undergrads commuting 67%

4. ADMISSIONS TO FIRST YEAR

Entry dates
Fall Full-time
Winter Part-time
Summer Part-time

First-year entries

	Fall (Sept)
Applications	6743
Admissions	3440
Enrolments	1155

Admissions offered to qualified candidates before early admission
Yes

Community-college transfer requirements
2-year CAAT, minimum B average

Advanced standing granted
Depends on overall average and program

Mature students admission requirements
Age 21, out of school for 2 years; may be admitted outright or on probation, either full- or part-time for one session

5. ADMISSIONS CONTACT

Alan P. Saxby
Registrar and Director of Admissions
Trent University
Peterborough, Ontario K9J 7B8
(705) 748-1215

6. STRUCTURE AND DEGREES

Board of Governors
26 members (M 20, F 6); 2 faculty, 2 students, 2 alumni)

Teaching faculty
Full-time 216 (M N/A, F N/A)
Part-time N/A

Faculty/Student ratio (FTE basis)
1:19

Undergraduate degrees conferred
Administrative Studies, Arts, Science

7. TEACHING FACILITIES

Largest first-year class 50
First-year courses with tutorials more than 90%

Lab places for first-year students
Biology 24, Chemistry 24, Computers 20, Languages 48, Physics 24

Research grants and contracts
$1,586,000

Graduate programs
Number of programs 5
Enrolment in master's programs 90

Libraries
With open stacks 90%
With closed stacks 10%
Total holdings 410,500 volumes

8. STUDENTS

Undergraduates
1st year 1115
2nd to 4th years 2500

Entering as Ontario Scholars 25%
Entering with scholarships 13%
Entering with OSAP help 37%

9. ENTRANCE SCHOLARSHIPS

Most prestigious
1. Champlain Scholarship (1):
Renewable
No application necessary
Deadline May 15
Requirements: 90% plus; supporting documentation; interview

2. Brian Heeney Scholarship (1):
Renewable
Awarded to runner-up for Champlain
No application necessary
Deadline May 15
Requirements: 90% plus; supporting documentation; interview

Full-tuition scholarships
Twenty-fifth Anniversary Scholarships (25):
Renewable
No application necessary
No deadline
90% plus required

Partial-tuition scholarships (variable)
No application necessary
No deadline
88% plus required

Scholarships for entering students
Offered 136
Accepted 47
Total budget for undergraduate scholarships $152,000

10. INTERNATIONAL STUDENTS

Students from outside Canada 12%
Scholarships awarded 44 (CIDA)
Services available Adviser; Academic Counsellor; Trent International Program
Language requirements for admission TOEFL score 550; MELAB score 85

11. ATHLETIC FACILITIES

Gym
Playing fields
Squash courts
Swimming pool
Tennis courts (outdoor)
Track centre (outdoor)
Weight/workout rooms

Inter-university sports
Cross-country running M, F
Curling F
Fencing M, F
Golf M
Hockey, field F
Rowing M, F
Rugby M, F
Skiing (Alpine) M, F
Skiing (Nordic) M, F
Soccer M, F
Squash M
Swimming M, F
Synchronized swimming F

Intra-mural organized sports
Badminton
Basketball
Cross-country running
Cycling
Hockey
Rowing
Soccer

Softball
Squash
Swimming
Tennis
Touch football
Track
Triathalon
Volleyball

Recreation and fitness programs

12. STUDENT LIFE

Student councils 6
Student clubs N/A

Pubs 6
Drinking awareness program

First-year orientation
1st week in September; parent sessions

13. STUDENT SERVICES

Counselling
Psychological, Career

Medical
Nurses 2; Doctors M (1), F (1)

Special needs
65-70% accessible, classes can be moved to accommodate

Other
Learning disability program
Essay writing/study skills program
Mature student association
Off-campus housing registry

14. RESIDENCES

Residence places
M and F limited; over 90% Co-ed
Some apartments/townhouses

First-year students
Places reserved 50% (20% single, 80% double)
Application deadline June 1
Ontario Scholars guaranteed residence place if deadlines met; 80% minimum required, lottery in July otherwise
Eligibility limitations based on student's home location
80% of allocations announced with offer of admission; others as processed

Upper-year students
Places reserved 50%
Allocations announced: varies

Wheelchair-accessible rooms 4

Meal-plan options
3 meals per day, 7 days per week

15. PROGRAMS OF UNDERGRADUATE STUDY

15.1 FACULTY OF ARTS AND SCIENCE

Degree
Bachelor of Arts, B.A.
Bachelor of Science, B.Sc.
Bachelor of Administrative Studies B.A.S.

Level
Ordinary 3 years
Honours 4 years

Programs
Administrative and Policy Studies
Anthropology
Biology
Biochemistry
Canadian Studies
Chemical Studies
Chemistry
Classical Studies
Comparative Development Studies
Computer Studies
Cultural Studies
Economics
English Literature
Environmental and Resource Studies
Geography
History
Mathematics
Modern Languages and Literatures (French, German, Spanish)
Native Studies
Philosophy
Physics
Political Studies
Psychology

Sociology
Women's Studies

First-year entry
Yes; 2nd-year entry for Canadian Studies, Comparative Development Studies and Women's Studies

Entry requirements
Minimum average: 70%
B.Sc.: OAC Mathematics
Chemistry: OAC Chemistry, Calculus
B.A.S.: Grade 12 Mathematics
Mathematics majors: OAC Calculus, Algebra and Geometry recommended
Biology majors: OAC Biology recommended
Physics majors: OAC Physics recommended
Special requirements: Unspecified OAC English

Students accepted 1100
Total in faculty 3500

Co-op (work/study) available
No; no correspondence or self-paced study

Graduation requirements
Minimum GPA: N/R
Full credits/courses: Honours 19–20, General 15; other requirements vary

Graduating students 902

15.6 FACULTY OF EDUCATION
(Trent-Queen's Concurrent Teacher Education Program)

Degree
Bachelor of Education, B.Ed., concurrent with a B.A., B,Sc. or B.A.S. (B.Ed. granted from Queen's)

Level
General, Honours

Programs
Primary-Junior
Junior-Intermediate
Intermediate-Senior

First-year entry Yes

Entry requirements
Minimum average: 75%
6 OACs including an unspecified OAC English
Primary-Junior, Junior-Intermediate: advanced Grade 12 Mathematics recommended
Demonstrated leadership, initiative in working with children

Students accepted 125
Total in faculty 375

Co-op (work/study) available
No; no correspondence or self-paced study; class-room teaching assistance necessary

Graduation requirements
Minimum GPA: N/R
Full credits/courses: Honours 19–20, General 15
Teaching practicum and education courses required each year

Graduating students N/A

16. FUTURE PLANS

Buildings
Environmental Sciences building for Geography, Biology, Environmental and Resource Studies programs, and for graduate program in Watershed Ecosystems, January 1991

University of Waterloo

1. OVERVIEW
The University of Waterloo was founded in 1957 on Co-operative Education and today boasts the world's largest co-op enrolment of more than 9,600 students. Waterloo's full-time and part-time undergraduate students are registered in six faculties: Applied Health Sciences, Arts, Engineering, Environmental Studies, Mathematics and Science. Situated in the City of Waterloo, the university offers bachelor's, master's and Ph.D. programs.

2. PRESIDENT
Douglas T. Wright

3. ENROLMENT
(1990 Fall semester; totals rounded to nearest 100)

Registration
Undergraduate full-time 15,600 (M 9200, F 6400)
Undergraduate part-time 8400 (M 2600, F 5800)
Graduate 2000 (M 1400, F 600)

Residence
Undergrads in residence approx. 30% (M 57%, F 43%)
Undergrads in off-campus housing N/A
Undergrads commuting 70%

4. ADMISSIONS TO FIRST YEAR

Entry dates
Fall, Winter, Spring, Summer

First-year entries

	Fall (May 1)	Winter (Dec 1)	Spring (Mar 1)
Applications	19,382	405	72
Admissions	11,097	115	20
Enrolments	4,128	35	12

Admissions offered to qualified candidates before early admission
Yes

Community-college transfer requirements
2 CAAT years with 1st-class honours or high 2nd-class honours

Advanced standing granted
1st-class or high 2nd-class honours in each of 3 CAAT years may be considered for admission to year 2.

Mature students admission requirements
2 to 5 (Arts) years away from formal education; do not meet normal requirements

5. ADMISSIONS CONTACT

Ken Lavigne
Associate Registrar
Admissions and Student Awards
Office of the Registrar
University of Waterloo
Waterloo, Ontario N2L 3G1
(519) 885-1211, ext. 2268

6. STRUCTURE AND DEGREES

Board of Governors
36 members (M 26, F 10; 7 faculty, 5 students, 2 support staff, 3 alumni)

Teaching faculty
Full-time 841 (M 734, F 107)
Part-time 119 (M 92, F 27)

Faculty/Student ratio (FTE basis)
1:20

Undergraduate degrees conferred
Applied Science, Architecture, Arts, Environmental Studies, Independent Studies, Mathematics, Optometry, Science

7. TEACHING FACILITIES

Largest first-year class 400
First-year courses with tutorials 50%
Lab places for first-year students N/R

Research grants and contracts $42,930,000

Graduate programs
Number of programs 70
Enrolment in master's programs 1216; doctoral programs 778

Libraries
With open stacks 4
With closed stacks N/R
Total holdings 2,400,000 volumes

8. STUDENTS

Undergraduates (full-time)

1st year	4300
2nd year	4382
3rd year	3902
4th year	2575

Entering as Ontario Scholars 61% (1990/91)
Entering with scholarships N/A
Entering with OSAP help N/A

9. ENTRANCE SCHOLARSHIPS

Full-tuition scholarships (approx. 147)
Application necessary; see Waterloo calendar for specifics
Deadline May 1
Requirements: 80% minimum normally; Engineering and Mathematics applicants must write Descartes exam; Physics applicants must write Sir Isaac Newton exam

Partial-tuition scholarships (approx. 493)
Application necessary; see Waterloo calendar for specifics
Deadline May 1
Requirements: 80% minimum normally; Engineering and Mathematics applicants must write Descartes exam; Physics applicants must write Sir Isaac Newton exam

Scholarships for entering students
Offered 1600
Accepted 640
Total budget for undergraduate scholarships $82,300

10. INTERNATIONAL STUDENTS

Students from outside Canada 2%
Scholarships awarded None
Services available Adviser; Academic; Other
Language requirements for admission TOEFL score 600

11. ATHLETIC FACILITIES

Gym
Ice rink
Jogging trails
9-hole golf course
Playing fields
Squash courts
Stadium
Swimming pool
Tennis courts (indoor/outdoor)
Track centre (outdoor)
Weight/workout rooms

Inter-university sports
Badminton M, F
Basketball M, F
Crew M, F
Cross-country M, F
Curling M, F
Field Hockey F
Figure skating F
Football M
Golf M
Hockey, field F
Hockey, ice M
Hockey, ice (indoor) F
Lacrosse M
Rugby M
Skiing (Alpine) M, F
Skiing (Nordic) M, F
Soccer M, F
Squash M, F
Swimming M, F
Swimming (synchro) F
Tennis M, F
Track and field M, F
Volleyball M, F

Intra-mural organized sports
Archery
Badminton
Baseball
Basketball
Broom-ball
Crew
Curling
Cycling
Diving
Equestrian
Fencing
Figure skating
Fitness classes
Flag football
Golf
Hockey, ball
Hockey, floor
Hockey, ice
Inner-tube water polo
Kendo
Land and water fitness
Martial arts
Orienteering
Power skating
Power walking
Racquetball
Rock and roll dance
Sailing
Scuba diving
Skiing (Alpine)
Skiing (Nordic)
Sky diving
Soccer
Social dance
Speed skating
Squash
Swimming
Table tennis
Tennis
Volleyball
Weight training
Wind surfing

Recreation and fitness programs

12. STUDENT LIFE

Student councils 1 main council plus 12 academic, 7 residence, 2 athletic
Student clubs 30+
Pubs 3
Drinking awareness program

First-year orientation
1 week before lectures begin; parent sessions

13. STUDENT SERVICES

Counselling
Psychological, Career, Peer

Medical
Nurses 10; Doctors M (5), F (5)

Special needs
Service/Resource Office for all disabilities
95% of campus wheelchair accessible

Other
Essay writing/study skills program
Mature student services
Off-campus housing registry

14. RESIDENCES

Residence places 2907
131 M, 126 F, 2650 C
1400 apartments/townhouses

First-year students
Places reserved: 500 single, 960 double
Application deadline early May
Places reserved for scholarship winners 205; minimum % varies by faculty
No eligibility limitations based on student's home location
Allocations announced August 1–15

Upper-year students
Places reserved 763
Allocations announced August 1–15

Wheelchair-accessible rooms
M(12), F(12)

Meal-plan options
3 meals per day, 7 days per week

15. PROGRAMS OF UNDERGRADUATE STUDY

15.1 FACULTY OF ARTS

Degree
Bachelor of Arts, B.A.

Level
General, Honours, Honours Co-op, Honours Applied Studies Co-op, Honours Accountancy Studies / Master of Accounting, Professionally Accredited Stream

Programs
Accountancy (Honours Co-op only)†
Anthropology*†
Classical Studies*
Drama and Theatre Arts (Acting, Technical, Academic Streams)*
Economics*†
English (Literature, Rhetoric and Professional Writing)*†
Fine Arts (Studio, History, Film Studies specializations)*
French*
Geography
German*
Greek (General only)
History*
Latin*
Medieval Studies*
Music*
Philosophy*
Political Science*†
Political Science (Honours Administrative Studies)*†
Psychology*†
Religion Studies*
Russian
Slavic Studies (Honours only)*
Social Development Studies
Social Development Studies (diploma in Social Work)
Sociology*†
Spanish*
* Honours major available in Applied Studies Co-op
† Departmental Co-op program available with Honours major

First-year entry Yes

Entry requirements
Minimum average: 60%; Accountancy Studies 80%, Applied Studies Co-op 80%, Arts Regular 70%
Arts Regular and Applied Studies Co-op: OAC English and 1 other Arts-related course
Recommended for
- Social Development Studies: OAC in Mathematics
- Arts Accountancy Studies: OAC Calculus, 1 other Mathematics, preferably Finite Mathematics
- Arts Applied Studies Co-op: 1 OAC Arts-related course, plus Mathematics and Science

Students accepted 2707
Total in faculty 4159

Co-op (work/study) available
Optional; required in Accountancy and Applied Studies programs
Correspondence and self-paced study

Graduation requirements
Minimum GPA: varies by program
Full credits/courses: Honours 20, General 15

Graduating students 1178

15.2, 15.9 FACULTY OF SCIENCE

Degree
Bachelor of Science, B.Sc.
Doctor of Optometry, O.D.

Level
General, Honours, Honours Co-op

Programs
Biochemistry
Boochemistry, Biotechnology Option
Biology
Biology and Environment and Resource Studies
Biology and Geography
Biology/Business Economics
Honours Science Program 2 (Pre-Health Professions Option)
Chemistry
Chemistry and Environment and Resource Studies
Chemistry (with Options)
Environmental Studies
Mathematics
Physics

Earth Sciences (Geology)
Earth Sciences (Geophysics)
Earth Sciences
  Geography Option
  Economics Option
Environmental Hydrogeology Option
Environmental Science
General Science
Honours Psychology/Science
Honours Science and Business
Liberal Science
Optometry
Physics
Physics (Geophysics Option)

First-year entry
Yes; year 2 for Optometry

Entry requirements
Minimum average: 60%; recent minimum average of successful candidates is mid-60% for Regular, low 70% for Co-op
OAC Calculus and either Algebra and Geometry or Finite Mathematics, 2 of Biology, Chemistry or Physics
Biology, Earth Sciences, Geography: OAC Chemistry
Chemistry, Biochemistry, Optometry or other Earth Science programs: OAC Chemistry and Physics
Physics: OAC Physics
Recommended for
- Sciences: OAC Chemistry, Physics
- Co-operative Applied Chemistry and Physics: OAC Finite Mathematics and Algebra and Geometry
- Geophysics option within Co-op Applied Earth Sciences: Algebra and Geometry
- Course requiring writing skills

Students accepted 2969
Total in faculty 2297

Co-op (work/study) available
Optional; correspondence and self-paced study

Graduation requirements
Minimum GPA: varies by program
Full credits/courses: Honours approx. 22, General 15

Graduating students 606

15.3, 15.5 FACULTY OF MATHEMATICS

Degree
Bachelor of Mathematics, B.Math.

Level
General, Honours, Honours Co-op

Programs
Actuarial Science
Applied Mathematics
Combinations and Optimization
Computer Science
Pure Mathematics
Statistics
Division of Mathematics for Industry and Commerce:
Computer Science / Information Systems
Mathematics / Chartered Accountancy
Mathematics / Management Accounting
Mathematics / Business Administration
Operations Research

First-year entry Yes

Entry requirements
Minimum average: 60%; majority of admissions are 75% or higher
OAC Algebra and Geometry, Calculus, English, with a minimum 60% in each required course
Finite Mathematics recommended
Mathematics and Accounting: at least 1 accounting course

Students accepted 1640
Total in faculty 3309

Co-op (work/study) available
Optional; no correspondence or self-paced study

Graduation requirements
Minimum GPA: N/A

Full credits/courses: Honours 20, General 15

Graduating students 549

15.7 FACULTY OF ENGINEERING

Degree
Bachelor of Applied Science, B.A.Sc.

Level
Honours Co-op

Programs
Chemical Eng.
Civil Eng.
Computer Eng.
Electrical Eng.
Geological Eng.
Mechanical Eng.
Systems Design Eng.

First-year entry Yes

Entry requirements
Minimum average: 60%; most admissions have averages of 75% or higher
OAC Algebra and Geometry, Calculus, Physics, Chemistry, English
OAC Finite Mathematics, 1 or more Computer Science courses recommended
Personal Information Form

Students accepted 1809
Total in faculty 3009

Co-op (work/study) available
Required; no correspondence or self-paced study

Graduation requirements
Minimum GPA: N/A
Full credits/courses: N/A

Graduating students 572

15.8 FACULTY OF ENVIRONMENTAL STUDIES

Degree
Bachelor of Architecture, B.Arch.
Bachelor of Environmental Studies, B.E.S.

Level
General, Honours, Honours Co-op, Pre-professional Architecture, Professional Architecture

Programs
Environment and Resource Studies
Geography
Pre-professional Architecture
Professional Architecture
Urban and Regional Planning

First-year entry Yes

Entry requirements
Minimum average: 60%
Pre-professional Architecture 75%; other programs 70%
Pre-professional Architecture: OAC English, or French, Physics, Calculus, Algebra and Geometry, interview and portfolio
Other programs: OAC English
Recommended for
- Pre-professional Architecture: OAC Finite Mathematics
- Environment and Resource Studies: OAC Science and Mathematics
- Geography: OAC Mathematics
- Urban and Regional Planning: OAC Mathematics

Students accepted 714
Total in faculty 1494

Co-op (work/study) available
Optional, required in Architecture; correspondence and self-paced study

Graduation requirements
Minimum GPA: N/A
Full credits/courses: Honours 40, General 30
Pre-professional Architecture 46
Professional Architecture 28

Graduating students 275

15.14 FACULTY OF APPLIED HEALTH SCIENCES

Degree
Bachelor of Arts, B.A. (Dance, Recreation and Leisure Studies)

Bachelor of Science, B.Sc.
(Kinesiology, Health Studies)

Level
General, Honours, Honours Co-op

Programs
Dance
Health Studies
Gerontology (minor)
Kinesiology
Recreation and Leisure Studies

First-year entry Yes

Entry requirements
Minimum average: 60%
Dance: audition
Health Studies: OAC Biology, Chemistry
Kinesiology: OAC Calculus, Chemistry, either Biology or Physics
Recommended for
- Dance: OAC English
- Health Studies: OAC Calculus
- Kinesiology: OAC Physics
- Recreation and Leisure Studies: at least 1 OAC Mathematics

Students accepted 1248
Total in faculty 1304

Co-op (work/study) available
Optional, no Co-op in Dance; no correspondence or self-paced study

Graduation requirements
Minimum GPA: N/A
Full credits/courses: General 15; Honours: Kinesiology, Recreation and Leisure 20; others 22

Graduating students 177

16. FUTURE PLANS

Buildings
Addition to Humanities for School of Accountancy
Addition to Optometry facilities
Science/Engineering building

University of Western Ontario

1. OVERVIEW

The University of Western Ontario is one of Canada's oldest, largest and most beautiful universities which has earned an enviable tradition of excellence. Affiliated with it are Brescia, Huron and King Colleges. It has 17 faculties and professional schools. It offers more than 40 degrees, diplomas and certificates to over 26,000 students.

2. PRESIDENT

G. Pedersen

3. ENROLMENT

(1990/91 Fall semester; undergraduate totals rounded to nearest 100)

Registration

Undergraduate full-time 19,700 (M 9700, F 10,000)
Undergraduate part-time 6400 (M 2000, F 4400)
Graduate 2794 (M 1576, F 1218)

Residence

Undergrads in residence 21.9%
Undergrads in off-campus housing N/A
Undergrads commuting N/A

4. ADMISSIONS TO FIRST YEAR

Entry dates

Fall

First-year entries (includes affiliates)

	Fall
Applications	29,230
Admissions	N/A
Enrolments	5,069

Admissions offered to qualified candidates before early admission

No

Community-college transfer requirements

2- or 3-year completed CAAT program; minimum overall average of C+ (2.3 GPA)
Contact admissions office for specific requirements

Advanced standing granted

3-year CAAT graduates, up to 5 courses depending on program and GPA

Mature students admission requirements

Age 21; out of school for 4 years; 60% in previous academic work
Number of courses allowed N/R

5. ADMISSIONS CONTACT

Mr Robert J. Tiffin
Director, Department of Admissions and Academic Records
Room 180, Stevenson-Lawson Building
University of Western Ontario
London, Ontario N6A 5B9
(519) 661-2120

6. STRUCTURE AND DEGREES

Board of Governors

31 members (M 26, F 4); 4 faculty, 3 students, 2 support staff, 4 alumni)

Teaching faculty

Full-time 1468 (M 1210, F 258)
Part-time 430 (M 282, F 148)

Faculty/Student ratio (FTE basis)

1:17

Undergraduate degrees conferred

Applied Health Sciences, Arts, Business Administration, Dentistry, Engineering, Law, Medicine, Music,

Nursing, Physical Education, Science, Social Science; degrees also offered by Brescia, King's and Huron colleges

7. TEACHING FACILITIES

Largest first-year class 400
First-year courses with tutorials 77%
Lab places for first-year students Biology 1716, Chemistry 1832, Computers 2776, Geography 600, Languages 1709, Physics 1350, Psychology 2486

Research grants and contracts $51,521,000

Graduate programs
Number of programs 45
Enrolment in master's programs 1945; doctoral programs 719

Libraries
With open stacks 8
With closed stacks N/R
Total holdings 4.4 million volumes

8. STUDENTS

Undergraduates (includes affiliates)

1st year	5069
2nd year	5441
3rd year	5166
4th year	2305

Entering as Ontario Scholars 60%
Entering with scholarships 10%
Entering with OSAP help 30%

9. ENTRANCE SCHOLARSHIPS

Most prestigious
President's Entrance Scholarships (5):
Renewable
Application necessary
Deadline March 1
Requirements: 90% minimum; essay or creative writing; proof of Canadian citizenship or permanent residency; transcript, interview

Full-tuition scholarships
Faculty Entrance Scholarships (11):
Renewable
Requirements same as for President's Scholarships
Ashbaugh Entrance Scholarships (up to 20):
Renewable
Application necessary
Deadline March 1
Requirements: 90% minimum, broad interests and leadership capabilities

Partial-tuition scholarships (409)
No application
No deadline
Minimum % varies (85–90%)

Scholarships for entering students
Offered 425
Accepted 425
Total budget for undergraduate scholarships $1,133,467

10. INTERNATIONAL STUDENTS

Students from outside Canada 4%
Scholarships awarded None
Services available Adviser; Academic Counsellor
Language requirements for admission TOEFL score 550; MELAB score 85

11. ATHLETIC FACILITIES

Combatives room
Curling rink
Dance studios
Gun range
Gym
Ice rink (indoor/outdoor)
Playing fields
Racquetball courts
Squash courts
Stadium
Swimming pool
Tennis courts (indoor/outdoor)
Track centre (indoor/outdoor)
Weight/workout rooms

Inter-university sports
Badminton M, F
Basketball M, F
Cross-country M, F
Curling M, F

Diving M, F
Fencing M, F
Figure skating F
Football M
Golf M
Gymnastics M, F
Hockey, field F
Hockey, ice M
Hockey, ice (indoor) F
Rowing M, F
Rugby M
Skiing (Nordic) M, F
Soccer M, F
Squash M, F
Swimming M, F
Tennis M, F
Track M, F
Volleyball M, F
Water polo M
Wrestling M

Intra-mural organized sports
Badminton M, F
Basketball M, F, C
Broom-ball C
Curling C
Football (touch) M
Frisbee tournament C
Hockey, ball M
Hockey, ice M, F
Inner-tube water polo C
Mountain bike relay M, F
Racquetball M, F
Slow-pitch softball M
Snow-pitch softball C
Soccer (outdoor/indoor) M, F
Squash M, F
Tennis M, F, C
3-pitch softball C
Wally-ball C
Volleyball M, F, C

Recreation and fitness programs

12. STUDENT LIFE

Student councils 1
Student clubs more than 100

Pubs 2
Drinking awareness program

First-year orientation
May–October; parent sessions

13. STUDENT SERVICES

Counselling
Psychological, Career, Peer

Medical
Nurses; Doctors

Special needs
Handicapped/special needs centre
30% of campus wheelchair accessible

Other
Essay writing/study skills program
Mature student association
Off-campus housing registry

14. RESIDENCES

Residence places
305 M, 305 F, 1888 C
240 apartments/townhouses

First-year students
Places reserved 1600 double, 200 single
Application deadline May 31
Places reserved for scholarship winners
80% minimum
No accommodation for London residents
Allocations guaranteed in June, announced in August

Upper-year students
Places reserved 700
Allocations announced in Spring

Wheelchair-accessible rooms 10

Meal-plan options
8 plans: 5-day and 7-day

15. PROGRAMS OF UNDERGRADUATE STUDY

15.1 FACULTY OF ARTS

Degree
Bachelor of Arts, B.A.

Level
3 years, 4 years (Honours)

Programs
Classical Studies
English

Film
French
German
Greek
Latin
Philosophy
Russian
Spanish
Visual Arts
Western Literature and Civilization
Women's Studies

First-year entry
Yes; enter most specialized programs in year 2

Entry requirements
Minimum average: mid 70%
OAC English, 2nd language recommended

Students accepted
1865 (combined 1st-year target of Arts, Social Science, Physical Education)
Total in faculty 2262

Co-op (work/study) available
No; no correspondence or self-paced study

Graduation requirements
See Western's calendar.

Graduating students 505

15.1 FACULTY OF SOCIAL SCIENCE

Degree
Bachelor of Arts, B.A.
Bachelor of Arts (Honours), B.A.
Bachelor of Arts, Administrative and Commercial Studies, B.A.
Bachelor of Science (Honours), B.Sc.

Level 3 years, 4 years (Honours)

Programs
Administrative and Commercial Studies:
Administrative and Information Studies
Financial and Economic Studies
Public Administration and Public Policy
Social Organization and Human Relations

Social Science:
Anthropology
Anthropology (Linguistics)
Economics
Geography
History
Political Science
Psychology
Sociology
Women's Studies

First-year entry
Yes; enter most specialized courses in year 2

Entry requirements
Minimum average: General mid 70%; Administrative and Commercial Studies high 70%
OAC English 1
Subjects required and recommended vary

Students accepted
2095 (combined 1st-year target of Arts, Social Science, Physical Education)
Administrative and Commercial Studies 375
Total in faculty 6152

Co-op (work/study) available
No; no correspondence or self-paced study

Graduation requirements
See Western's calendar.

Graduating students 1595

15.2 FACULTY OF SCIENCE

Degree
Bachelor of Science (Honours), B.Sc.
Bachelor of Science (Honours Home Economics), B.Sc.(H.Ec.)
Bachelor of Arts (Honours), B.A.
Bachelor of Science, B.Sc.
Bachelor of Science (Home Economics), B.Sc.(H.Ec.)
Bachelor of Arts, B.A.

Level
3 years, 4 years (Honours)

Programs
Actuarial Science
Applied Mathematics
Astronomy
Biochemistry
Biology
Biophysics
Cell Biology
Chemistry
Computer Science
Ecology and Evolution
Genetics
Geology
Geophysics
History of Science
Home Economics
Mathematics
Microbiology and Immunology
Pharmacology and Toxicology
Physics
Physiology
Planetary Science
Plant Sciences
Statistics
Zoology

First-year entry
Yes; enter most specialized programs in year 2

Entry requirements
Minimum average: low 70%
OAC English 1, Calculus, Algebra and Geometry

Students accepted 1250
Total in faculty 3125

Co-op (work/study) available
No; no correspondence or self-paced study

Graduation requirements
See Western's calendar.

Graduating students 695

15.3 FACULTY OF BUSINESS ADMINISTRATION

Degree
Bachelor of Arts (Honours) in Business Administration, H.B.A.

Level
Honours

Programs
Business Administration

First-year entry
No; enter year 3 with 10 university credits

Entry requirements
Minimum average: 70% in 10 university credits
OAC English 1, 1 OAC Mathematics to enter 1st university year; 1st-year Economics, 1 half course Computer Science, 1 half course Statistics; 2nd-year Business 257 or an equivalent senior accounting course
Extracurricular activities strongly recommended

Students accepted 145
Total in faculty 286

Co-op (work/study) available
No; no correspondence or self-paced study

Graduation requirements
See Western calendar.

Graduating students 143

15.7 FACULTY OF ENGINEERING SCIENCE

Degree
Bachelor of Engineering Science, B.E.Sc.

Level
Professional

Programs
Chemical and Biochemical Eng.
Civil Eng.
Electrical Eng.
Materials Eng.
Mechanical Eng.

First-year entry Yes

Entry requirements
Minimum average: 70%
OAC English 1, Calculus, Algebra and Geometry, Chemistry, Physics

Students accepted 325
Total in faculty 942

Co-op (work/study) available
No; no correspondence or self-paced study

Graduation requirements
See Western's calendar.

Graduating students 125

15.9 FACULTY OF DENTISTRY

Degree
Doctor of Dental Surgery, D.D.S.

Level
Professional

Programs
Dentistry

First-year entry
No; enter year 3 with at least 10 university courses

Entry requirements
Minimum average: A– in undergraduate studies
OACs same as for Faculty of Science
Year 1: full laboratory courses in Biology, Chemistry, Physics
Year 2: Honours science program including Organic Chemistry
Dental Aptitude Test

Students accepted 40
Total in faculty 159

Co-op (work/study) available
No; no correspondence or self-paced study

Graduation requirements
See Western's calendar.

Graduating students 39

15.10 FACULTY OF MUSIC

Degree
Bachelor of Music (Honours), B.Mus.
Bachelor of Musical Arts, B.Mus.A.
Bachelor of Arts (Honours Music), B.A.
Bachelor of Arts, Music, B.A.

Level
3 years, 4 years (Honours)

Programs
Music Education
Music History
Performance
Theory and Composition

First-year entry Yes

Entry requirements
Minimum average: C
OAC English 1, Grade 13 Music or equivalent; or equivalent conservatory certificates
Conservatory Grade VI piano proficiency highly recommended
Personal interview/audition; performing ability on principal instrument

Students accepted 125
Total in faculty 386

Co-op (work/study) available
No; no correspondence or self-paced study

Graduation requirements
See Western's calendar.

Graduating students 108

15.12 FACULTY OF LAW

Degree
Bachelor of Laws, LL.B.

Level
Professional

Programs
Law

First-year entry
No; enter year 3 with minimum 10 university courses

Entry requirements
Law: minimum B+ average in 10 unspecified university courses
3-year degree recommended
Law School Admission Test (LSAT)

Students accepted 165
Total in faculty 470

Co-op (work/study) available
No; no correspondence or self-paced study

Graduation requirements
See Western's calendar.

Graduating students 157

15.13 FACULTY OF APPLIED HEALTH SCIENCES

Degree
Bachelor of Science, Occupational Therapy, B.Sc.O.T., and Physical Therapy, B.Sc.P.T.

Level
Professional

Programs
Occupational Therapy (O.T.)
Physical Therapy (P.T.)

First-year entry
No; enter year 2

Entry requirements
Minimum average: mid-70s
P.T.: OAC English 1, Calculus, Algebra and Geometry required
O.T.: OAC English 1, Biology, Calculus, Algebra and Geometry recommended
O.T.: 1st-year university Biology and Psychology or Sociology
P.T.: 1st-year university Biology, Calculus, Chemistry and Physics; 1 of Anthropology, Psychology or Sociology
Applicant must be Canadian citizen or permanent resident.

Students accepted 45 in O.T., 60 in P.T.
Total in faculty 252 in each

Co-op (work/study) available
No; no correspondence or self-paced study

Graduation requirements
See Western calendar.

Graduating students 89

15.13 FACULTY OF MEDICINE

Degree
Doctor of Medicine, M.D.

Level
Professional

Programs
Medicine

First-year entry
No; enter in year 3

Entry requirements
Minimum average: A in undergraduate courses
OACs same as Faculty of Science
Year 1: full laboratory courses in Biology, Chemistry and Physics; 2 courses from arts or social science
Year 2: Honours science program including Organic Chemistry
3-year degree recommended

Students accepted 105
Total in faculty 415

Co-op (work/study) available
No; no correspondence or self-paced study

Graduation requirements
See Western calendar.

Graduating students 100

15.13 FACULTY OF NURSING

Degree
Bachelor of Science in Nursing, B.Sc.N.

Level
3-year Post R.N. program, 4-year program

Programs
Nursing

First-year entry Yes

Entry requirements
Minimum average: mid 70%
at least 60% in OAC or OSSD Advanced Mathematics, OAC Biology, Chemistry
OAC Calculus, Algebra and Geometry recommended

Students accepted 60
Total in faculty 311

Co-op (work/study) available
No; no correspondence or self-paced study

Graduation requirements
See Western calendar.

Graduating students 92

15.14 FACULTY OF KINESIOLOGY

Degree
Bachelor of Arts, B.A.

Level
3 years, 4 years (Honours)

Programs
Physical Education

First-year entry Yes

Entry requirements
Minimum average: mid 70%
Honours: OAC Biology
OAC or OSSD Physics and Mathematics recommended

Students accepted
1865 (combined 1st-year target of Arts, Social Science, Physical Education)
Total in faculty 636

Co-op (work/study) available
No; no correspondence or self-paced study

Graduation requirements
See Western calendar.

Graduating students 157

15.16 FACULTY OF SOCIAL WORK (King's College)

Degree
Bachelor of Social Work, B.S.W.

Level
Honours

Programs
Social Work

First-year entry
No; enter in year 3 with 10 completed university courses

Entry requirements
Minimum average: 70% in year 2
OACs for undergraduate program selected
Year 1 and 2, 3 Social Work courses, 3 Social Science courses and at least one Arts course; personal suitability assessed

Students accepted 45
Total in faculty 90

Co-op (work/study) available
No, field placement; no correspondence or self-paced study

Graduation requirements
See Western calendar.

Graduating students 45

16. FUTURE PLANS

Programs
Effective September 1992, OAC 1 (or Grade 13) English will be required by all faculties

Buildings
New Science Centre providing conference, laboratory, classroom and lecture space; new facilities in Molecular Biology, Biotechnology, Environmental Science as well as related fields; scheduled opening 1991

Wilfrid Laurier University

1. OVERVIEW
Wilfrid Laurier University has distinguished itself as a small university where excellence is cultivated. In 1990, more than 50% of its first-year students were Ontario Scholars. With an emerging reputation for research, the university is well known for studies at the undergraduate level in arts, science, business, economics and music.

2. PRESIDENT
John A. Weir

3. ENROLMENT
(1990 Fall semester; totals rounded to nearest 100)

Registration
Undergraduate full-time 5100 (M 2600, F 2500)
Undergraduate part-time 4300 (M N/A, F N/A)
Graduate full-time 328 (M N/A, F N/A)

Residence
Undergrads in residence 21.8% (M N/A, F N/A)
Undergrads in off-campus housing 63.2%
Undergrads commuting 15%

4. ADMISSIONS TO FIRST YEAR

Entry dates
Fall, Winter

First-year entries

	Fall (Sept)	Winter (Jan)
Applications	13,510	98
Admissions	5,554	2
Enrolments	1,537	1

Other entry dates
5 other dates; check with university

Admissions offered to qualified candidates before early admission
Yes

Community-college transfer requirements
Cumulative average of B- or better; or a B- average or better in last 2 semesters of a 3-year CAAT program

Advanced standing granted
5 full credits depending on CAAT program

Mature students admission requirements
Grade 12, 2 years work experience; or age 21, 2 years work experience

5. ADMISSIONS CONTACT

Mr George Granger
Associate Registrar, Admissions
Admissions Office
Wilfrid Laurier University
75 University Avenue West
Waterloo, Ontario N2L 3C5
(519) 884-1970, ext. 2099

6. STRUCTURE AND DEGREES

Board of Governors
33 members (M 26, F 7); 3 faculty, 2 students, 2 support staff, 3 alumni)

Teaching faculty
Full-time 317 (M N/A, F N/A)
Part-time 283 (M N/A, F N/A)

Faculty/Student ratio (FTE basis)
2:17

Undergraduate degrees conferred
Administration, Arts, Commerce, Music, Music Therapy, Science

7. TEACHING FACILITIES

Largest first-year class N/A

First-year courses with tutorials 57%
Lab places for first-year students
Biology over 40, Chemistry approx. 22, Computers over 100, Languages 24, Physics approx. 22

Research grants and contracts
$3.2 million

Graduate programs
Number of programs 9
Enrolment in master's programs 282; doctoral programs 19

Libraries
With open stacks 1
With closed stacks N/R
Total holdings 1,190,000 volumes

8. STUDENTS

Undergraduates

1st year	1520
2nd year	1298
3rd year	1308
4th year	436 (not including co-op)

Entering as Ontario Scholars 50%
Entering with scholarships 10%
Entering with OSAP help N/A

9. ENTRANCE SCHOLARSHIPS

Most prestigious
Centennial-Anniversary Scholarships (20):
No application necessary
No deadline
90%+ required

Full-tuition scholarships N/A

Partial-tuition scholarships (134)
No application necessary
No deadline
86% required

Scholarships for entering students
Offered approx. 450
Accepted 150
Total budget for undergraduate scholarships approx. $300,000

10. INTERNATIONAL STUDENTS

Students from outside Canada 1%
Scholarships awarded N/A

Services available Dean of Students; AIESEC; Chinese Students Association
Language requirements for admission TOEFL score 560; MELAB score 90

11. ATHLETIC FACILITIES

Gym
Playing fields
Saunas
Squash courts
Swimming pool
Tennis courts (outdoor)
Weight/workout rooms

Inter-university sports
Basketball M, F
Cross country M
Figure skating F
Football M
Hockey M
Rugby M
Soccer M, F
Swimming M, F
Track M, F
Volleyball M, F

Intra-mural organized sports
Basketball M
Hockey, ball M
Hockey, ice M
Soccer M, F
Squash (singles) M, F
Tennis M, F
Touch football M, F
Volleyball M, F

Recreation and fitness programs

12. STUDENT LIFE

Student councils 1
Student clubs 52

Pubs 2
Drinking awareness program

First-year orientation
1st week of September

13. STUDENT SERVICES

Counselling
Psychological, Career, Peer

Medical
Nurses 3; Doctors M (2), F (4)

Special needs
Special needs co-ordinator
Handicapped/special needs centre
Campus mostly wheelchair accessible

Other
Essay writing/study skills program
Mature student association
Off-campus housing registry

14. RESIDENCES

Residence places
574 M, 539 F, 60 C
6 apartments/townhouses for married students

First-year students
Places reserved 36 single, 774 double
Application deadline July 1
Approx. 40 places reserved for scholarship winners; minimum 90% required
No eligibility limitations based on student's home location
Allocations announced August 1

Upper-year students
Places reserved 63
Allocations announced March 15

Wheelchair-accessible rooms Yes

Meal-plan options
Declining balance, minimum; per 8 months

15. PROGRAMS OF UNDERGRADUATE STUDY

15.1 FACULTY OF ARTS AND SCIENCES, ARTS

Degree
Bachelor of Arts, B.A.

Level
General, Honours

Programs
Anthropology
Archaeology
Biology
Canadian Studies*
Classical Studies
Communication Studies*
Computing*
Economics
English Language and Literature†
English Literature*
English Literature and Rhetoric*
Film Studies*
Fine Arts*
French
Geography
German
Greek
History
Humanities Studies†
Latin
Mathematics
Music*
Philosophy
Political Science
Physical Education
Psychology
Religion and Culture
Sociology
Spanish
Third World Studies*
Urban Studies*
* General only
† Honours only; all others are both

First-year entry Yes

Entry requirements
Minimum average: 60% General, 65% Honours
OAC English with appropriate OAC language for language disciplines
Check requirements with each department

Students accepted N/A
Total in faculty 2678

Co-op (work/study) available
Internship available in Honours Anthropology, English, Geography, History, Political Science, Psychology, Sociology

No correspondence or self-paced study

Graduation requirements
Minimum GPA: General 4.5 in major; Honours 7.00 in major; 4.00 in others
Full credits/courses: Honours 20–23; General 15–16.5

Graduating students 754

15.2 FACULTY OF ARTS AND SCIENCES

Degree
Bachelor of Science, B.Sc.

Level
General, Honours

Programs
Biology
Chemistry
Computing*
Computing and Computer Electronics†
Mathematics
Physics*
* General only
† Honours only; all others are both

First-year entry Yes

Entry requirements
Minimum average: 60% General, 65% Honours
OAC English, Calculus (except for Chemistry); Mathematics and Sciences depending on program
Check requirements with each department.

Students accepted N/A
Total in faculty 2678

Co-op (work/study) available
Internship available in Honours Biology, Computing and Computer Electronics, Mathematics
No correspondence or self-paced study

Graduation requirements
Minimum GPA: 4.50 in major; Honours 7.00 in major; 4.00 in all others
Full credits/courses: Honours 20–22; General 15–16.5

Graduating students 51

15.3 SCHOOL OF BUSINESS AND ECONOMICS

Degree
Business Administration, B.B.A.

Level
Honours

Programs
Honours Business Administration
Honours Business Administration Co-op option, which may include options in Biology, Chemistry, Economics, Mathematics or Physics

First-year entry Yes

Entry requirements
Minimum average: 65%
OAC English, Calculus

Students accepted 400
Total in school 1660

Co-op (work/study) available
Yes; no correspondence or self-paced study

Graduation requirements
Minimum GPA: 7.0 in business courses; 5.00 in 4th-year non-business courses
Full credits/courses: Honours 22

Graduating students 323

15.3 SCHOOL OF BUSINESS AND ECONOMICS

Degree
Bachelor of Arts, B.A. (Economics)

Level
General, Honours

Programs
General: Economics
Honours:
Economics
Economics with Finance and Accounting option or Co-op option

Economics with Administration option
Economics with Mathematics option

First-year entry Yes

Entry requirements
Minimum average: 65% Honours, 60% General
OAC English, Calculus

Students accepted 250
Total in school 1660

Co-op (work/study) available
Yes, in Honours Economics; no correspondence or self-paced study

Graduation requirements
Minimum GPA: General, 4.5 in all major subjects; Honours, 7.00 in senior economics courses and minimum cumulative GPA of 4.00 in other subjects
Full credits/courses N/A

Graduating students 323

15.10 FACULTY OF MUSIC

Degree
Bachelor of Music, B.Mus.

Level
Honours

Programs
Baroque and Early Music
Church Music
Composition
Comprehensive
Comprehensive Music Education with Administration Option (business)
Music History
Performance
Theory

First-year entry Yes

Entry requirements
Minimum average: 65%
OAC English
Audition/interview; theory placement test

Students accepted 60
Total in faculty 224

Co-op (work/study) available
Practicum available in 3rd and 4th year; no correspondence or self-paced study

Graduation requirements
Minimum GPA: 7.00 in 4th-year music courses; minimum 4.00 in other subjects
Full credits/courses N/A

Graduating students 32

15.10 FACULTY OF MUSIC

Degree
Bachelor of Music Therapy, B.M.T.

Level
Honours

Programs
Music Therapy

First-year entry
No; enter in year 3 after 2 years Honours Bachelor of Music

Entry requirements
See Bachelor of Music requirements
Minimum GPA of 7.00 in required university Music and Psychology courses
Personal interview; faculty recommendation

Students accepted 10-12
Total in faculty 224

Co-op (work/study) available
No; no correspondence or self-paced study

Graduation requirements
Minimum GPA: 7.00 in 4th-year Psychology and Music courses; 4.00 in other courses
Full credits/courses: Honours 23

Graduating students 10

16. FUTURE PLANS

Buildings
250-bed apartment-style undergraduate residence, completed by Spring 1991. When completed,

residence places will be available for virtually all 1st-year students who request it.
Planning underway for new science building

University of Windsor

1. OVERVIEW

Canada's southernmost university, the University of Windsor is located at the most heavily travelled border point between Canada and the United States. Unique programs in Law (M.B.A./LL.B. and J.D./LL.B.), communication studies, music, music therapy, theatre, drama in education, planning and co-operative engineering, among others, distinguish Windsor as one of Canada's outstanding medium-sized universities.

2. PRESIDENT

Ronald W. Ianni

3. ENROLMENT

(1990 Fall semester; totals rounded to nearest 100)

Registration

Undergraduate full-time 9715 (M 4823, F 4892)
Undergraduate part-time 4849 (M 1529, F 3320)
Graduate 620 (M 393, F 227)

Residence

Undergrads in residence 17%
Undergrads in off-campus housing N/A
Undergrads commuting 83%

4. ADMISSIONS TO FIRST YEAR

Entry dates

Fall

First-year entries

	Fall (Sept)
Applications	10,000
Admissions	6,200
Enrolments	3,195

Other entry dates

January (Winter Semester), May (Intersession), July (Summer Session)

Admissions offered to qualified candidates before early admission

Yes

Community-college transfer requirements

2-year CAAT diploma; advanced standing with 3-year CAAT diploma depending on program

Mature students admission requirements

Age 21; younger applicants out of school for 2 years considered with 66% average in 4-year university-oriented secondary-school program

5. ADMISSIONS CONTACT

Mr Orville Houser
Assistant Registrar, Admissions
University of Windsor
Windsor, Ontario N9B 3P4
(519) 253-4232

6. STRUCTURE AND DEGREES

Board of Governors

32 members (M 22 F 10; 4 faculty, 2 students, 2 alumni)

Teaching faculty

Full-time 508 (M 406, F 102)
Part-time N/A

Faculty/Student ratio (FTE basis)

1:18

Undergraduate degrees conferred

Applied Science (engineering), Arts, Commerce, Computer Science, Fine Arts, Human Kinetics, Law, Music, Music Therapy, Musical Arts, Public Administration, Science, Science in Nursing, Social Work

7. TEACHING FACILITIES

Largest first-year class 450
First-year courses with tutorials 10%
Lab places for first-year students As necessary

Research grants and contracts $6 million

Graduate programs
Number of programs 44
Enrolment 620

Libraries
With open stacks 3
With closed stacks N/R
Total holdings 1.8 million volumes

8. STUDENTS

Undergraduates

1st year	3200
2nd year	2000
3rd year	2000
4th year	1900

Entering as Ontario Scholars 17%
Entering with scholarships 9%
Entering with OSAP help 45%

9. ENTRANCE SCHOLARSHIPS

Most prestigious
Open scholarships (4):
Renewable
No application necessary
Deadline May 31
Requirements: 80% plus

Partial-tuition scholarships
Competition scholarships (available in several departmental areas):
Application necessary
No deadline
Requirements: 75% or more; supporting documentation, contact Windsor

Awards: varying amounts
Application necessary
No deadline
Requirements: % average varies; supporting documentation, contact Windsor

Scholarships for entering students N/A

10. INTERNATIONAL STUDENTS

Students from outside Canada 7%
Scholarships awarded None
Services available Adviser; Academic Counsellor
Language requirements for admission TOEFL score 550; MELAB score 88

11. ATHLETIC FACILITIES

Gym
Playing fields
Stadium
Swimming pool
Tennis courts (indoor/outdoor)
Track centre (indoor/outdoor)
Weight/workout rooms

Inter-university sports
Basketball M, F
Cross-country M, F
Curling M, F
Fencing M
Football M
Golf M
Hockey M
Soccer M, F
Swimming M, F
Tennis F
Track and field M, F
Volleyball M, F

Intra-mural organized sports
Badminton
Basketball
Curling
Golf
Hockey
Slow Pitch
Volleyball
Water polo

Recreation and fitness programs

12. STUDENT LIFE

Student councils 1
Student clubs 50

Pubs 3
Drinking awareness program

First-year orientation
Last 2 weeks in August; parent sessions

13. STUDENT SERVICES

Counselling
Psychological, Career, Peer

Medical
Nurses 2; Doctors M, F (part-time)

Special needs
Handicapped/special needs centre
99% of campus wheelchair accessible

Other
Learning disability program
Essay writing/study skills program
Mature student association
Off-campus housing registry
Planning and Placement Service

14. RESIDENCES

Residence places 1650
M, F, C; varies depending on breakdown of applicants
Apartments/townhouses 225

First-year students
Places reserved 860 double
No places reserved for scholarship winners
No eligibility limitations based on student's home location
Allocations announced mid-June

Upper-year students
Places reserved 1014
Allocations announced Summer

Wheelchair-accessible rooms 40

Meal-plan options
3 plans that operate on declining credit

15. PROGRAMS OF UNDERGRADUATE STUDY

15.1, 15.10 FACULTY OF ARTS

Degree
Bachelor of Arts, B.A.
Bachelor of Fine Arts, Acting, B.F.A.
Bachelor of Fine Arts, Music Theatre, B.F.A.
Bachelor of Fine Arts, Visual Arts, B.F.A.
Bachelor of Music, B.Mus.
Bachelor of Music therapy, B.Mus.Th.
Bachelor of Musical Arts, B.M.A.

Level
General, Honours

Programs
Art History
Asian Studies
Clasical and Modern Languages
Drama in Education
Dramatic Art
English
French Language and Literature
Literatures and Civilizations
Music
Music Theatre
Music Therapy
Philosophy
Religious Studies
Visual Arts

First-year entry Yes

Entry requirements
Minimum average: high 60%, low 70%
OAC English; corresponding OAC for Languages
Drama in Education; interview
Acting, all Music programs: audition

Students accepted 550
Total in faculty 1487

Co-op (work/study) available
Limited co-op; no correspondence or self-paced study

Graduation requirements
Minimum GPA: Honours B, General C
Full credits/courses: Honours 20, General 15

Graduating students 200

15.1 15.15 FACULTY OF SOCIAL SCIENCE

Degree
Bachelor of Arts, B.A.
Bachelor of Public Administration, B.P.A.
Bachelor of Social Work, B.S.W.

Level
General, Honours

Programs
Anthropology
Canadian Studies
Communication Studies
Criminology
Economics
Family Studies
Geography
History
International Relations
Latin American Studies
Media Practices
Planning
Political Science
Psychology
Public Administration
Resource Management
Social Work
Sociology
Urban Studies

First-year entry Yes

Entry requirements
Minimum average: high 60%, low 70%
OAC English
OAC Mathematics required for Honours Geography, Urban Studies, Planning

Students accepted 1200
Total in faculty 3840

Co-op (work/study) available
Internship in Public Administration, Media Practices, no correspondence or self-paced study

Graduation requirements
Minimum GPA: Honours B, General C
Full credits/courses: Honours 20, General 15

Graduating students 600

15.3 FACULTY OF BUSINESS ADMINISTRATION

Degree
Bachelor of Commerce, B.Comm.
Bachelor of Commerce in Economics, B.Comm.Ec.

Level
Honours

Programs
Accounting
Administrative Studies
Finance
Management Science
Marketing and Policy and Strategy

First-year entry Yes

Entry requirements
Minimum average: high 60%, low 70%
B.Comm.: OAC English, and either Algebra and Geometry, Calculus, or Finite
B.Comm.Ec.: OAC English, Algebra and Geometry, or Finite

Students accepted 500
Total in faculty 1559

Co-op (work/study) available
No; no correspondence and self-paced study

Graduation requirements
Minimum GPA: B average
Full credits/courses: Honours 20

Graduating students 300

15.2, 15.5, 15.13 FACULTY OF SCIENCE

Degree
Bachelor of Science, B.Sc.
Bachelor of Computer Science, B.C.S.
Bachelor of Science in Nursing, B.Sc.N.

Level
Honours

Programs
Biological Sciences
Chemistry and Biochemistry
Computer Information Systems
Computer Science
Geology
Great Lakes Biology
Mathematics and Statistics
Nursing
Physics
Science, Technology and Society

First-year entry Yes

Entry requirements
Minimum average: high 60%, low 70%
OAC English, Algebra and Geometry, Calculus; 2 of Biology, Chemistry or Physics

Students accepted 450
Total in faculty 1186

Co-op (work/study) available
Yes, Great Lakes Biology; no correspondence or self-paced study

Graduation requirements
Minimum GPA: B average
Full credits/courses: Honours 20

Graduating students 250

15.7 FACULTY OF ENGINEERING

Degree
Bachelor of Applied Science, B.A.Sc.

Level
Honours

Programs
Civil Eng.
Electrical Eng.
Environmental Eng.
Industrial Eng.
Mechanical Eng.
Mechanical Eng. with Materials option

First-year entry Yes

Entry requirements
Minimum average: 70%
OAC English, Algebra and Geometry, Calculus, Physics, Chemistry, plus 1 other subject

Students accepted 160
Total in faculty 402

Co-op (work/study) available
Yes; no correspondence or self-paced study

Graduation requirements
Minimum GPA: C average
Full credits/courses: Honours 44

Graduating students 85

15.12 FACULTY OF LAW

Degree
Bachelor of Laws, LL.B.

Level
Professional

Programs
Law

First-year entry
No; after 10 undergraduate courses

Entry requirements
Minimum average: B+ to A+ in undergraduate studies
OACs as required for undergraduate study
Contact faculty for special requirements

Students accepted 146
Total in faculty 404

Co-op (work/study) available
No; no correspondence or self-paced study

Graduation requirements N/R

Graduating students 125

15.14 FACULTY OF HUMAN KINETICS

Degree
Bachelor of Human Kinetics, B.H.K.

Level
Honours

Programs
Human Movement
Leisure Studies
Sports Administration

First-year entry Yes

Entry requirements
Minimum average: mid to high 70%
OAC English
OAC Chemistry, Biology recommended

Students accepted 100
Total in faculty 330

Co-op (work/study) available
Yes; no correspondence or self-paced study

Graduation requirements
Minimum GPA: C average
Full credits/courses: Honours 40

Graduating students 70

16. FUTURE PLANS

Buildings
Faculty of Business Administration building, Fall 1992

Programs
Concurrent Bachelor of Education/ Bachelor of Science

York University

1. OVERVIEW

Founded in 1959, York University has rapidly achieved an international reputation for excellence in teaching and research. Students choose York because of this renowned reputation, but also for its close student-faculty relationships and innovative programmes. York's reputation and commitment to education is reflected in its motto, "Tetanda Via" ... The Way Must Be Tried.

2. PRESIDENT

Harry W. Arthurs

3. ENROLMENT

1990/91 Fall semester

Registration
Undergraduate full-time 21,460
Undergraduate part-time 15,051
Combined M 13,890, F 22,621
Graduate 3479 (M 1951, F 1528)

Residence
Undergrads in residence 8.5% (M N/A, F N/A)
Undergrads in off-campus housing N/A
Undergrads commuting 91.5%

4. ADMISSIONS TO FIRST YEAR

Entry dates
September, February

First-year entries

	Fall (Sept)	Winter (Feb)
Applications	22,400	2,244
Admissions	12,700	1,159
Enrolments	5,349	908

Admissions offered to qualified candidates before early admission
Yes

Community-college transfer requirements
Minimum GPA over 8 CAAT academic-semester courses: 2.6/4.00

Advanced standing granted
Depending on academic content of CAAT program

Mature students admission requirements
Age 21, out of school 2 years, no unfavorable academic record within past 2 years, Ontario resident; number of courses allowed varies

5. ADMISSIONS CONTACT

Sandra Millar
(secondary school applicants)
Barbara Lynch
(all other applicants)
Suite B, West Office Building
York University
4700 Keele Street
North York, Ontario M3J 1P3
(416) 736-5100

6. STRUCTURE AND DEGREES

Board of Governors
29 members (M 24, F 5; 2 faculty, 2 alumni, 2 students)

Teaching faculty
Full-time 1200 (M N/A, F N/A)
Part-time 1417 (M N/A, F N/A)

Faculty/Student ratio (FTE basis)
1:16

Undergraduate degrees conferred
Administrative Studies, Arts, Education, Environmental Studies, Fine Arts, Law, Science

7. TEACHING FACILITIES

Largest first-year class 500
First-year courses with tutorials over 50%

Lab places for first-year students
Biology 400, Chemistry 500, Physics 450, Languages 1765

Research grants and contracts
$24,882,000

Graduate programs
Number of programs 32
Enrolment in master's programs 2635; doctoral programs 818

Libraries
With open stacks 5
With closed stacks 0
Total holdings 6 million volumes

8. STUDENTS

Undergraduates (1989-90)

1st year	6837
2nd year	5466
3rd year	5240
4th year	2134

Entering as Ontario Scholars 25%
Entering with scholarships 11%
Entering with OSAP help 24%

9. ENTRANCE SCHOLARSHIPS

Most prestigious
Proctor Entrance Scholarship (1): $16,000 over 4 years
Application necessary
Deadline March 15
Requirements: 90% or more; nomination letter from principal; record of community service

Full-tuition scholarships (1415)
No application necessary
No deadline
85% required by Faculty of Arts, Glendon College, Environmental Studies; 87% Faculty of Science
Faculty of Fine Arts Talent Awards given on basis of Performance Evaluation

Partial-tuition scholarships (1202)
No application necessary
No deadline
Requirements: 78%; no supporting documentation

Scholarships for entering students
Offered 2617
Accepted 1127

Total budget for undergraduate scholarships N/A

10. INTERNATIONAL STUDENTS

Students from outside Canada 4.5%
Scholarships awarded None
Services available Adviser; Academic Counsellor, English-as-a-second-language courses
Language requirements for admission TOEFL score 580; MELAB score 90; York English Language Test (YELT) requires Pass (50%) on both oral and written parts.

11. ATHLETIC FACILITIES

Cricket pitch
Fitness Assessment lab
Gym
Ice rink
Playing fields
Softball diamonds
Sport therapy clinics
Squash courts
Swimming pool
Tennis courts (indoor/outdoor)
Track centre (indoor/outdoor)
Weight/workout rooms

Inter-university sports
Badminton M, F
Basketball M, F
Cross-country M, F
Field hockey F
Figure skating F
Football M
Gymnastics M, F
Hockey, ice M, F
Hockey, indoor F
Rugby M
Soccer M, F
Squash M, F
Swimming M, F
Synchronized swimming F
Tennis M, F
Track and field M, F
Volleyball M, F

Water polo M
Wrestling M

Intra-mural organized sports
Badminton M, F, C
Bowling M, F, C
Basketball M, F, C
Broom-ball C
Cross-country M, F
Curling M, F, C
Flag football M, F
Golf M, F
Hockey, ball F
Hockey, ice M
Inner-tube water polo C
Soccer (indoor) F
Soccer M
Softball C
Squash M, F, C
Swimming M, F, C
Table tennis M, F, C
Tennis M, F, C
Volleyball M, F, C

Recreation and fitness programs

12. STUDENT LIFE

Student councils 14
Student clubs 86

Pubs 10
Drinking awareness program

First-year orientation
Week before classes begin in September; parent sessions

13. STUDENT SERVICES

Counselling
Psychological, Career, Peer

Medical
Nurses 2; Doctors M (3), F (4)

Special needs
Handicapped/special needs centre
Over 50% of campus wheelchair accessible

Other
Learning disability program
Essay writing/study skills program
Mature student association
Off-campus housing registry

14. RESIDENCES

Residence places 2130
Approx. 50% M, 50% F

First-year students
Places reserved 50% (232 single, 546 double)
No application deadline but spaces fill up quickly
Places reserved for scholarship winners; minimum average required: 85% for Faculties of Arts and Science; Fine Arts based on Performance Evaluation
Eligibility limitations based on student's home location
Allocations announced mid-July

Upper-year students
Places reserved 786
Allocations announced July 1

Wheelchair-accessible rooms N/A

Meal-plan options
$1695, buys in-house currency for campus facilities

15. PROGRAMS OF UNDERGRADUATE STUDY

15.1 FACULTY OF ARTS

Degree
Bachelor of Arts, B.A.

Level
Ordinary, Honours, Specialized Honours

Programs
African Studies
Anthropology
Canadian Studies
Chinese
Classics
Classical Studies
Communication Arts
Computer Science
Creative Writing
East Asian Studies
Economics
Economics and Business
English

French
Geography
German
Greek
Health and Society
Hebrew
History
Humanities
Individualized Studies
Italian
Japanese
Labour Studies
Latin
Latin American and Caribbean Studies
Law and Society
Linguistics
Mass Communications
Mathematics
Mathematics for Commerce
Philosophy
Polish
Political Science
Psychology
Public Policy and Administration
Religious Studies
Russian
Science, Technology, Culture and Society
Social and Political Thought
Sociology
Spanish
Ukrainian
Urban Studies
Women's Studies

First-year entry Yes

Entry requirements
Minimum average: 70%
OAC English plus 1 of Classical Studies, *Français*, French, Geography, History, Mathematics, a modern language
OAC Mathematics recommended

Students accepted 5290
Total in faculty 15,206

Co-op (work/study) available
No; no correspondence or self-paced study

Graduation requirements
Full credits/courses: Honours 20, Ordinary 15

Graduating students 2646

15.2 FACULTY OF PURE AND APPLIED SCIENCE

Degree
Bachelor of Science, B.Sc.

Level
Ordinary, Honours, Specialized Honours

Programs
Applied Mathematics
Atmospheric Chemistry
Biology
Biotechnology
Chemistry
Computer Science
Earth and Atmospheric Science
Ecology
Geography
Mathematics
Physical Education
Physics and Astronomy
Psychology
Science (undeclared major)
Space and Communication Sciences
Statistics

First-year entry Yes

Entry requirements
Minimum average: 68%
2 OAC Sciences, 1 or 2 OAC Mathematics (depending on course)
Physical Education, 1 OAC Science and Mathematics

Students accepted 605
Total in faculty 1376

Co-op (work/study) available
No; no correspondence or self-paced study

Graduation requirements
Full credits/courses: Honours 20, Ordinary 15

Graduating students 227

15.3 FACULTY OF ADMINISTRATIVE STUDIES

Degree
Bachelor of Business Administration, B.B.A.

Level
Honours

Programs
Specialization in:
Accounting
Combined B.B.A. / Computer Science
Economics
Finance
Management Science
Marketing
Organizational Behaviour / Industrial Relations
Policy

First-year entry
Yes

Entry requirements
Minimum average: high B average
1 OAC English, 1 OAC Math (Calculus recommended) supplementary application required

Students accepted N/A
Total in faculty N/A

Co-op (work/study) available
No; no correspondence or self-paced study

Graduation requirements
Minimum GPA N/A
Full credits/courses N/A

Graduating students 107

15.6 FACULTY OF EDUCATION

Degree
Bachelor of Education, B.Ed.

Level
Ordinary, Honours

Programs
B.Ed. Concurrent:
Primary/Junior
Junior/Intermediate
Intermediate/Senior
Judaic Studies option

First-year entry
No; minimum 1 year university study required

Entry requirements
Minimum average: 70% in 1st year university study
Requirements: No special subjects; experience working with children in an organized setting

Students accepted 285
Total in faculty N/A

Co-op (work/study) available
Practicum required; no correspondence or self-paced study

Graduation requirements
Minimum GPA: C+ average
Full credits/courses: Honours 20; Ordinary 15, education courses

Graduating students 265

15.8 FACULTY OF ENVIRONMENTAL STUDIES

Degree
Bachelor in Environmental Studies, B.E.S.

Level
Honours only

Programs
Environmental Policy and Action
Nature, Technology and Society
Human Settlement and Population
Global Development, Peace and Justice

First-year entry Yes

Entry Requirements
Minimum 70%
requirements:
1 OAC English; Biology and Mathematics recommended, supplementary application

Students accepted 80
Total in faculty N/A

Co-op (work/study) available
No; 12 week practicum work experience in final years, no correspondence of self-paced study

Graduation requirement
Minimum GPA N/A
Full credits/courses 20

Graduating students N/A

15.10 FACULTY OF FINE ARTS

Degree
Bachelor of Fine Arts, B.F.A.
Bachelor of Arts, B.A.

Level
Honours, Specialized Honours

Programs
Dance
Film and Video
Fine Arts Studies
Music
Theatre
Visual Arts

First-year entry Yes

Entry requirements
Minimum average: 70%
Requirements: No special subjects; English recommended; Performance Evaluation (contact faculty for specific information)

Students accepted 432
Total in faculty 1441
Co-op (work/study) available
No; no correspondence or self-paced study

Graduation requirements
Full credits/courses: Honours 20

Graduating students 220

15.12 OSGOODE HALL LAW SCHOOL

Degree
Bachelor of Laws, LL.B

Level
3-year professional program

Program
Law

First-year entry
No; minimum two years of undergraduate study

Entry requirements
Minimum average: 75% over 2 years of university study
Requirements: No special subjects; high score on Law School Admission Test (LSAT); letters of reference

Students accepted 332
Total in faculty 960

Co-op (work/study) available
No; no correspondence or self-paced study

Graduation requirements N/A

Graduating students 298

16. FUTURE PLANS

Buildings
Centre for Fine Arts, Phase 3
New Student Centre, Spring 1991
Calumet College and Residence, Spring 1991
New Academic Building, Spring 1992

Glendon College, York University

1. OVERVIEW

Located on its own beautiful campus close to downtown Toronto, Glendon is the bilingual liberal-arts faculty of York University. Approximately 1800 students study towards a Bachelor of Arts degree. Courses are taught in both French and English. The large number of francophone students provides a milieu in which students can improve their level of bilingualism.

2. PRINCIPAL

Roseann Runte

3. ENROLMENT

1990 Fall semester

Registration
Undergraduate full-time 1365 (M 295, F 1070)
Undergraduate part-time 350 (M 61, F 265)

Residence
Undergrads in residence 23% (M 27%, F 73%)
Undergrads in off-campus housing N/R
Undergrads commuting 77%

4. ADMISSIONS TO FIRST YEAR

Entry dates
Fall, Winter

First-year entries

	Fall	Winter
Applications	1406	105
Admissions	1067	60
Enrolments	414	47

Admissions offered to qualified candidates before early admission
Yes

Community-college transfer requirements
Advanced standing granted
See York University section.

Mature students admission requirements
See York University section.

5. ADMISSIONS CONTACT

Julie Parna-Stief
Co-ordinator of Advising & Liason
Glendon College, York University
2275 Bayview Avenue
Toronto, Ontario M4N 3M6
(416) 487-6710

6. STRUCTURE AND DEGREES

Board of Governors
See York University section

Teaching faculty
Full-time 133 (M 84, F 49)
Part-time 86 (M N/A, F N/A)

Faculty/Student ratio (FTE basis)
1:10

Undergraduate degrees conferred
Bachelor of Arts

7. TEACHING FACILITIES

Largest first-year class 150
First-year courses with tutorials 18%
Lab places for first-year students
Computers 49, Languages 60, Natural Science 75

Research grants and contracts
$60,399

Libraries
With open stacks 1
With closed stacks 0
Total holdings 240,000 volumes

8. STUDENTS

Undergraduates

1st year	530
2nd year	440
3rd year	437
4th year	210

Entering as Ontario Scholars 31%

Entering with scholarships 14%
Entering with OSAP help N/A

9. ENTRANCE SCHOLARSHIPS

Most prestigious
1. Proctor Entrance Scholarship (1): $16,000 over 4 years; see York University section.

2. President's Scholarship (1): $4,000, renewable
No application necessary
No deadline
High academic standing required

Full-tuition scholarships
Entrance Scholarship:
No application deadline
No deadline
Requirements: 85%; 87% for renewable scholarship; may differ for non-Ontario applicants

Partial tuition scholarships (3)
Friends of Glendon Entrance Award ($600):
No application necessary
No deadline
High academic standing required

Glendon Merit Awards
No application necessary
no deadline
83% and Certificate of Bilingualism or 78% (85% OAC English, French)

Scholarships for entering students
Offered 125
Accepted 45
Total budget for undergraduate scholarships N/A

10. INTERNATIONAL STUDENTS

Students from outside Canada 1%
Scholarships awarded None
Services available Adviser; Academic Counsellor
Language requirements for admission
See York University section

11. ATHLETIC FACILITIES

Fitness studio
Jogging trails (outdoor)
Gym
Playing fields
Squash courts
Swimming pool
Tennis courts (outdoor)
Weight/workout rooms

Inter-university sports
See York section.

Intra-mural organized sports
See York section.

Recreation and fitness programs

12. STUDENT LIFE

Student council 1
Student clubs 16

Pubs 1
Drinking awareness program

First-year orientation
Week prior to start of classes; parent sessions

13. STUDENT SERVICES

Counselling
Psychological, Career

Medical
Nurses 1; Doctors M (2), F (1)

Special needs
Wheelchair accessibility N/A

Other
Learning disability program linked to York campus program
Essay writing/study skills program
Mature student association
Off-campus housing registry

14. RESIDENCES

Residence places 401
42 M, 150 F, 209 C

First-year students
Places reserved
166 single, 74 double
Application deadline None
Places reserved for scholarship winners
Eligibility limitations: priority to

students outside Metropolitan Toronto
Allocations announced July 1

Upper-year students
Places reserved 160
Allocations announced July 1

Wheelchair-accessible rooms 2

Meal-plan options
In-house currency to purchase meals on campus, or small amounts of currency plus kitchen access (60 places)

15. PROGRAMS OF UNDERGRADUATE STUDY

15.1 FACULTY OF GLENDON COLLEGE

Degree
Bachelor of Arts, B.A.
Bachelor of Education, B.Ed.

Level
Ordinary, Honours

Programs
Canadian Studies
Computer Science
Economics
English
French Studies
Hispanic Studies
History
International Studies
Linguistics and Language Studies
Mathematics
Multidisciplinary Studies
  Art in Society
  Drama Studies
  18th Century Studies
  Environmental and Health Sciences
  Individualized Programs
Philosophy
Political Science
Psychology
Sociology
Translation
Women's Studies

First-year entry
Yes, except Translation (enter year 2, entrance exam required) and Education (enter year 2 or 3)

Entry requirements
Minimum average: 68%
No special subjects required
OAC French or *Anglais* recommended
Non-Ontario applicant requirements will differ

Students accepted N/A
Total in faculty 1723

Co-op (work/study) available
No; no correspondence or self-paced study; Translation and Computer Science have possibility of internship; Work and Study option of academic and work experience available

Graduation requirements
Minimum GPA: 4.0 Ordinary, 5.0 Honours on scale of 9.0
Full credits/courses: Ordinary 15, Honours 20
Second language requirement prior to graduation

Graduating students 328

Glossary

Bachelor's degree The first university degree, for which a student follows a specific undergraduate program (e.g., B.A. = Bachelor of Arts).

Co-op Or work/study programs, which provide paid work terms as well as academic sessions to integrate practical experience with theory. Co-op programs often require a higher academic standard and undergraduate degrees may take longer to complete.

Course A unit of study identified by a course title and a unique course number within an academic program.

Credit A unit of academic value earned within a particular program. Usually, 15 full, or 30 half, or 30 semester credits are required for a general, ordinary pass degree.

Doctoral degree The highest academic degree granted in an area of study (e.g., Ph.D. = Doctor of Philosophy).

Elective Also called an option, it is a non-major course, not specifically required in a program. Credit for the course will be counted toward the student's degree program.

FTE Full-time equivalent: a conversion of total number of students to an equivalent number of full-time students depending on their course load (differs from university to university).

Full-time student A student who is registered in four or more undergraduate per year or per semester is usually considered a full-time student, though there are variations among universities.

General degree Also called an ordinary or pass degree, it is an undergraduate requiring a minimum of 15 full, or 30 half, or 30 semester credits.

International students Students who enter university on a foreign passport.

Internship Internship programs enhance a student's program of study with relevant, paid work usually during vacation periods. Finding employment may be either the university's or the student's responsibility.

LSAT Legal Standard Admissions Test results must be presented to law faculties within Ontario as an admission requirement.

Major A primary area of specialization within a degree program; a specific number of courses must be taken.

Master's degree A graduate degree earned after a Bachelor's degree and prior to a Doctor of Philosophy degree (e.g., M.A. = Master of Arts).

Mature student An applicant to a university who does not have a grade 13/OAC basis for admission. Often the term is used broadly to signify anyone enrolling in university studies after a significant absence from formal education.

MCAT Medical College Admission Test results must be presented to most medical faculties in Ontario as an admission requirement. There are also other standardized admission tests for pharmacy (PCAT) and graduate business programs (GMAT)

MELAB The Michigan English Language Assessment Battery is a test of English proficiency accepted by some Ontario universities.

Minor A secondary area of specialization that requires fewer courses than a major but includes sufficient courses to meet university standards for a thorough knowledge of a subject area.

Non-traditional students Same as Mature students.

OAC An Ontario Academic Credit is a secondary-school credit required by Ontario universities for entry into degree programs. Grade 13 credits are still an acceptable equivalent at this time for applicants who are not graduating from the current system.

Option Same as elective

OSAP Ontario Student Assistance Program. Information can be obtained through guidance offices, any Ontario university or from Ministry of Colleges and Universities, Student Awards Branch, P.O. Box 4500, Thunder Ontario P7B 6G9; telephone 1-800-465-3013 (toll free) or 1-807-345-4830.

OUAC The Ontario Universities Application Centre dispenses university application forms for daytime undergraduate programs at Ontario universities. Contact: Ontario Universities Applications Centre, 90 Woodlawn Rd. W., Guelph, Ontario N1H 7P4; telephone 1-800-265-8341 (toll free) or 1-519-823-1940.

Part-time student A student who is not enrolled into a full-time program as defined by a university and to whom special restrictions may apply.

Practicum Time spent during the course of study in a practical situation on a regular basis, usually unpaid. It combines theory with practice (e.g., education students spending time in a class-room to gain experience).

Prerequisite A course that must be successfully completed in preparation for entering another course.

Program A combination of courses in a subject area (or areas) that fulfils the requirements for a degree.

Registration The choosing of courses, often in consultation with university staff and/or faculty, that meet program requirements. Payment of fees is also made at this time.

Semester An academic period, usually 13 weeks, but there are variations (e.g., six weeks of intensive study).

Standing A specific requirement set by faculties that must be met by students to continue in their programs. Standing usually includes the maintenance of specific minimum cumulative and major averages.

TOEFL The Test of English as a Foreign Language is a test of English proficiency required by Ontario universities.

Appendix One

Ontario Colleges of Applied Arts and Technology

Algonquin College
1385 Woodroffe Ave.
Nepean, ON K2G 1V8
(613) 727-9400

Cambrian College
1400 Barrydowne Rd.
Sudbury, ON P3A 3V8
(705) 566-8101

Canadore College
1300 Gormanville Rd.
P.O. Box 5001
North Bay, ON P1B 8K9
(705) 474-7600

Centennial College
P.O. Box 631, Station A
Scarborough, ON M1K 5E9
(416) 694-3241

Conestoga College
299 Doon Valley Dr.
Kitchener, ON N2G 4M4
(519) 748-5220

Confederation College
P.O. Box 398
Thunder Bay, ON P7C 4W1
(807) 475-6110

Durham College
P.O. Box 385, Simcoe St. N.
Oshawa, ON L1H 7L7
(416) 576-0210

Fanshawe College
1460 Oxford St. E.
P.O. Box 4005
London, ON N5W 5H1
(519) 452-4100

George Brown College
Box 1015, Station B
Toronto, ON M5T 2T9
(416) 967-1212

Georgian College
1 Georgian Dr.
Barrie, ON L4M 3X9
(705) 728-1951

Humber College
P.O. Box 1900
Etobicoke, ON M9W 5L7
(416) 675-3111

Lambton College
1457 London Rd.
P.O. Box 969
Sarnia, ON N7T 7K4
(519) 542-7751

La Cité collegiale
1400 place Blair, piece 707
Gloucester, ON K1J 9B8
(613) 786-2483

Loyalist College
Wallbridge-Loyalist Rd.
Box 4200
Belleville, ON K8N 5B9
(613) 962-9301

Mohawk College
Fennell Ave. and West 5th
Box 2034
Hamilton, ON L8N 3T2
(416) 575-1212

Niagara College
Woodlawn Rd.
P.O. Box 1005
Welland, ON L3B 5S2
(416) 735-2211

Northern College
P.O. Box 2002
South Porcupine, ON P0N 1H0
(705) 235-3211

St. Clair College
2000 Talbot Rd. W.
Windsor, ON N9A 6S4
(519) 966-1656

St. Lawrence College
2288 Parkedale Ave.
Brockville, ON K6V 5X3
(613) 345-0660

Sault College
P.O. Box 60
Sault Ste. Marie, ON P6A 5L3
(705) 759-6774

Seneca College
1750 Finch Ave. E.
North York, ON M2J 2X5
(416) 491-5050

Sheridan College
1430 Trafalgar Rd.
Oakville, ON L6H 2L1
(416) 845-9430

Sir Sandford Fleming College
Brealey Dr.
Peterborough, ON K9J 7B1
(705) 743-5610

Responses

If you would like to offer comments or suggestions for future editions of *The Student's Guide to Ontario Universities*, please complete and detach this page. Send it to:

Dyanne Gibson
The Student's Guide to Ontario Universities
c/o University of Toronto Press
10 St Mary Street, Suite 700
Toronto, Canada M4Y 2W8

Suggestions____

Comments____

If you are willing to provide further information, please include your name and address.

Thank you.

ORDER FORM

You can order additional copies of *Student's Guide to Ontario Universities*, 1992 edition by Dyanne Gibson from your bookseller or by mail from University of Toronto Press. For mail orders, fill in this order form and mail to:

Manager, Direct Mail Marketing,
University of Toronto Press,
10 St. Mary Street, Suite 700,
Toronto, Canada M4Y 2W8

Please send me ____ copy(ies) *Student's Guide to Ontario Universities*, 1992 editition (0-8020-6884-7) at $16.95 each. $_____

Postage and handling $2.50 for one, $1.00 each additional $_____

8% NY sales tax if applicable $_____

TOTAL $_____

Name (Print)

Street

City

Province / State Postal / Zip Code

Country

Payment, purchase order, or charge account *must* accompany this order.
Make cheque payable to *University of Toronto Press.*
Outside Canada prices are in US dollars.
New York residents please add 8% sales tax.

- ☐ Enclosed please find cheque / money order
- ☐ Institutional purchase order (please attach to order form)
- ☐ VISA
- ☐ MasterCard

Expiry date of credit card month year

Signature (order not valid without it)

Prices subject to change without notice.